CHUCK & KATHIE

The POWER OF Hospitality

An open heart, open hand and open home
will change your world

LIFE CHANGING WORDS OF PRAISE

"The POWER of Hospitality is not only good reading, but biblical, inspiring and true. For Chuck and Kathie Crismier, hospitality is a way of life. I know this book is true because of our own past experiences together. Chuck is my dear brother and friend, and this book reflects his character. It also reveals what true Christians need to be like. This book is both biblical and practical. Read it!"

Dr. John Perkins
Founder—Christian Community Development Association
President—John M. Perkins Foundation for Reconciliation and
Development

"Here is a very powerful book! This is one we all need to read. It will be life changing."

Emilie Barnes, Author
Founder—*More Hours in My Day* Seminar

"The POWER of Hospitality identifies a major, but neglected strategy for reaching the lost. I am very encouraged by the depth of thinking, clarity of writing, and practicality of challenge to believers to demonstrate hospitality."

Dr. Bill Gothard, Founder
Institute in Basic Life Principles

"Chuck and Kathie Crismier have touched a nerve—an issue to which every leader needs to be sensitized. They make clear what the Bible says: To fully qualify for ministry leadership, my home must have an open door. I am not called to tolerate an invasion of privacy, but I am called to live with an openness to hospitality."

Jack W. Hayford, Litt. D.
Pastor/Chancellor, The Church on the Way
The King's Seminary

"If we look at the Bible seriously, we will discover it is hard to avoid the mandate of 'being given to hospitality.' From its very first pages where God extends an invitation to man and woman to enjoy the garden with Him to its last pages with the grand banquet of the Lamb, the Bible is a handbook on hospitality. Both Old and New Testaments extend God's open-hearted welcome.

The POWER of Hospitality is a book to be taken seriously. Chuck and Kathie Crismier have compellingly drawn attention to the Scriptural mandate that hospitality is a central part of the divine plan to show forth God's heart to a world filled with lonely, wandering and homesick people. Here is the most natural of church-growth tools, of evangelism outreach; here is the key to creating healing centers for battered and weary folk...a way to show whole neighborhoods what God is really like."

Karen Burton Mains, Author
Co-host, Radio Chapel on the Air

"This strikes a responsive chord with God's people. What could be simpler, yet more profound, than to love our neighbors—in the church, in the neighborhood, in our sphere of influence—as ourselves? We have made both discipleship and personal witnessing so complicated that we don't do either one well anymore—and feel enormously guilty in the process.

Brilliantly researched and very well presented, this is the message Christians of our land **must** heed if we are to see revival in the Church and in America. I wish every believer in the United States would read...and implement the message of this book."

Jim Montgomery, President
Dawn Ministries

"In a warm and timely book, Chuck and Kathie Crismier are reviving the long-neglected calling to hospitality. They demonstrate that hospitality is not necessarily found in a cook book or in one on manners, but in the heart of believers. It is, therefore, a natural outflow of the Holy Spirit. Hospitality is a place where community develops and God's family grows. Invite an unbeliever into your home and treat them like royalty. It will make it so much easier for them to invite Jesus into their hearts."

Che Ahn, Senior Pastor
Harvest Rock Church
Pasadena, California

"Chuck and Kathie Crismier tackle one of the most crucial issues of 21st century America. As millions of people come to our shores and one-fifth of all Americans change addresses each year, the cry for community and hospitality is often heard, but rarely answered. Here, at last, is a handy resource that will guide every believer and church to practice the principle of being "given to hospitality." This book has challenged my outlook, and its inspiring and practical approach should be in every practicing Christian's personal library."

Rajendra Pillai, Author
Reaching the World in Our Own Backyard

"What timing! In a society that is becoming increasingly fragmented, because of broken relationships, comes a manual of hope and help. The Power of Hospitality will challenge contemporary church philosophy to its core while offering a biblical model of body life that could impact generations to come. I commend this resource to you as a vital work and at a critical time to reach a hungry world in search for the heart of Christ."

Byron Paulus, President
Life Action Ministries
Buchanan, Michigan

The POWER OF Hospitality

An open heart, open hand and open home
will change your world

CHUCK & KATHIE CRISMIER

elijah books

Richmond, Virginia

All Scripture quotations are from the King James Version. The choice of the King James Version was based upon its continued prominence as the most quoted, read, remembered, and published version in the historical life of Western Christianity. Emphasis is indicated by bold-faced type to highlight portions of the text for particular focus throughout.

The Power of Hospitality
Copyright © 2005 by Charles and Kathleen Crismier

Published by Elijah Books
P.O. Box 70879
Richmond, VA 23255

ISBN 0-9718428-2-5

Interior design by Pine Hill Graphics
Cover design by Fresh Air Media

Library of Congress Cataloging-in-Publication Data
(Provided by Cassidy Cataloguing Services, Inc.)

Crismier, Charles.

   The power of hospitality : an open heart, open hand and open home
will change your world / Chuck and Kathie Crismier. -- 1st ed. --
Richmond, Va. : Elijah Books, 2005.

   p. ; cm.
   ISBN: 0-9718428-2-5

   1. Hospitality—Religious aspects. 2. Christianity. 3. Christian life.
I. Crismier, Kathie. II. Title.

BV4501.3 .C75 2005
248.4—dc22   0503

Printed in the United States of America.

In Memory

This book is dedicated to the memory of our dear friend, Steve Smith, who, together with his wife, Wanda, wooed us persistently through their open heart of hospitality nearly thirty years ago. As a successful businessman, Steve's heart, hand and home were always open, making strangers welcome. May the faithful example of this godly couple, who so lovingly invested in our lives, now reach into your heart, transforming your home, that many may experience *The Power of Hospitality.*

Contents

PART II:
The Art and Practice of Hospitality
by Kathie Crismier

APPENDIX

Preface

YOU ARE ABOUT TO EXPERIENCE *THE POWER OF HOSPI-TALITY*. The pages you hold in your hand will change your life forever. You will gain new eyes, acquire a new heart, and be gripped by an entirely new and exciting life purpose. For many people it has been like being born-again...again. Your marriage will take on a new dimension, binding you closer in Kingdom purpose. Your children's lives will be greatly expanded. Singles will have new hope and purpose. And your congregation will be empowered with new life. You are about to experience *The Power of Hospitality*! May your life never again be the same!

This Book Is Important To Your Christian Walk.
Here's why.

THE AMAZING POWER OF HOSPITALITY may well be one of the most misunderstood and under-taught topics in the Church. The Apostle Paul stated that it is essential for all Christian living and leadership. Contrary to popular belief, nowhere is hospitality presented as a "gift I have" but rather as a "gift I give." And refusal to offer hospitality brought severe judgment from a loving God.

Paul, giving instruction to the Body of Christ as to how genuinely to live out our faith, reminds we must be "given **to** hospitality." Peter includes hospitality as an essential for end-time living. And the prophets, beginning with Moses, made clear that God's heart is for the stranger. The very heart of the gospel reveals and exemplifies God's own heart of hospitality. His sons and daughters, therefore, must exemplify that same heart of hospitality.

WE ARE ABOUT TO OPEN THE DOOR to an entirely new world, seeing your life as a follower of Christ from a new and fresh perspective. This book will revolutionize your life and thinking, giving new perspective on what it means to be a Christian. It will provide for you, as it has for us, practical reality to the rhetoric of agape love so easily talked about but so seldom walked.

AN UNDERSTANDING OF HOSPITALITY has, for us and our family, opened an entirely new world, given us new eyes, and helped us to become better carriers of the gospel as "good news." It has empowered families, healed marriages and transformed entire congregations. We trust it will do the same for you and that your life, church and community will forever be transformed by *The POWER of Hospitality*. It has the power to change your world, too.

A KEY IS BEING PLACED in your hands that will open the door of your life to opportunities and experiences you never dreamed possible. That same key will do what you've thought was impossible—open the heart's door of others.

Here are practical and powerful tools for pastor and people alike. May the Lord bless you as much as He has us as you step into the new world of *The POWER of Hospitality*.

Yours for an open heart, an open hand and an open home.
Chuck and Kathie Crismier

PART I

The Heart and Power of Hopitality

by Chuck Crismier

God's divine plan for hospitality will be unfolded and His divine power through hospitality will be unleashed to forever transform your heart, mind and life.

Chapter *1*

Whatever Happened to Hospitality?

You can tell a lot

about a town by how

it treats its visitors.

THERE WAS A TIME when hospitality was at the heart of the American home. There was a time when hearts and homes that practiced hospitality welded families into community with an invisible glue that let people know they belonged and were welcome and accepted. And there was a time twenty centuries ago when one of the hallmarks of the Church was "behold how they love one another." They broke bread together *from house to house* with gladness and singleness of heart," and the Church exploded (Acts 2:41-47).

Something dramatic has happened, however, since those times. In fact, palpable changes have taken place in our time, in just one generation. So widespread is this change of heart reflected in the closing of our homes that *Christianity Today* (May 22, 2000) asked the head-line question, "Whatever Happened to Hospitality?" The writer notes, "For Christians, a lack of hospitality toward strangers has crept into our churches." He laments visiting "dozens of evangelical churches and few have shown hospitality beyond a simple greeting of *hello*."

There is a growing and pervasive sense throughout our land that hospitality is becoming discouragingly scarce as an *art* and as an expression of the *heart*. So let me ask you, *Whatever happened to hospitality?*

Alone in a Crowd

The world's population is being funneled rapidly from scattered farms and agrarian country settings to cities and teeming metropo-lises. This sociological phenomenon has been taking place for a cen-tury in America. Faceless people now pass us by the hundreds without identity or affinity. We connect only of necessity for work or worship and then flee to the haven of home to catch our breath in personal peace, only to repeat the cycle of human anonymity the next day, intent on getting to, through and from work.

Even pastors now have few friends; only 30 percent of them will admit having any friends at all. Many folk are experiencing what one sociologist called "crowded loneliness"—they are surrounded by people but "lost in the crowd." There is an absence of heart connect-edness, a deep feeling that no one knows my name, or even cares. This is true for both men and women. The collective effect is the col-lapse of all sense of community, a conclusion now validated almost universally by both secular and spiritual sociological observers.

This rapidly growing social development was demonstrated to us with a rather dramatic revelation one Sunday afternoon in 1983. We had recently moved to a new neighborhood consisting of two blocks on one street. We had been welcomed only by "Mama Rosa", the self-appointed street captain who knew everything about everybody any-where. Since we had for several years given ourselves to hospitality as a way of life, we determined to invite the neighbors on these two blocks for a Christmas open house.

In true lawyerly fashion, I prepared an appropriate "subpoena." Kathie and I walked the street, personally serving these subpoenas on our unmet "friends," inviting them to join us. We were pleasantly shocked when fifty-two responded, insisting upon crowding into our dining room to revel in a decade-long-sought opportunity for collective fellowship. One couple reported that after seventeen years they had finally met their neighbors as they walked to our home, even though they lived directly across the street from each other, less than two hundred feet away.

But the same patterns persist in our worshiping congregations. In one congregation we attended for several months, the worship service was interrupted weekly for a time of welcoming and greeting in purported hospitality. Almost without exception, we noticed that as someone would reach out to shake the hand, they would look at someone else. The greetings were largely empty, and little genuine hospitality was extended. Although mixed numerically, the races clearly did not mix relationally. They mixed only in music. Something essential was missing that could pour life into an empty cup of fellowship.

Being given to hospitality, Kathie and I invited the pastor and his wife for dinner. After complimenting his message and ministry, we expressed our hearts' concern over the deficiency in hospitality and what a difference it could make. The next Sunday, the pastor addressed the congregation, calling them to hospitality and inquiring as to the experience of his members in opening their homes to one another. What happened was indeed shocking to pastor and people alike. One by one, people stood and lamented that no one had ever had them into their home. White folk were troubled that they had never been in the homes of their black brothers and sisters. Black folk complained that they had never been invited to break bread in a "white" home. They were in *covenant* with God but not in *community* with one another. They were strangers in a large congregation with little fellowship, strangers in the "commonwealth of faith."

I do not tell this story to be critical, but it reveals a heart condition that has been increasingly characteristic of our culture. The roots are much deeper and more widespread than one might think. So I ask you to look with me over the shoulder of history for a moment, back to a time just one generation after the birth of our nation.

Habits of the Heart

America grew and prospered after her Revolution for Independence. Fueled by the spirit of liberty and trusting in God's guidance, her abundance dwarfed her need. Hers was an open heart. As her citizens rejoiced in plenty, she opened her doors to the world. And the world came knocking. Never had there been such an expression of hospitality from a nation to the world. "Give us your tired, your poor, your huddled masses yearning to breathe free," wrote Emma Lazarus. There is "an open door." As a Jew, she had experienced America's extraordinary open heart to the stranger.

The spirit of liberty had bound us together. Blessing flowed. But gradually a mutant form of liberty began to emerge. It grew. Having not been recognized for its deadly nature, its roots were not pulled up. It went to seed and multiplied. America became proud. And the Spirit of the Lord in the land yielded ground to another spirit—the spirit of men and women exulting in their new independence.

Independence took on new meaning. No longer seeking freedom from political oppression, independence began to claim freedom from personal responsibility to fellow citizens. This mutant form of independence spread rapidly across the land, went to seed, and mutated again, producing a wayward child named "Individualism." Individualism took on an identity of its own. Its resemblance to the grandparent brought acceptance to the heart of the nation. A generation arose that knew not the nature of liberty and independence as conceived in the hearts of our fathers.

Many people noted that Americans were fiercely independent. But it was really individualism that had taken hold. It was the new "right" to "be my own man," to "do it my way" without regard to others. Secular "sociologist" and political observer, Alexis de Tocqueville, came from France to America in 1830 to discover what made America great. Lurking in the shadows of our prosperity, he discovered a dangerous "habit of our hearts." To describe it, he coined the term *INDIVIDUALISM*. He warned in *Democracy in America* that unless this twisted form of liberty were brought under control, it would jeopardize the very future of the Republic and destroy her.

Writing in their bestseller, *Habits of the Heart* (1985), sociologists Robert Bellah et al., discuss de Tocqueville's observations at great length, describing this "habit of the heart."

> Individualism is a calm and considered feeling which disposes each citizen to isolate himself from the mass of his fellows and withdraw into the circle of family and friends; with this little society formed to his taste, he gladly leaves the greater society to look after itself.

What would you expect to be the consequences of this "habit" of our national "heart?"

Alienated from the Whole

Things produce after their kind, and individualism has proved to be no exception. Openness of heart prompting open hands and open homes of hospitality began to disappear from common practice.

In their revealing study *The Day America Told the Truth*, advertising executives Patterson and Kim, describe the ultimate consequences of America's embracing the cult of individualism. These findings sound a warning to pastor and people alike.

> Americans are disengaging their personal futures from
> our national destiny. Most Americans think that their own
> futures will be fine and dandy. They have become so alienated

from the whole that they think they will be individually immune from the fate that they believe will befall the nation as a whole.

Virtually every social problem that plagues America today can be traced, in whole or in part, to the perversion of liberty known as *individualism*. Illegitimacy, divorce and broken families, AIDS, violent crime, abortion—the highest rates in the industrialized world—are all traceable to individualism. Our "culture of violence" is due to "violent individualism." Spiritually speaking we might call it "raw selfishness." That something has happened in the *Habits of the Heart* is no longer a matter of debate. "Viewed From Right or Left, Cultural Trend Lines are Alarming," declared an editorial headline. The writer admits, "Because the facts of social disintegration are…so staggering, this is no longer a matter of ideological argument." He concludes, "It is no longer possible to pretend that the values by which people live their lives don't matter."

Hope for Healing

"Are You Prepared For What the Future May Hold?" That is the question heading pollster George Gallup's final chapter in *Forecast 2000*. They are intrinsically words of warning from one of America's most respected researchers and reporters of the life of our nation. Gallup minces no words, stating, "We now face serious dangers that threaten our future and perhaps our very existence as a nation."

We are hurting and we know it. America's heart is broken. We need a message of genuine hope and healing. We need a prescription designed by the Creator Himself for the very problems that ail us.

What you are about to read is not another "culture-war" analysis. It is not a book lamenting all of the dark statistics that glower at us daily. Rather, it is a heart-felt exploration into the very heart of God for those who profess to be Christians. It is a book of help and hope for pastor and lay people. In its pages are keys that will expand your personal horizons and open a whole new world to you as a Christian. We believe it will change the way you think about life and ministry. It may well bring healing and hope to your marriage and family. It could revolutionize your congregation. We trust that as you walk out its pages, it will bring needed healing to our land. Join us now as we look at life through the divinely ground lense of *The POWER of Hospitality.*

Heart-Opening Questions
For Personal and Group Reflection

Chapter 1

1. When you read that the early church "broke bread together from house to house with gladness and singleness of heart," does it stir any desires in your own heart for such fellowship?

2. Can you relate at all to the headline of the *Christianity Today* article that asks, "Whatever Happened to Hospitality?" How does it connect in your life? In your home? In your neighborhood? In your congregation?

3. Have you ever felt alone in a crowd? Why?

4. When was the last time you invited a neighbor into your home? Have you been invited into a neighbor's home in the last twelve months?

5. Would you consider your congregation hospitable? Why, or why not?

6. Americans pride themselves on individualism, yet a foreign observer, Alexis de Tocqueville, who actually coined the word *individualism,* warned as far back as 1830 that it was a dangerous "habit of our hearts" that threatened the very future of the Republic. In what ways might this "habit of our hearts" threaten our future?

7. In what ways might individualism be tied to most of the social ills plaguing America?

8. Do you agree that America's heart is broken? Why, or why not?

9. Can you see ways in which hospitality might help to heal our nation's broken heart?

10. How might a new and fresh application of hospitality in the life of Christians restore credibility to the Christian church in America?

God's Heart for Hospitality

Hospitality, in the fullest

meaning of that word,

is as close as we can ever

get to the face of God.

GOD'S PLAN FOR YOU INCLUDES HOSPITALITY! No man, woman, or child of accountable age is exempted from this overarching plan and purpose of God for His people. It is so simple, so basic. It is an essential part of being made in the image of God Himself. And its secrets are revealed as our hearts become tuned to the heart of God.

Blessed to Be a Blessing

Abraham, the "father of the faith," was called the friend of God (James 2:23). He seemed to connect with the heart of God. He was

21

a man who was deeply committed to his own family, leading them in the ways of the Lord (Gen. 18:19). But he was also a man who reached out to strangers (Gen. 18:1-8).

As Abraham fed and fellowshipped with strangers in his tent, God chose to renew His promise of a son to this desert sojourner. God also gave Abraham a warning of the impending destruction of the wicked society around him during this hospitality interlude between the Divine and a desert nomad. And when the angelic guests had gone, Abraham, with a heart of divine hospitality, "stood yet before the Lord" on behalf of his neighbors whose lives were subject to impending judgment (Gen. 18:20-33).

The God who would be friend to man, reaching to span heaven and earth, promised to his friend Abraham, "I will bless thee...and thou shalt be a blessing" (Gen. 12:2). So that the message would not be missed, the Lord who would become known as the "God of Abraham, Isaac, and Jacob," prophesied of his friend, "all the nations of the earth shall be blessed in him" (Gen. 18:18). Yet, when his wife, the mother of many nations died, Abraham revealed to the inhabitants of the land, "I am a stranger and a sojourner" (Gen. 23:4).

Believe it or not, you and I are blessed to be a blessing. We are blessed with faithful Abraham (Gal. 3:9). If you are Christ's, if you are a born-again, Bible-believing Christian or a Jewish believer in the Messiah, "then are ye Abraham's seed and heirs according to the promise" (Gal. 3:29). Put these words on your tongue: "I am blessed to be a blessing." Say them out loud by faith and in humility. Agree with God, and you, too, can be called a "friend of God" (John 15:14-15).

Why, then, did Abraham lament, "I am a stranger and a sojourner"? Planet earth is not a "friend to grace." Neither are its inhabitants, unless they accept God's extension of divine hospitality through His plan of reconciliation and salvation. Earth can be a lonely place. It requires the power of hospitality to restore life-giving relationships.

Commanded to Hospitality

Hospitality is at the heart of agape love. It is the activating disposition of heart and mind that translates agape love into practical language understandable by every man, woman, or child. It requires no further explanation. True hospitality speaks for itself. It is understood with the mind yet communicates to the heart. **Hospitality is the language of the heart of God.** For this reason, a Jewish rabbi noted, "Hospitality, in the fullest meaning of that word, is as close as we will ever get to the face of God."

Hospitality is required content in the life expression of every Christian believer. It is a course requirement in "Christianity 101." No discipleship effort, however limited or distilled, is complete without teaching by precept and example in hospitality. This may sound a bit foreign to our practice and strangely absolute, yet it is absolutely true, because hospitality is not a suggestion but a command.

"Use hospitality one to another without grudging," warns Peter (I Peter 4:9). This affirmative statement immediately follows Peter's exhortation, "And above all things have fervent charity among yourselves" (I Peter 4:8). Peter considers this area of our lives to be a deeply spiritual expression of the essence of our faith. And indeed it is. "Fervent charity," observes the apostle, "covers a multitude of sins" (I Peter 4:8). Neither charity nor hospitality will save us **from** sin, but they **cover** many of our failures in relationships with others that occur as a result of the weakness of our own flesh.

Prerequisite for Leadership

Hospitality lies at the heart of all legitimate leadership! Why? Because it is the very heart of God. It is impossible to truly *lead* with the heart of God unless you *share* the heart of God. And no man or woman can honestly, with full integrity of faith, extend his or her hand as the "hand of God" unless he or she possesses God's heart of hospitality and acts accordingly. Therein lies the healing and restoring power of true godly relationship.

Consider these strong words of the Apostle Paul to his ministry disciple, Timothy:

> If a man desire the office of a bishop [overseer or leader],
> he desireth a good work. A bishop [overseer, elder, or leader]
> must be blameless,...**given to hospitality** (I Tim. 3:1-2).

Notice! The person aspiring to a position of leadership or being considered for such a position must be "**given** to hospitality." Notice again. Paul does not say "gifted in" but "given to" hospitality. Failure to honestly and accurately read and apply this requirement for leadership—yes even pastoral leadership—lies at the heart of much of our failure as the Church both to equip the saints for true ministry and to accurately transmit the gospel to an unbelieving world.

We have found it necessary to replace this quintessential requirement of hospitality with a host of gospel gimmicks ranging from the sublime to the ridiculous. Our "covenant communities" of faith are neither in covenant nor community. And the fracture of covenant and community in God's house has led to massive fracture of community in our national "house." Individualism reigns supreme from the Church house to the White House and from pulpit to pew. We must restore "hospitality from the heart" to the heart of our lives and ministry if we would see God's hand move in power among us.

A cry has gone up across America and the world for authentic Christianity. Some of us claim to bear the absolute truth; others of us claim to offer Christian compassion. But the time has come for "mercy and truth to meet together" (Ps. 85:10). Hospitality is the enabling force, the connecting link.

In the discipleship of Titus, Paul confirmed again the absolute necessity of hospitality for leadership. He instructs Titus to "ordain elders in every city" (Titus 1:5). He then describes the behavior, spirit, and heart of a bishop, elder, or overseer (these terms are synonymous).

A bishop must be blameless… **a lover of hospitality**… sober, just, holy, temperate; Holding fast the faithful word…" (Titus 1:7-9).

The great Apostle Paul does not say one who is in leadership must be "gifted in" hospitality. Rather, he or she must be a "lover of hospitality." To be a lover, one must set his or her mind and heart to the task. This is God's "affirmative action" plan. Ours has been a poor substitute.

Leaders who love hospitality will have a profound effect on those they lead. Their message will be massaged naturally by the heart and spirit in both the delivery and in the entire life expression of the messenger. The collective heart and life of hospitality displayed by disciples authenticates the message that we "may be able by sound doctrine both to exhort and to convince the gainsayers" (Titus 1:9). Never has there been a greater need or a greater opportunity.

Widows Warranting Welfare

Welfare is a term fraught with much political and religious baggage. The Scriptures, however, clearly define situations and classifications of persons for whom God's covenant community, the Church, (not the government) should make provision. While we are always to reach to the poor, providing not only fish but also the ability to fish, the widows are specifically singled out for care.

"Honor widows that are widows indeed," says the Apostle Paul in his instructions to Timothy (I Tim. 5:13). Some widows, he says, are not entitled to assistance; others are. How do we determine who is entitled to care as a widow and how they should be cared for?

First, children are to provide care for their own mothers. If they fail to do so within their ability, they have "denied the faith" and are "worse than an infidel" (I Tim. 5:8). It is a display of gross inhospitality toward one's own flesh. Isaiah calls it hiding "from thine own flesh" (Isa. 58:7).

A widow is not to be taken into the care of the Church, if her extended family is able to provide full care, until she is at least sixty years old and the wife of one man (i.e., not a polygamist). She must then be "well reported for good works" (I Tim. 5:10). What are those good works?

> ...if she have brought up children, **if she have lodged strangers,** if she have washed the saints' feet, if she have relieved the afflicted, if she have diligently followed every good work (I Tim. 5:10).

Note carefully! A widow entitled to welfare consideration by the covenant community of believers must have displayed an observable and diligent ministry of hospitality reflected in humble service. The resurgence of such a heart and hand of hospitality would be a salutary step toward restoring New Testament Christianity for the twenty-first century.

No Believer is Exempt

Every believer in Jesus as Messiah must be "given to" hospitality! Christ came as an extension of divine hospitality. Likewise, we, as "Christ-ones," must extend divine hospitality. No believer is exempt.

The apostle to the gentiles was a stickler on the absolute essential of hospitality gracing the life and ministry of the believer. In his letter to the Church at Rome, he pleaded with the fledgling church: "I beseech you therefore, brethren, by the mercies of God, that ye present your bodies a living sacrifice, holy, acceptable unto God, which is your reasonable service" (Rom. 12:1). He followed this plea with a list of seven ministry gifts that broadly define the various motivational and ministry functions of the Church. The list of gifts is then followed by a list of behaviors and attributes that are to characterize **all** believers in Christ.

At least twenty-one items are on Paul's list. Of these twenty-one, at least eleven are directly related to hospitality and its expression:

- "Let love be without dissimulation" [phoniness];
- Be kindly affectioned one to another…in honor preferring one another;
- Distributing to the necessity of saints;
- **Given to hospitality;**
- Bless them that persecute you;
- Rejoice with them that do rejoice;
- Weep with them that weep;
- Be of the same mind one toward another;
- Condescend to men of low estate;
- Live peacefully with all men;
- If thine enemy hungers, feed him; if he thirst, give him drink (Rom. 12:9-20).

It is important again to see how carefully Paul chooses his words. He says we must be "given to hospitality," not "gifted in" hospitality. Peter confirms Paul's viewpoint when he exhorts us, "Use hospitality one to another without grudging" (I Pet. 4:9). Hospitality is a holy expectation from a holy people who profess to be the servants of a holy God. As it is written, "…as he which hath called you is holy, so be ye holy in all manner of conversation [life]" (I Pet. 1:15).

Hospitality—the Heart of Revival

The *mind* of revival is an awakening to truth leading to repentance. The *heart* of revival is an awakening of agape (unselfish, godly) love reflected in hearts of hospitality, extending hands of hospitality, and opening homes of hospitality.

When ancient Israel, the covenant people of God, forgot their Maker, they also forgot the heart of their Maker as it was to be expressed tangibly in their dealings with one another. Having abandoned God's truth, they soon abandoned their godly commitments to each other. God then sent prophets to woo and to warn them. Although the prophets never used the word *hospitality*, they warned the people of the broken heart of God as they thundered the truth that would restore the heart.

Isaiah is a classic case. In Isaiah 58, the prophet lifts up his voice "like a trumpet" to show God's people their transgressions. He speaks of a people who "seek me daily," of a "nation that **did** [past tense] righteousness," and of a people who seem spiritual as reflected in regular fasting. But Isaiah pierces to the heart of their worship, revealing a total lack of God's heart of hospitality for those who were made in His image. Isaiah cries out,

> Is not this the fast that I have chosen? Is it not to deal thy bread to the hungry, and that thou bring the poor that are cast out to thy house? When thou seest the naked, that thou cover him; and that thou hide not thyself from thine own flesh (Is. 58:6-7)?

Isaiah then describes one of the most thrilling pictures of what God will do among a covenant people who truly have His heart, allowing mercy and truth to "kiss each other." It is a glowing depiction of what Christian Americans yearn for at the turn of the millennium after a generation of pleading with the Lord of the Church for revival. If you will obey God's Word, reflecting real-life agape love and holy hospitality…

> Then shall thy light break forth as the morning, and thine health shall spring forth speedily; and thy righteousness shall go before thee; the glory of the Lord shall be thy reward.

> Then shalt thou call, and the Lord shall answer; thou shalt cry, and He shall say, Here I am.

If thou draw out thy soul to the hungry, and satisfy the afflicted soul; **then** shall thy light rise in obscurity, and thy darkness be as noonday:

And the Lord shall guide thee continually, and satisfy thy soul in drought,…and thou shalt be like a watered garden, and like a spring of water, whose waters fail not.

And they that shall be of thee shall build the old waste places: thou shalt raise up the foundations of many generations; and thou shalt be called the repairer of the breach, the restorer of paths to dwell in (Is. 58:8-12).

Promises do not come much better than that, do they? A renewed heart of biblical hospitality is both a prerequisite *for* revival and a result *of* revival. Not only personal, family and community life are dramatically affected by such change of heart but also the entire nation. America—yes any nation—can move from being a nation that "did" righteousness to being a nation that "does" righteousness. The rest will be HIS-story.

Personal and Family Blessings

Imagine your family as doers of righteousness with a holy heart of hospitality. "The liberal soul shall be fat (fulfilled and prosperous): and he that watereth shall be watered also himself" (Prov. 11:25).

You and your family can be blessed with faithful Abraham, for "they which be of faith are blessed with faithful Abraham" (Gal. 3:9). In Abraham, God's friend, were all the nations and families of the earth to be blessed. But that can be fulfilled only through you and me as his seed, in Christ, as we reveal the mind and heart of Christ. That will require *The POWER of Hospitality*. And to grasp its meaning and vast implications, we must look more closely over the shoulder of history at the meaning of hospitality.

Heart-Opening Questions
for Personal and Group Reflection
Chapter 2

1. Do you have any trouble believing that God's plan for you includes hospitality?

2. God told Abraham that He would bless him so that he might be a blessing. Do you see yourself and your family as a conduit of God's blessing for others? Recall some recent examples.

3. Why do you think the Jewish rabbi said, "Hospitality, in the fullest meaning of that word, is as close as we will ever get to the face of God?" If that is indeed true, how close do you think you are to the face of God?

4. Are you able to agree that hospitality is an absolute essential in the life of every true believer? Why, or why not?

5. Did it surprise you to find that the Apostle Paul considered hospitality to be essential for all true Christian leadership? Do you agree or disagree? Why?

6. Has hospitality ever been discussed as one of the essential qualifications for pastor, elder, deacon, church school teacher or home group leader in your congregation?

7. Were you surprised to learn that the Apostle Paul does not describe hospitality as a "gift" but rather as something we must be "given to?" If so, why does this surprise you? Does it change the way you should look at hospitality? If so, how?

8. In what ways might hospitality be both a prerequisite *for* revival and a result *of* revival?

We're All Strangers Here

The Lord your God loveth

the stranger Love ye

therefore the stranger.

(Deuteronomy 10:17-19)

CROWDED LONELINESS IS FRIGHTENING. It is nearly inescapable in our modern world, unless, of course, you radically and persistently give yourself to hospitality. Men, women, and young people flee isolation and even strangerhood in their homes and workplaces for the malls. At least in the mall we have a remote, yet almost perverted sense of togetherness. Even our church buildings are now being designed like malls , breeding grounds for artificial relationships. We belong to the club of strangers yearning desperately for fellowship.

Moses, Midian, and Modern America

Moses had a similar problem. He was renowned in Egypt yet felt like a stranger, to both Egyptian society and the Hebrew people. His personal struggle resulted in the killing of an Egyptian, for which he fled for his life. He became personally estranged from both Hebrew and Egyptian. He could no longer entertain even the thought of fellowship with either slave or slave owner.

Stephen, the first martyr of the Church, spoke of a seldom-emphasized memory of Moses, the great deliverer. Moses fled Egypt and "was a stranger in the land of Midian..." (Acts 7:29).

Moses, once noted and promoted by the pomp of Egypt, became a nobody, a stranger in a strange land. Stephen told us that in his strangerhood, Moses "begat two sons" (Acts 7:29). Forty years Moses lived as a stranger from the comforts of Egypt. All who live godly in Christ Jesus today will live as strangers and pilgrims in this world. But must we live as strangers from each other?

Pastors and Parishioners at Risk

George Barna, in his book *Virtual America,* revealed the following astounding statistics. They should break your heart but may also reveal your heart.

- Fifty-five percent of all non-Christian Americans believe it is getting harder and harder to make lasting friendships.
- Sixty-two percent of "born-again" Christians claim it is getting hard to make lasting friendships.
- Seventy-three percent of all "evangelical" Christians are finding it difficult to make real friends.[1]

Do we dare put it in print? It seems that the stronger the apparent commitment to scriptural authority, the more severe the problem of our relationships. Conclusion: the more RELIGION, the less RELA-TIONSHIP. Something is desperately wrong! Do you agree? Divided and in a state of dissolution, we stand. Individualism reigns supreme.

On my daily broadcast, *VIEWPOINT*, I interviewed H. B. London, head of pastoral ministries for Focus on the Family. Our focus was on the topic "Pastors at Risk." He disclosed that at least 70 percent of pastors in America claim they have NO friends. One listening pastor later told me he thought the figure was really much higher.

Whatever happened to Christian community? Whatever happened to the "covenant community" in America? Are we destined to be strangers in the "Commonwealth of Faith?"

Secular and religious observers alike agree on at least one thing: the overarching social problem in America is not AIDS or abortion, but the total fracture of all sense of community. AIDS and abortion did not create the fracture but reflect it. As we have entered the seventh millennium, we are neither committed to one another, nor to life itself. Our increasing commitment seems to be to SELF and self alone.

The fracture of community is also revealed in the widening chasm that divides our families. The divorce rate among Christians exceeds that of the nation at large. The divorce rate among pastors equals that of their congregations (Hartford Seminary Study), and divorce among fundamentalist Christians exceeds the nation at large by seven percent (according to the premier issue of the *Barna Report*). Christ may be our Savior, but SELF is king. Believe it or not, a Rutgers University Study titled "The State of Our Unions" reveals that the Bible Belt now has the highest divorce rate in America outside of Nevada, fifty percent higher than the nation as a whole. Could it be that the Church has taken the lead even in estranging the family?

William Hendricks, author of *Exit Interviews*, also appeared on *VIEWPOINT*. He revealed that 53,000 people per week are leaving through the "backdoor" of America's churches. To find out why, he interviewed two dozen frustrated parishioners from coast to coast, people who no longer darken church doors but remain committed to Christ.

Among the various concerns given, Hendricks confirmed the following three basic reasons why Christians with ten years or more of church experience are fed up.

- They do not believe their pastors and leaders are telling them the "gospel truth."
- **They do not believe the Church provides true Christian fellowship and community** but is rather a "gospel country club" of Sunday back-slappers who couldn't care less about one another after the noon hour on Sunday.
- **They do not believe their individual giftedness and spiritual purpose on earth, as part of a body, is recognized** beyond the cry for tithes and offerings.

In short, American Christians increasingly feel like strangers WITHIN the Church that is supposed to be a single body—the BODY of Christ.

A Cry for Community

America, from the Church house to the White House, is crying out for genuine community. We cannot live without it. Jesus' cry to the Father before His crucifixion was "That they may be one." The hallmark of the early church was "Behold how they love one another." And our nation was born of a vision for genuine covenant community of the New Testament variety.

Is there hope for a revival of true "covenant community" in this land where our fathers died? I believe there is. Our hope lies not in tirades against Washington but in trumpeting the truth to God's people; not in crystallized religion but in Christian relationship; not in "Churchianity" but in a twenty-first century display of "the Word made flesh" and dwelling among us. It is called "hospitality."

Zipporah bore Moses a son, "…and he called his name Gershom: for he said, I have been a stranger in a strange land" (Ex. 2:22). But it was never God's intent that Moses find himself a stranger among his own people.

In the Congregation, but Not OF IT!

It's Tough to Be a Stranger

An estimated three million Israelites fled Egypt. Cries of anguish pierced the night as the Egyptians lamented for their firstborn stricken as a result of Pharaoh's rebellion against God. Four hundred years the Israelites had languished as slaves and strangers in a pagan land. As they came out, Moses delivered the warning word of the Lord:

> Thou shalt neither vex a stranger, nor oppress him: for ye were strangers in the land of Egypt (Ex. 2:21).

Six hundred thousand adult male descendants of Abraham, besides women and children, fled from Pharaoh's dominating grasp (Ex. 12:37). Most found identity and comfort among their twelve tribes. "Strangers" also joined Israel's march, believing the God of Jacob yet alien to the sons of promise (Ex. 12:38). Gentiles. Apparently, God expected such strangers to join the children of Israel by faith or fellowship (though not by lineage), for He specifically included them to be blessed along with the descendants of Abraham (see Ex. 12:48-49).

It is fascinating to note that exactly seventy times the "I AM" spoke to the stranger through Moses during Israel's sojourn from Egypt to the Promised Land—in Exodus, Leviticus, Numbers, and Deuteronomy. In Moses' final instructions to Israel (in Deuteronomy) before they crossed over Jordan, he spoke twenty-four times of God's heart for the stranger—twice for each of the twelve tribes. Interestingly, Moses expressed Yahweh's heart for the stranger, even in declaring a believing stranger as being one in covenant with the congregation:

Keep therefore the words of this covenant, and do them, that ye may prosper in all that ye do. Ye stand this day all of you before the Lord your God…men of Israel, your little ones, your wives, and **thy stranger that is in thy camp**…. That thou shouldest enter into covenant with the Lord thy God…(Deut. 29:9-12).

Israel knew what it was to be a stranger. It's tough! And God would not let Israel forget it. He commanded Israel to open her heart, her hand, and her home in hospitality. Hospitality reaches to strangers. And all of us are susceptible to strangerhood in an alienated sea of crowded loneliness.

CRISIS OF LONELINESS

"He died of a broken heart" is a phrase often heard, but it is difficult to grasp the mechanism of how such a thing might occur. If a man can die of a broken heart, how about a family, a Church, or even a nation?

My attention was captured by two letters to the editor of *TIME* magazine in response to a feature article titled "Twentieth-Century Blues." A Michigan woman lamented, "What we crave is people—the closeness of relatives…a neighbor…an unexpected guest. These are not Darwin's social instincts…. They are gained by reaching out." But a New York man cut the festering sore of loneliness amidst twenty-first century blues wide open: "Feeling miscast in our own lives, we experience depression almost as a moral stand, a protest against a world we do not understand."

I interviewed author and commentator, J. Kerby Anderson, on my daily broadcast. In discussing his excellent book *Signs of Warning—Signs of Hope*, he warned that the "baby boom" generation (those born between 1946 and 1964) is headed for a crisis of loneliness. Since the "baby boomers" comprise the single largest generation in American history, our entire society is in for a revelation of the consequences of fractured community, a revelation beyond anything yet experienced or even comprehended.

The children of baby boomers provide an early taste. Although referred to as "baby busters," they more commonly bear the label "Generation X." They have been crossed out by their parents and crossed off by society, rooted neither in family, culture, nor community. They are the "alone" generation. Strangers.

Legacy of Loneliness

Loneliness can truly break the heart. A Harvard sociologist warned that, emotionally, one of the social consequences of the fragmentation of social groups would be loneliness and a legacy of coldness. Another consequence is insecurity and the nagging question "Who cares for me?"

In *The Broken Heart: The Medical Consequences of Loneliness*, James Lynch documented, "The price we are paying for our failure to understand our biological needs for love and human companionship may be ultimately exacted in our own hearts and blood vessels." According to studies at both the University of California and the University of Michigan, adults who do not belong to nurturing groups or relationships have a death rate twice as high as those with frequent, caring contact.

Small Group Inclusion

As church congregations increasingly shift toward megachurches, the most nurturing relationships outside the family increasingly fade into "crowded loneliness." Small groups, relationally based rather than organizationally driven, can be wonderful bridges for the Body. But often such groups, when organizationally driven, create the illusion of satisfying relational needs but are lacking in underlying covenant commitment because they often serve more the needs of organizational management than the needs of relational ministry. Organizational programs will never resolve relational pain and emptiness. The Church house in America faces a crisis of loneliness, and our hearts are bleeding and broken. Where can we find hope?

THE COVENANT CONNECTION

John Winthrop (1588–1649) was the most prominent of the first Puritans to land on our shores. As a godly attorney, he described the "city set on a hill" that he and his fellow Puritans intended to found. His words have remained a model for what life in America was intended to be:

> We must delight in each other, make others conditions
> our own, rejoice together, mourn together, labor and suffer
> together, always having before our eyes our community as
> members of the same body.

Before the Puritans landed at Massachusetts Bay in 1630, John Winthrop penned perhaps the clearest expression of the "American vision." He called it "A Model of Christian Charity." It is so foundational to our country as a "Christian" nation that I provide a copy in the Appendix. A few short excerpts should be sufficient to set the tone.

> We are a company professing ourselves fellow members
> of Christ,…we ought to account ourselves knit together by
> this bond of love, and live in the exercise of it….

Reflecting on the weakness of Christians in implementing true Christianity, Winthrop declared, "That which most people in churches only profess as truth, we bring into familiar and constant practice. We must love…without pretense…with a pure heart and fervently; we must bear one another's burdens; we must not look on our own things but also on the things of our brethren." What a vision!

But Winthrop also warned, "Nor must we think that the Lord will bear with such failings at our hands as He does from those among whom we have lived…." He sounds like Moses warning Israel, doesn't he?

THE PRICE OF A BROKEN COVENANT

The early Puritans believed the gospel was truly good news. But they were equally convinced that toying with God's plan was bad news. "If we neglect to observe these articles," wrote Winthrop, "and—dissembling with our God—shall embrace this present world…seeking great things for ourselves…the Lord will surely break out in wrath against us…and make us to know the price for the breach of such a covenant."

And so we have it! We have seen the great blessing that flowed for nearly four hundred years from the fountain of our fathers' holy faith, expressed in a covenant community. Yet, in the same fashion, we have reaped the devastating whirlwind of our own progressive rebellion against that covenant in this last century—a century that has been euphemistically called "The American Century." We have exchanged the covenant community for independence and individualism. We are now totally free—free from God and free from each other—and America's heart is broken. What can repair the breach? Only *The POWER of Hospitality.*

HOPE FOR A BROKEN HEART

America's only hope includes a restored covenant community. We must again become a people committed to active, sacrificial relationship with one another as a demonstration of our covenant with God. It begins at your home and in the Church. It begins with holy hospitality. It is formed in an open heart, an open hand, and an open home. With broken homes come broken hearts. With a divided church comes a divided community. A nation divided against itself cannot stand.

A people committed only to themselves will starve physically, emotionally and spiritually. Similarly, church congregations committed only to their own programs, without active commitment to the body at large in their own city, are incubators of isolationism. God is calling you and me to a renewed understanding of Christian covenant and a restored commitment to Christian community. It is our only hope! And it is born in a heart of hospitality.

Heart-Opening Questions
for Personal and Group Reflection

Chapter 3

1. Why would 70 percent of American pastors admit they have no friends? Is this a desirable condition?

2. How might hospitality be related to 53,000 people per week leaving the back door of America's congregations?

3. Do the words *covenant community* have meaning for you? In what way did these words describe the first century church? Do you think they describe the church in America today? What about your congregation?

4. Why do you think God was so adamant about Israel's reaching to strangers?

5. Many have heard the phrase "he died of a broken heart." Can you see how, if a man or woman can die of a broken heart, a family, a congregation, or even a nation could similarly die? Describe how that might happen.

6. Do you think that God is concerned about loneliness? Are you lonely? Do you purposely seek to satisfy the loneliness in others? Do you reach to strangers?

7. Do you believe Christians in America today are living so as to fulfill or "flesh out" the American Vision of a "covenant community" as described by John Winthrop in his "Model of Christian Charity"?

8. Why do you think both spiritual and secular observers agree that one of the most serious problems facing our nation is the total fracture of all sense of community?

9. Are you willing to be part of the solution in healing America's broken heart?

What Is Hospitality?

Hospitality is not a gift

I have, but a gift I give.

Hospitality is not primarily a

matter of ART, but of HEART.

HOSPITALITY IS EASIER CAUGHT than taught. Hospitality also creates lasting memories. One of our first such memories as a married couple takes us back more than thirty years to our second year of marriage. We had recently become involved in the young-married's class of a large congregation, but we really knew few people. One can feel rather lonely among so many—like a stranger.

Our crowded estrangement was broken one Sunday as a young seminary student and his wife invited us over for lunch. We did not hesitate to accept, but we wondered how they could afford to extend their hand and home to us. As a fledgling teacher at that time, I was struggling to make ends meet and figured their situation must be at least as tight as ours, or worse.

As the congregation dispersed to the privacy of their homes, our invitors led us across a parking lot and a small street to the rough exterior of a wooden staircase that ascended to their "penthouse" quarters above what appeared to be an ancient garage. Furnishings were simple and Spartan at best, but clean. After we men enjoyed a time of gentlemanly conversation, the ladies beckoned us to a small table covered by an inexpensive red-and-white-checkered tablecloth, where we dined sumptuously on hot dogs.

The details of memory were not cemented by finery but by fellowship which left an indelible impression spanning a lifetime. God forbid that seminary training or theological specialization ever supplanted the practical touching of strangers for this dear couple. No preaching could ever replace the practice of holy hospitality. Our paths have never again crossed since that year of brief fellowship borne of hospitality, but Kathie and I will be forever indebted to Don and Jeannie Schutt for opening a window of grace to a theologically-prepared but relationally-impaired couple. They opened to us a vision for hospitality.

Ministry's Missing Link

Contrary to much popular opinion, all of us who profess Christ as Savior and walk with Him as Lord are called to be ministers. This may come as a shock to many, since our Western application and interpretation of the faith following the reign of the Roman emperor, Constantine, around 327 A.D. has revealed itself in a profound separation of pastor from parishioner, clergy from laity, and "minister"from those "ministered unto." But from Exodus to Revelation, God has revealed a very contrary intention. Those hierarchical classifications have preserved and perpetuated an *organizational* view of the faith but have largely paralyzed the Hebraic or *relational* expression of the faith. In short, we have exchanged the Hebraic **heart-set** for the Greco-Roman **mindset**.

With a mighty arm God led Israel out of Egypt, declaring from the beginning His holy intentions:

> **Ye shall be unto Me a kingdom of priests, and an holy nation** (Ex. 19:6).

Who are the ministers of our God? Who are the "priests" in God's eyes? Are they pastors, popes and bishops? No! They are ALL of God's people who will obey His voice. Isaiah proclaimed a kingdom of priests, beginning with Christ as our example, but including you and me: "…that they might be called trees of righteousness, the planting of the Lord, that He might be glorified" (Is. 61:3). Consider the practical implications of these profound words:

> **But ye shall be named Priests of the Lord:**
> **Men shall call you the Ministers of our God** (Is. 61:6).

Can you fathom the massive consequences for the effective ministry of the end-time church if we truly believed this and conducted ourselves accordingly? It would be nothing short of revolutionary! The Protestant Reformation may have pronounced the "priesthood of all believers," but it never truly promoted or practiced it.

Peter understood this principle of the kingdom in the New Covenant when he said, "Ye…as lively stones, are built up a spiritual house, an **holy priesthood,** to offer up spiritual sacrifices, acceptable to God by Jesus Christ (I Pet. 2:5). Peter continues with words so well-known that they have been put to music:

> Ye are a chosen generation, **a royal priesthood,** a holy nation…(I Pet. 2:9).

The words of the Apostle John complete the picture, from the beginning of the book to its end. This is "The Revelation of Jesus Christ" (Rev. 1:1):

Jesus Christ, who is the faithful witness, and the first begotten from the dead, and the prince of the kings of the earth…**hath made us kings and priests** unto God and His Father, to Him be glory and dominion for ever and ever (Rev. 1:5-6).

The Lamb "took the book out of the right hand of Him that sat on the throne. And twenty- four elders fell down before the Lamb…saying, Thou art worthy… And **hast made us unto our God kings and priests**: and we shall reign on the earth (Rev. 5:6-10).

The Apostle Paul made clear that pastoring, along with other enumerated ministry callings, are not *positions* but *functions* for the "perfecting," or equipping, of the saints "for the work of the ministry" (Eph. 4:11-12). The same apostle then makes expressly clear that anyone aspiring to function in an "overseeing" capacity in the Body must be "given to hospitality" (I Tim. 3:2) and that the entire Church (all followers of Christ) must be "given to hospitality" (Rom. 12:13).

Hospitality may well be the "missing link" of ministry. I am convinced hospitality is an essential functioning ingredient for all legitimate ministry. It is elementary, indeed foundational. It may well be the key the Holy Spirit has put in our hands to reveal the "good news" of the Gospel to what may well be the most skeptical generation to inhabit planet earth on the near edge of the Second Coming.

The Universal Ministry

Hospitality is not only the "missing link" of ministry for all who call themselves by the name of the Lord but also the universal ministry. Interestingly, while there are "diversities of gifts," "differences of administrations" (I Cor. 12:46), and varying public leadership roles in the Body (I Cor. 12:28; Eph. 4:11), as well as seven distinct "motivational" gifts (Rom. 12:6–8) and "all have not the same office" (Rom. 12:12), the entire Body and its members in particular are to be "given to hospitality" (Rom. 12:12).

Hospitality is a non delegable duty. It is the opportunity of every Christian believer. There are no exceptions for differences in race, class, culture, status, office, or personality type. **Hospitality is the universal ministry. Confession of faith reveals Christ in our convictions, but hospitality reveals Christ moving in our hearts.**

Reaching to Strangers

The word *hospitality* is found only in the New Covenant, but its manifestation is clearly shown back in the book of Genesis with father Abraham. It is an expression of the very character and ways of God. "God is love," declares the Apostle John (I Jn. 4:8), but God tangibly expresses that love by reaching to strangers.

Hospitality comes from the Greek word *philoxenos*. Its functional definition is "to reach to strangers." Christianity is the consequence of God's hospitality to man. Christ was God's hospitality incarnate or made flesh. "The Word was made flesh, and dwelt among us," declared John, so that we could "behold His glory, the glory as of the only begotten of the Father, full of grace and truth" (John 1:14).

Hospitality enables grace and truth or mercy and truth to meet in a holistic manifestation of the fullness of the Good News. The Father reached across the "tracks of time" to a "God-forsaken" planet called earth to enable us who were "without Christ, being **aliens from the commonwealth of Israel, and strangers from the covenants of promise,** having no hope and without God in this world" to come near Him through "the blood of Christ" (Eph. 2:12–13). Just before His ascension back to the Father, Jesus exhorted the five hundred disciples gathered on the Mount of Olives to continue that holy display of divine hospitality, declaring, "As My Father hath sent me, even so send I you" (John 20:21).

Hospitality lies at the heart of the Christian faith. Christianity is God's reaching out to man. All other religions reveal man grasping for God or gods. If we are truly Christ-ones, hospitality must necessarily be a central reality of both our message and our manner. We see this displayed consistently in the life of Christ:

- Jesus reached to outcast lepers;
- Jesus reached to a despised tax collector;
- Jesus reached to a despised Samaritan woman;
- Jesus reached to a blind man;
- Jesus reached to a prostitute.

Openness to Others

If I am to reach to strangers, I must be open to others. That runs entirely counter to the grain of modern American society.

Back in 1835, French observer Alexis de Tocqueville warned us as a people that a plague which he called "individualism" was beginning to eat at the heart of the nation. "Individualism," he said, "is a calm and considered feeling which disposes each citizen to isolate himself from the mass of his fellows…he gladly leaves the greater society to look after itself." Then he warned us with a vivid picture of individualistic destiny: "Such folk owe no man anything…They form the habit of thinking of themselves in isolation and imagine that their whole destiny is in their hands." Finally, they "forget their ancestors." They isolate themselves both from their descendants and from their contemporaries. "Each man is forever thrown back on himself alone, and there is danger he may be shut up in the solitude of his own heart."

Was he a prophet? Robert Bellah, et al., in the best seller *Habits of the Heart*, concluded, "Tocqueville saw the isolation to which Americans are prone as ominous for the future of our freedom." The same isolation threatens both the message and the mission of American Christians. Listen with your heart to Paul addressing the Philippian Church on this issue:

If there be any consolation in Christ, if any comfort of love, if any fellowship of the Spirit…

…in lowliness of mind let each esteem other better than themselves. **Look not every man on his own things, but every man also on the things of others.**

Let this mind be in you which was also in Christ Jesus (Phil. 2:1–5).

This requires heart surgery. It may also require some hammer-and-chisel work on the mind, as it did in my own life as a man and a husband. God used two political campaigns to begin the process of opening my own heart, hand and home to people. His method was simple. Over a period of three years from the Fall of 1975 to the Spring of 1978, I walked more than one thousand miles door-to-door. The process was simple and repetitious: knock on the door, introduce yourself, let them know you want to represent them, thank them, and send them a personal follow-up note. It was a secular pursuit with a spiritual purpose, although I was unaware of the purpose at the time. The doors of my heart began to swing outward rather than inward. I discovered, as the psychiatrist Paul Tournier once said, that "Happiness is a door opening outward."

The essence of hospitality is revealed in openness rooted in love. It is expressed by an open heart, an open hand, and an open home.

- OPEN HEART—the heart of Christ—LOVE
- OPEN HAND—the mind of Christ—SERVICE
- OPEN HOME—the life of Christ—GIVING

Have you noticed that the loving heart of God was revealed by the Father's open hand in the sending of Jesus, the only-begotten Son? The love of the Father, revealed through Christ, was displayed in an open hand of service, for our Lord reminds His disciples, "…whosoever of you will be the chiefest shall be servant of all"

(Mark 10:44). But the ultimate goal of Christ's coming was to reconcile us so we would no longer be estranged from God (strangers) but become "friends" (John 15:13–15), so that we could be welcomed into the Father's home. Here is ultimate hospitality. Listen to Jesus' comforting words of hope:

> Let not your heart be troubled: in my Father's house are
> many mansions [rooms]: **I go to prepare a place for you.**
> And if I go and prepare a place for you, **I will come again**
> **and receive you** unto myself; that where I am, there ye may
> be also (John 14:1–3).

I cannot say I have opened my heart if I am unwilling to open my hand in service and my home in hospitality. Neither will the mere presence of people in my home be perceived as hospitality if my heart and hand are not first open. It is no accident that we say, "Home is where the heart is." Hospitality is not primarily a matter of *ART* but of *HEART*.

Whether my home is open is not dependant upon my social status, my financial status, my racial or cultural status, or even my ministry status but on my heart status. An open heart opens the hand that opens the home. So what is the condition of your heart? A hand or home closed to others reveals a heart closed to others. Are you known for your open hand and open home? If not, God is knocking on your door, even at this moment. Speaking to His Church at the close of His book, Christ yearns for your relationship in mutual exchange of hospitality. Listen to His call:

> **Behold, I stand at the door and knock**: if any man hear
> my voice, and open the door, I will come in to him, and will
> sup with him, and he with me.

> He that hath an ear, let him hear what the Spirit saith
> **unto the churches** (Rev. 3:20–22).

Heart-Opening Questions
for Personal and Group Reflection

Chapter 4

1. Can you think of practical and meaningful ways in which hospitality might truly be seen as the "missing link" of ministry? How has the absence of genuine hospitality diminished the effect of the gospel in your life?

2. In what ways might hospitality empower you to be a more effective "minister of our God?"

3. How might an *organizational* view of the faith differ from a *relational* view or expression of the faith?

4. In what way is hospitality the "universal ministry?"

5. Why does hospitality lie at the very heart of the Christian faith?

6. If hospitality, in its simplest expression, means to "reach to strangers," who might such "strangers" be in your life? What makes someone a stranger?

7. Why is happiness a door opening outward?

8. Why did Jesus use expressions of hospitality in His final, end-time plea to the Church at Laodicea (Rev. 3:20–22)?

9. Why is hospitality not primarily a matter of *ART* but of *HEART*?

10. In what three ways is hospitality expressed? An open _____, an open_____, and an open _____.

Chapter 5

What If I Am Not Hospitable?

Hospitality is to

the Christian life

what breathing is

to human life.

THE WORLD, AND YES, THE KINGDOM OF GOD are filled with extroverts and introverts, talkers and listeners, public folk and private folk, and every other personality type imaginable. Some appear to be extraordinarily gifted, and others of us wonder where we were when gifts and talents were disbursed. Therefore, it is entirely possible—even likely—that you are thinking, *But what if I am not hospitable?*

I can relate! When Kathie and I were first married thirty-eight years ago, she was the "life of the party," and I was the "party pooper." (Please, don't any of our friends say "Amen" too loudly.) Kathie thoroughly enjoyed talking and being with people. I, on the other hand, although not unsociable, was much more quiet, sedate, private and focused on my studies and "things that really mattered," in my estimation.

Kathie yearned for an open home of hospitality, having not come from such a home. She wanted our home to be graced by people, following examples she had witnessed. It was a deep and continually erupting desire which caused me perpetual frustration. It was not that I hated people, but rather that I valued other things— the world of ideas, thinking, and personal peace and privacy. I was totally contented with my wife and a couple of friends… "Us four, no more, Amen!" The rest was meaningless frivolity from my viewpoint.

Kathie's hopes were perpetually crushed. She increasingly acquiesced to my more forcefully expressed views. Her yearning was seldom satisfied, and my home remained my castle—unwelcoming to strangers. I had no vision for hospitality. My wife's dreams were destroyed, and her plans were perishing. We learned an important lesson: hospitality must happen in the heart before it can happen in the home.

Vision Is Linked to What I Value

You have heard it a hundred times: "Where there is no vision, the people perish:" (Prov. 29:18). It is absolutely true. God Himself said so. But how are we to understand it? How does it apply to our lives in the area of hospitality?

Value and vision go hand in hand. If I have "vision" for something, I must first place high value upon it. The dimension of "vision" I have for hospitality will correspond to the degree of value I place on it. Our experience reveals that while people appreciate experiencing the hospitality of others, they really place little value on hospitality other than sentimentally, reflected in phrases such as "Southern hospitality."

If we truly desire a vision for hospitality to be birthed in our hearts, perhaps conception will take place as we open ourselves to the historical and eternal value that our Creator has placed upon hospitality. We have seen it displayed by Christ, the "Word made flesh," the express image of God translated from heaven to earth. We have heard the apostles, who spent three and a half years with Jesus, call for it. Consider these words by Peter:

> Above all things have fervent charity. **Use hospitality one to another** without grudging (I Pet. 4:8–9).

These words inspire vision by establishing value. Paul, the apostle to the gentiles, reinforced that value when he made clear that no one should even be considered for church leadership who was not "given to hospitality" (I Tim. 3:2). But when Paul required all of us who claim Christ's name not only to display His love but also be "given to hospitality," he placed a preeminent value on something that many of us have considered both optional and relatively unimportant.

Where in Christ's claims on your life does hospitality fit? Do you value reaching to strangers as highly as God does, or as Christ's apostles do? Is your vision for hospitality beginning to open?

How Do You See Yourself?

My *vision* for hospitality will never extend beyond the degree to which I see its *value*. But neither will my vision for hospitality become a reality beyond the point I see myself as God's earthly agent of heavenly hospitality. If I see no real kingdom value in hospitality, I will never see myself as God's agent of hospitality. On the other hand, if I admit its value intellectually but cannot, or will not, embrace my role as "God's hand extended" through hospitality, vision will never be fully born despite lip service of desire. As a man, conception in my heart for holy hospitality occurred only when appreciation of its value met and "kissed," in Christ-like compassion, my personal willingness to be an earthly carrier of His heavenly heart.

This is what James calls being a "doer of the word" and not a "hearer only." Failure to see myself as "God's hand extended" in hospitality results in a *creedal* Christianity that is not *credible.* James calls it "deceiving your own selves" (James 1:22). Others call it hypocrisy.

Hospitality will breathe credibility into your creedal faith. It will require, however, that you see both its kingdom value and yourself as having kingdom responsibility to be a kingly carrier of the divine nature of hospitality. Are you willing? Remember, "I can do all things through Christ which strengthens me" (Phil. 4:13).

Gifted "In" or Given "To"?

"I am not hospitable because I am not *gifted in* hospitality." Does that have a familiar ring? Lack of being "gifted in" hospitality is undoubtedly the number *one* excuse and barrier to acting in hospitality. It is convenient but incorrect.

This last generation has seen considerable and encouraging emphasis placed on "gifts" in the Scriptures. There is, however, much confusion in the discussion. Gifts of "operation" are confused with gifts of "office." Talents, personality types, and even tongues join the mix. Paul tells us, "…concerning spiritual gifts, brethren, I would not have you ignorant" (I Cor. 12:1). We may not be ignorant, but we are deeply confused collectively as a Body. Some categorize the gifts, others prioritize them, and some have chronicled hundreds of them.

Most pastors, teachers, and parishioners list "hospitality" as a "gift." Yet, in not a single place in Scripture, from Genesis to Revelation, is hospitality itemized, referenced, or even broadly discussed as a "gift." This is critically important if you and I, and the Body as a whole, are to discuss this matter obviously dear to God's heart with spiritual and intellectual integrity.

If I can convince myself that hospitality is a "gift" and conclude that I am not "gifted" in it, I can affirm its value while rejecting any personal responsibility to be an earthly carrier. "That's for those who are *gifted in* hospitality," I reason. And so the Church has, in primary measure, missed application and operation of what appears to be an absolute essential to the Christian experience and message. We have missed *The POWER of Hospitality* in both our preaching and our practice. The vacuum has been filled by many unbiblical substitutes.

Hospitality is to the Christian life what breathing is to human life. A heart of hospitality produces the spiritual breath carrying agape love, being kindly affectioned one to another, preferring one another, distributing to the necessity of saints, blessing them that persecute, and living peaceably with all men (Rom. 12:9–18).

Hospitality is not a gift I have, but a gift I give. My gift of hospitality to others flows from God's gift of hospitality to me. My heart for hospitality is an earthly expression of God's heart of hospitality. His character is carved on the membranes of my mind and heart.

For this reason, Paul tells all of the saints (that's all of us who are born again in Christ) that we should be "given to" hospitality (Rom. 12:13). For the same reason, Paul requires as a minimum standard for anyone considered for leadership that the person be "given to" (not gifted in) hospitality (I Tim. 3:2). More importantly, giving ourselves "to" hospitality is to be "without grudging" (I Pet. 4:9). Elders, pastors, and all in functional positions or spiritual offices are to be "lovers of hospitality" (Titus 1:5–8). It is an essential ingredient enabling us to "hold fast the faithful word…" that we "may be able by sound doctrine both to exhort and to convince gainsayers" (Titus 1:9). God leaves us no wiggle room, does He?

God's Hand Extended

God gave dominion to man in the earth (Gen. 1:27–28). He created man in His own image (Gen. 1:26–27). He created man for relationship with Himself (Gen. 3:8-10) and for relationship with other humans made in God's image (Gen. 2:19–24). This was a permanent commitment on God's part, putting all things under man's feet in the earth (Ps. 8:4–6). God sovereignly designed for man to exercise dominion and to do His will out of a loving and obedient relationship.

But Adam failed and gave dominion to Satan, the Deceiver, as the "prince of this world" (John 12:31).

Because God had given dominion to man in the earth, He looks for men and women who share His heart and will extend His hand in the earth. He sought for a man to "stand in the gap" for the land but could find none (Ezek. 22:30). "He saw that there was no man, and wondered that there was no intercessor" (Is. 59:16). Therefore, "when the fullness of the time was come, God sent forth His Son, made of a woman...that we might receive the adoption of sons" (Gal. 4:4–5). "Since by man came death, by man came also the resurrection..." (I Cor. 15:21). "The first man Adam was made a living soul; the last Adam was made a quickening spirit" (I Cor. 15:45). And Christ, the "last Adam," just before His ascension, exhorted the disciples then gathered, "as My Father hath sent Me, even so send I you" (John 20:21).

Jesus told His disciples during His ministry, "As long as I am in the world, I am the light of the world" (John 9:5). Jesus is not physically in the world today; therefore, He must work through His men and women who are in this world by His Holy Spirit. This is why He warned His followers not to attempt ministry in His name "until ye be indued with power from on high" (Luke 24:49; Acts 1:4–8). Jesus made clear, "Ye are the salt of the earth;" "Ye are the light of the world" (Matt. 5:13-14). And John, the beloved disciple, pointedly declared, "Beloved, **now** are we the sons of God" (I John 3:2).

God's heart is one of divine hospitality. His son, Adam, instead of opening the earth to the eternal hope and hospitality of God as planned, gave authority and an open door to the Deceiver to become the "prince of this world." The sinless "only-begotten Son," as God-made-flesh, reclaimed that authority in the earth, restoring dominion to man. Therefore, Paul says of Christ that God "hath put all things under His feet" (Eph. 1:22).

It is now your opportunity and mine, as adopted sons, to be God's hand extended. Indeed, it is our divine mandate to extend His holy hospitality to an estranged world, but "especially unto them who are of the household of faith" (Gal. 6:10). If God is love, we must, as

His sons and daughters, be "love." If God's heart of love extends hospitality, then your heart of love and mine must extend hospitality. There is no opting out. Hospitality is not an expression of sentimentality but of salvation itself.

The Tangible Handle

We are continually reminded that there are two great commandments: to love the Lord with all of our heart, soul, mind and strength; and to love our neighbor as ourselves (Matt. 22:36–39). "On these two commandments hang **all** the law and the prophets," declared Jesus. That sounds incredibly important.

The word *love* in such passages where we are instructed to *love* God or *love* others, comes from the Greek word *agapao* which means to love "in a moral sense" revealed in tangible action, not issuing from feeling but from one's moral essence and character. Most of us have heard repeated sermons and teachings on the differences between *agape*, *phileo*, and *eros* love. We are exhorted to love with *agape* love or the God-kind of love. But have you noticed how difficult it is to get a handle on *agape* love?

Over the past thirty years, we have become increasingly convinced that *agape* love is often elusive because we so seldom operate in or understand hospitality. Hospitality is the heart-set and most openly-expressed evidence of *agape* love or the God-kind of love. The *phileo* or *eros* brands of love will embrace friends or stimulate sexual allure but will not reach to strangers without some ulterior motive. Biblical hospitality is the tangible expression of *agape* love that proceeds from an open heart that opens our hand to open our home. It gives us a "handle" on agape love. It leads us to "take compassion" as Jesus did rather than merely *feeling* compassionate.

Almost every disciple of Christ is familiar with the "Love" chapter, I Corinthians 13. Nine times in thirteen verses the word *charity* appears in the King James translation. Other versions translate *charity* as "love." But what is the nature of this love? Is it affection? No! It is an active form of love, *agape,* which is derived from *agapao,* the kind of love that issues from one's moral or spiritual essence or character and reveals itself in active form.

Try an experiment. Try reading the "Love" chapter of I Corinthians 13, and each time you find the word *charity* or *love,* replace it with the word *hospitality.* It works quite well. The reason is that whereas agape love is the essence and character out of which hospitality proceeds, hospitality is the most common public face on the agape love that resides within. Similarly, the word *charity* is probably a better or more functional translation of *agape* than is the word *love,* because of the implied action required to reveal the very existence of the God-kind of love.

It is no wonder, therefore, that we most commonly refer to our public expressions of practical love beyond ourselves as acts of *charity* and refer to organizations that collectivize our individual charitable acts as *charities.* Hospitality is the functional heart of agape love that opens our hands and homes to charitable acts for strangers. Interestingly, though, "charitable" acts are often rooted in motivations other than charity or agape love and are not always an expression of a heart of hospitality. Desire for tax benefits, recognition, power, control, and reputation are often the real motives of such acts, rendering them nothing but political, business, or social tools rather than heart expressions. Of people who act from such motives, Jesus noted, "They have their reward" (Matt. 6:1–4). Such acts are of no eternal value.

The Eternal Connection

Some might ask, "Are you suggesting our hospitality on earth has an eternal connection or consequence?" Absolutely! There are two such eternal connections. We will look at one here and the other in a later chapter.

Consider with me what is commonly referred to as Jesus' "Olivet Discourse." It begins with Matthew 24 and concludes with Matthew 25. During the week of His crucifixion, Jesus sat down with His disciples to brief them on what to expect looking toward the end of the age. You will find the oft-quoted words of Jesus' end-time prophecy in Matthew 24. In Matthew 25, Jesus then begins a series of three parables to reveal the nature of His eternal kingdom and those who would gain entrance.

The first two parables are the familiar "Parable of the Ten Virgins" and the "Parable of the Talents." The third is the "Parable of the Sheep and the Goats." This last parable is the most challenging of Jesus' parables. Many scholars have theorized over its meaning. No words of our Lord more deserve the Apostle Paul's admonition, "Behold therefore the goodness and severity of God," than these words (Rom. 11:22). They were spoken to provoke serious heart inspection by all of us who claim Christ as Savior and Lord. So serious is this passage that it is almost never fully read, quoted, or taught. Let's take a brief look. It begins with Matthew 25:31.

The scene is that of judgment. Jesus will "sit upon the throne of his glory." The King James Version states, "all nations" will be gathered before Him (Matt. 25:32). The word *nations* would better be translated "peoples, races and tribes." In other words, it is a way of saying that all persons, of whatever race, tribe, or nation will be there. None will be excluded for this momentous event.

We then read of those to whom the King, Christ Himself, will extend the open hand and heart of hospitality to welcome them into His home and kingdom—His Father's house (vv.34–40). This beautiful, heart-warming and oft-read passage concludes with one of the most frequently quoted verses of the Bible:

> Inasmuch as ye have done it unto the least of these my brethren, ye have done it unto me (Matt. 25:40).

What had these folks done to receive the hand of hospitality into the kingdom? They had opened their hearts, hands and homes in hospitality as a divine expression of agape love in the earth to strangers… the hungry, the thirsty, the stranger, the naked, the sick and the prisoner.

Now we must move to one of the least read or quoted passages of Scripture that is nevertheless an integral part of Jesus' end-time message. These words are so shocking, so unnerving, that we would prefer not to read them, convincing ourselves that "ignorance is bliss." But if Jesus meant what He said, ignorance will not mean bliss but eternal banishment from His eternal kingdom.

> Then shall he say unto them on the left hand, Depart
> from me, ye cursed, into everlasting fire, prepared for the
> devil and his angels (Matt. 25:41).

Who are those "on the left hand?" Who are those who will be told, "Depart from me, ye cursed"? It is those who failed to open their hearts, hands and homes in hospitality as a divine expression of agape love in the earth to strangers—the hungry the thirsty, the stranger, the naked, the sick and the prisoner.

The passage makes clear that many of these folk really believed they had a "ticket through the Pearly Gates." They argue and attempt to reason with the Lord (Matt. 25:44). One can almost hear them: "But I confessed Christ twenty-five years ago," "But you don't understand—I'm a deacon or pastor," "I taught seminary," "I taught Bible studies," "I believe in God, and Jesus, and the Apostles Creed," or "I was saved at that Billy Graham Crusade."

This is really tough stuff! This does violence to the "cheap grace" theology of modern America. It is even a frontal assault on much arm-chair theology. But these are the words of Jesus, the Anointed One, the Lord of the Church. Would we dare to disagree with Him? "Can two walk together except they be agreed?" (Amos 3:3).

Although we cannot be saved by our works (Eph. 2:8–9), can we be saved without practical outward evidence of the inward work? Will our creedal Christianity save us? Or must the creed be made credible by holy hospitality, revealing the agape love of the Father in our hearts? Could this have been what James meant when he said, "faith without works is dead"? (James 2:20). Perhaps this is what Jesus meant when He said,

> Not every one that saith unto Me, Lord, Lord, shall enter
> the kingdom of heaven; **but he that doeth the will of My
> Father** which is in heaven (Matt. 7:21).

Jesus concludes His Olivet Discourse to His disciples with some of the most terrifying words in the entire Scripture. He was about to die, and He knew it. He had invested His entire ministry time on earth with these men. He wanted to leave them with a balanced picture from the Father's viewpoint of that which was truly important. Immediately after these words, He departed with His disciples for their final Passover meal together before His crucifixion. These are the words He left to impress upon them the awesome and eternal consequences of the parable:

> **Verily I say unto you, Inasmuch as you did it not unto
> the least of these, ye did it not unto Me.**
> **And these shall go away into everlasting punishment: but
> the righteous into life eternal** (Matt. 25:45–46).

The heart of the matter is the heart. Hospitality issues from a holy heart and produces a happy heart. For a holy heart, hospitality is a pleasure. For a legalistic and religious heart, hospitality may be a pain. Which kind of heart do you have? What would Jesus say?

If this chapter has been difficult, don't get defensive. Take it up with Jesus. They were His words anyway. We are all in this together. Can you imagine what would happen in your home, your city, our nation, and even our world if all who profess the name of Christ truly walked in hospitality, toward both those within the Body and those outside? It would be like witnessing a revolution, a revolution of love revealing His truth. Isn't that what Jesus has in mind? Before His Second Coming, Christ is preparing a Bride that is demonstrating *The POWER of Hospitality*. Are you prepared? If not, are you willing to have His Holy Spirit birth in you a heart of holy hospitality? Eternal destiny—both yours and that of others—may await your decision.

Heart-Opening Questions
for Personal and Group Reflection

Chapter 5

1. Have you seen yourself as not "having the gift" of hospitality? Why?

2. Why do you think others have "the gift" of hospitality but you don't?

3. Since the Scriptures clearly indicate that hospitality is not a gift I *have*, but a gift I *give*, does this help to change your thinking on hospitality? If so, in what ways?

4. In what ways do you see yourself as God's hand extended in the earth? Is this concept hard for you to see? If you were more accustomed to practicing hospitality, would it be easier for you to see yourself truly as God's heart and hand extended to others?

5. How might hospitality provide a "tangible handle" for demonstrating the agape love of God?

6. Why do you think Jesus portrayed hospitality (or its lack) as having a serious eternal connection?

7. Since "the heart of the matter is the heart," what is the true condition of your heart? Do you truly have a genuine heart of hospitality? Is the Holy Spirit convicting you in this regard?

8. Are you willing to have the Holy Spirit birth in you a heart of holy hospitality?

9. Are you willing to begin to put hospitality into practice? If so, how might you take a first step? If not, why not?

Chapter 6

Breaking Bread—
Breaking Barriers

Breaking bread is

a divine design for

dissolving differences

and opening blind eyes.

BAFFLING BARRIERS ABOUND, but they are not insurmountable. God has created and ordained the perfect key to unlock the door to racial barriers, status barriers, misunderstanding barriers, revelation barriers, and, yes, even faith barriers.

BREAD! Breaking bread together is the key. In a very real sense, until we break bread together, we are virtual strangers. Jesus declared Himself to be the "bread of life" (John 6:35). He gave Himself to be "broken" that we might no longer be estranged from the Father.

Jesus, the same night in which He was betrayed, took bread,

> And when He had given thanks, He broke it, and said,
> Take, eat, **this is my body, which is broken for you:** this do in
> remembrance of me (I Cor. 11:23–24; Luke 22:19).

As we give ourselves as "bread to be broken," often in the actual breaking of bread with strangers as well as with those estranged, God's Spirit is given entré for healing, reconciliation, and revelation. This chapter has potent ramifications for many of the most serious issues that trouble the Church and our nation as well as our families and communities. It reveals the most powerful tool, other than preaching, for bringing others into relationship with Christ. Do not be deceived by its apparent simplicity. It is both simply profound and profoundly simple. Breaking bread is a divine design for dissolving differences and opening blind eyes.

All Strangers Here

The simple truth is that we are all strangers here on planet Earth. From birth, all men are estranged from God (Rom. 3:23; 6:23). Without Christ, we are "aliens from the commonwealth of Israel, and strangers from the covenants of promise" (Eph. 2:12). "But now in Christ Jesus," we "are no more strangers and foreigners, but fellow citizens with the saints, and of the household of God" (Eph. 2:13, 19).

Because we are born into estrangement from God, we carry that strangerhood into all of our earthly relationships. The sin nature breeds strangerhood because it is fundamentally selfish—*SELF*-centered. We make effort, in our flesh, to escape this predicament in many ways by doing various deeds of service and what some call "random acts of kindness." But history reveals the unpleasant reality that we neither love God nor his creatures but rather our*selves*.

This *self* focus and fixation is manifested in many ways that underlie some of the most serious problems facing our families, our congregations, our communities, our nation and even the world at large. Rather than allowing ourselves to become as "broken bread" with Christ, our fleshly natures seek to break others. Rather than giving of ourselves to break bread together naturally and relationally, our tendency is to short-circuit this relational commitment with programs and organizational structures. These become artificial substitutes for the reality of relationships, leaving a relational vacuum and even spiritual emptiness. We can see this pattern borne out even in our relationships with the Lord, using books *about* God to replace the "Word of Life," and religious activities to replace time spent with the "Bread of Life,"—Christ.

God, by His Spirit, is seeking to develop intimate relationship with His Bride, the Church, before the Second Coming of Christ. That "blessed hope" of the Church is rapidly approaching. You can almost feel it in the air. But the Bride is not ready. She neither loves God with all of her heart nor loves her neighbor as herself. These relationships demand both responding to God's heart of hospitality and reaching to others with an open heart, hand, and home of hospitality. God is wooing us to the relational simplicity of the Gospel.

The Communion Cup—The Broken Bread

No practice of the Church is deemed more solemn than that of "communion," or "the Lord's Supper." Some congregations experience it only occasionally, whereas for some entire denominations it is the central focus and is practiced every time the congregation gathers.

The first recorded communion meal with Christ was the evening before His crucifixion. Each of the four Gospels records that it was "the Passover." Jesus, being a Jew, had celebrated the Passover as the Scriptures required each year, but that year was different. It was to be the fulfilment of the original Passover when Israel was taken from Egypt, delivered by God's mighty arm from the "house of bondage."

Jesus was about to die, and He knew it. His heart yearned for the Twelve He had chosen and in whom He had invested three and a half years. And He chose to spend His last free hours *with* them over a meal. This was not a ritual to pass around a wafer and a small communion cup; it was a full Passover meal. Jesus had instructed Peter and John to prepare it "that we may eat" (Luke 22:8).

Those who would break barriers together must break bread together. But our breaking of bread must not be of *ritual* but of *relationship*, not of *form* but of *fellowship*. It was in the breaking of bread that Jesus broke the news of His betrayal (Matt. 26:21). It was in the breaking of bread, eating together, that selfish strife among the Twelve was revealed the very day before the crucifixion, and Jesus was able to bring correction "greased" by the God-ordained lubricant of a shared meal (Luke 22:23–30). It was the relational context of a common meal that gave Jesus entré to warn Simon Peter that "Satan hath desired to have you, that he may sift you as wheat" (Luke 22:31), yet to reveal from the depth of relationship, "But I have prayed for thee, that thy faith fail not" (Luke 22:32).

Imagine with me a black man and a white man who have invested, by faith, three years of weekly meals together building a "Kingdom friendship." Do you think they might be able to talk about things of the Kingdom and issues of their relationship in ways that would otherwise be impossible or considered off-limit? What might we expect of two pastors, one claiming himself of Calvin and the other of Arminius, who have decided to break bread together for the Kingdom's sake for three years? Might Christ rise above Calvin and Arminius, enabling the pastors to embrace "in Christ"? This is not the stuff of ecumenism or feeling-based unity but of unity born of relationship—first in Christ, then manifested with one another. Truth is wedded to trust in the breaking of bread. Mercy and truth are enabled to "kiss" each other.

Interestingly, it was in the context of the "Lord's supper" that the Apostle Paul chose to rebuke the Corinthian church for their abuse and cavalier treatment both of their relationship with the Lord and with each other. "When ye come together in the church," he reported, "I hear that there be divisions among you" (I Cor. 11:18). We conveniently extract our favorite "communion" passage from its context, losing much of its significance. This is a reason why Paul concludes the passage with one of the most dire warnings in the New Testament:

> Let a man examine himself, and so let him eat of that bread
> and drink of that cup. For he that eateth and drinketh
> unworthily, eateth and drinketh damnation to himself, not dis-
> cerning the Lord's body. For this cause many are weak and
> sickly among you, and many sleep [are dead] (I Cor 11:28–30).

Paul speaks of two fractured relationships which produce practical, even physical, consequences:

(1) A disrespect of God's loving promises carried in the very Body of Christ, reflecting cavalier treatment of our relationship with the Lord and His covenant;
(2) A disrespect of the Body of Christ revealed in our selfishness, even in the common meal together, perpetuating barriers rather than healing them.

For these reasons, Paul concludes, "If we would judge ourselves, we should not be judged."…"Wherefore, my brethren, when ye come together to eat, tarry for one another" (I Cor. 11:31, 33). This corrective word is given in the same spirit as Jesus' own words: "Therefore, if thou bring thy gift to the altar, and there rememberest that thy brother hath ought against thee; leave there thy gift before the altar, and go thy way; first be reconciled to thy brother and then come and offer thy gift" (Matt. 5:23–24).

The Father wants His sons and daughters reconciled, but on His terms. To be "in Christ" demands that those who claim His name agree with Him on what He has said. He desires that nothing come between us and Him. He insists that we allow **no barrier** to arise between us and our brothers and sisters in Christ to impede the flow of His grace. For we are Christ's Body, as it is written, "a body hast thou prepared me" (Heb. 10:5). The breaking of bread in the *communion* meal is the Father's powerfully simple yet profound way of maintaining open hearts with Christ and with His Body manifested in open hands and open homes, all revealing holy hospitality. Only then can we reach to others. While divisions and barriers remain, our "brothers in Christ" remain strangers.

The consequences for our failure to properly "discern the Lord's body" in this way are serious. In addition to broken and festering relationships comes bitterness, even sickness and death (I Cor. 11:30). Whole nations are affected, even destroyed. But most serious of all is the jeopardy resulting to our eternal destiny. John, the "beloved disciple," devotes five chapters, I John 1–5, to painting this picture.

> "He that loveth not his brother abideth in death"
> (I John 3:14).

> "He that saith he is in the light, and hateth his brother, is in darkness even until now" (I John 2:9).

> "Let us not love in word, neither in tongue, but in deed and in truth. And **hereby we know that we are of the truth and shall assure our hearts before him**" (I John 3:18–19).

Breaking Racial Barriers

"Can we all get along?" These are the classic words of Rodney King issuing from the Los Angeles riots. They are emblazoned on the historic front cover of *Time* (May 1, 1992). Notwithstanding good intentions, civil rights laws, affirmative action, rallies and evolving politically-correct notions, the simple biblical answer to King's simple question is "No!"

The carnal or fleshly nature of man—whether black or white, yellow or brown—will always seek to separate himself in one-upsmanship from others of God's creation. It began with Adam and Eve; was revealed in their sons, Cain and Abel; and will always assault our relationships until the Prince of Peace comes to reign. This is why our great and continuing efforts at organizational reconciliation repeatedly fail, showing only modest returns. The real problem is not *color* but *carnality*, commonly known as the "sin nature."

A Baffling Barrier

Armstrong Williams, the black syndicated columnist, declared, "You can't be Godly and Prejudiced." That's true! But, Ellis Close wrote in *Newsweek* (March 14, 1994), "It's hard to start a dialogue on race." He observed, "To write about race for an interracial audience is to sorely test one's faith."

U. S. News (October 23, 1995) noted, "A persistent stealth racism is poisoning black-white relations." Black orator, Dr. Cornell West, speaking on February 17, 1999, in the former capitol of the Confederacy, Richmond, Virginia, warned that the future of democracy is in the balance. "It behooves us to wrestle with it before we run into the wall of history." The reality is that we have already run into that wall. It is called the "carnal nature."

Evangelist Billy Graham, appearing on *Prime Time Live*, was asked by Diane Sawyer, "If you could wave your hand and make one problem in this world go away, what would it be?" Without pausing for breath, Dr. Graham replied, "Racial division and strife." It continues to be said that the most segregated hour in America is the Sunday morning worship hour.

The black pastor of the ten thousand-member Crenshaw Christian Center, having spent one entire year addressing racism on national television, declared to *Charisma*, "A few years of pulpit-swapping apparently haven't uprooted bigotry in the church." When I invited the pastor of one of the largest black congregations in America to join me live on my daily radio broadcast, *VIEWPOINT*, for a serious discussion of racial issues, he flatly refused after I had spent fifteen minutes pouring out my heart in concern. He declared, "I don't want to have any more to do with white pastors or leaders."

This was particularly shocking since I had interviewed more than six hundred national guests and had otherwise never received a flat-out rejection.

Dr. Tony Evans, a leading black pastor in Dallas, wrote in *The Alternative View* (September 1995), "Satan has split this coalition called the church. As a result, we are not seeing the revival in this country that everyone is praying for." "Why? Because God will not bring a white revival or a black revival or a Hispanic revival or an Asian revival. He is only going to bring a Holy Ghost revival." "Until we become a unified church, until being a Christian is more important that anything else," warns Evans, "you can forget revival." In other words, declares Dr. Evans, "God has not come to take sides, but to take over!"

I love that rhetoric! Don't you? It's very true! However, it remains just that—rhetoric, words. Our world—the Christian world—abounds in rhetoric. What we lack is relationship. We have substituted organizations, programs, conferences and a variety of methods for the simplicity of simple relationships built over meals.

What we share with you here is so simple as to perhaps sound almost sacrilegious. But we have found it proven in the fires of reality over and over again. It is not a formula but a walk of faith. Let me share just a few representative experiences.

DR. JOHN PERKINS

I first met Dr. John Perkins in the late 1970s. He had recently moved to Pasadena, California, where I was a fledgling trial attorney and had just concluded running twice for the California Assembly. Someone invited me to his home for a simple presentation of his planned ministry venture in drug-infested Northwest Pasadena. When no one showed up thirty minutes after the scheduled time, John said, "Chuck, we're on *CP* time—that's *colored person* time." That was news to me. John is black, but I am white.

For ten years, I spoke once a month at the Pasadena Christian Businessmen's Committee. Five of those years I served as president, continuing as a practicing attorney. Breakfast was always served, but to the group. Dr. Perkins heard me speak to that group dozens of times and frequently gave much appreciated affirmation. There was respect between us but little true relationship.

When I founded Save America Ministries in 1992 and began phasing out my law practice, I invited Dr. Perkins to dinner and asked if he would consider becoming an "advisory board" member, since I was convinced that racial reconciliation would be an integral part of any moral and spiritual revival. He agreed.

We began regular and lengthy meals together—at least once a month. The more we broke bread together, the more our hearts were knit. We were able to discuss difficult and challenging issues of every size and description. But something deeper than important rhetoric transpired. It was true relationship. We came to yearn for those times together. After a two or three hour mealtime, we did not want to leave.

Between John Perkins and me, race became an irrelevancy. We were "kingdom" men about kingdom purposes; besides, we had become friends. When John learned God was calling me to relocate to the former capital of the Confederacy, Richmond, Virginia, he extended a special invitation to join him on a speaking engagement there. When I left California, I deeply missed those times we invested together. It is now twelve years later, and I truly miss John's regular fellowship. He does too. We managed to squeeze in another of those valued meals when I spoke recently in John's current hometown of Jackson, Mississippi. It was like old times. I love him as my own brother. "How good and how pleasant it is for brethren to dwell together in unity" (Ps. 131:1)!

Bob King

Nine years ago, a kingdom-minded white brother came to me and said, "You've got to meet Bob King. He is a black pastor in town. I think you guys have to get together." And we did so over lunch. Neither of us will forget that first three hours together as the former Capitol of the Confederacy served as a backdrop for our common meal.

I had been asked to be a key participant in a racial reconciliation conference in Southern California. The thought occurred to me, *I think Bob King, my new friend, should join me and share my time.* The conference promoter received this idea as an exciting expression of reconciliation. So Bob and his wife, Yvonne, joined Kathie and me for a weekend flight, food and fellowship in California. The trip solidified our consciousness of jointly carrying the cross of covenantal commitment.

Breaking bread breaks barriers, but it also reveals barriers. Reality comes forth in true relationship. And so it did. Doctrinal differences began to threaten division. Racial sensitivities began to surface. Tensions rose. Weekly meals together produced both agony and ecstasy. While mutually longing for unified feelings, we were often unified only by faith and a conviction that we must be willing to be "broken bread" for the cause of the kingdom.

Unseen issues of power, position, and purpose began to surface. Looking good on the outside, we were "termite-ridden" on the inside with carnal concerns. The flesh foundered. But faith would rise in relationship and forgiveness was extended. As it is written, "the kingdom of heaven suffereth violence, and the violent take it by force" (Matt 11:12). We are convinced that there is a "violence" of intentionalized relationship, facilitated by the breaking of bread while allowing ourselves to be broken that will break every barrier in Christ.

That was precisely Christ's mission. "The Word was made flesh and dwelt among us" (John 1:14). He broke bread with men that they might be reconciled with God and with one another. And he "hath given to us the ministry of reconciliation" (II Cor. 5:18). The ministry of reconciliation is the ministry of breaking bread and becoming "broken bread" to reconcile others to God and to one another in holy hospitality.

After three-and-a-half years, Bob King and I were brothers in process, but so were the disciples with Christ. After five years, we shared holy and heart-felt communion together after four hours of prayer, praise, purifying forgiveness, and provoking discussion. Now we are strongly yoked without color barrier for Kingdom business.

The disciples, after three years, were still in strife, arguing at the Last Supper over who would be greatest (Luke 22:24). One betrayed Him. They all were offended in Him (Matt. 26:31), and Peter denied Him despite his protestations to the contrary (Matt. 26:33–35). Yet, Jesus bridged the barriers by breaking bread with them in the crucible of the crucifixion. He broke bread with them over breakfast to reveal His resurrection (John 21:9–14). And He desires to break bread with us today through His Body, the Bride.

CITY-WIDE PASTORS

As both a pastor and national broadcaster confronting the issues of our time, I developed a tremendous burden for the problems that are devastating the black family throughout our country and in our own city. I had to act as the Holy Spirit urged.

After preparing a comprehensive fact sheet and posting it to our web site, saveus.org, I was troubled about how, as a white man, to broach these serious issues with black pastors. The risk of rejection was great, as you might well understand, given our racially sensitive climate. But God came through again with His simple prescription: invite a dozen black pastors to your home to "break bread."

God, knowing what was coming, had paved the way in relationship through the breaking of bread with another black brother, Bill Carter. One morning, he walked into a restaurant where I was enjoying breakfast with another African-American pastor. He came over to our table, chatted for a few minutes, and we invited him to join us. Bill and I broke bread every Monday morning for the next three months as the Lord knitted our hearts. He affirmed, "Chuck, we've got to get more of the other black pastors together to talk about the horrendous problems devastating the black family."

For five weeks straight, God again knitted the hearts of black pastors and a white pastor over a shared meal in our home. Kathie, as usual, was a wonderful hostess. We invested from three to five hours together on each occasion, grapling with issues so provocative and potentially divisive they were likely to culminate in a nuclear reaction. But instead of a nuclear reaction, the Holy Spirit brought nearness of relationship. The resulting unity in Christ despite potentially explosive issues was nothing short of a modern miracle. And that miracle is now beginning to reach into the deepest recesses of the minds and hearts of leaders in our city in the midst of desperation, all facilitated by the powerful simplicity of breaking bread. We rejected organizational meetings for organismal relationship, and God did the rest.

THE RISK OF RELATIONSHIP

"So how can the problems of racism, culturism and classism in the Body of Christ be overcome?" asks Tony Evans. "By brothers and sisters who are willing to take the risk and build relationships across the racial and social lines that divide us," he responds. Are you willing to break bread and be "broken bread" as a true minister of reconciliation? Are you willing to take the risk of relationship? Are you willing to invest your time in one or twelve men or women for three or more years? Christ did. "As my Father hath sent me, even so send I you," declared our Lord (John 20.21). Do we really believe that?

"We have lost the focus of the Gospel—God's reconciling power," according to Dr. John Perkins in *Christianity Today* (October 4, 1993). "We have learned to reproduce the church without the message,"said Perkins. "There is no biblical basis for a black, white, Hispanic, or Asian church." "We need some living examples to stand up and be willing to accept the persecution that goes with preaching this message."

Corporate gatherings to banter about racial reconciliation will not bridge our racial divide. Seminars will not save us. Harping on past hurts will not heal us. Rhetoric will not reconcile us. Only the Word made flesh through *The POWER of Hospitality* will heal our broken hearts.

As I wrote in *Renewing the Soul of America* (2002), "A mournful cry issues from saint and sinner alike amidst the agony of the tearing of the flesh and fabric of our society." "The God who gave us liberty will no longer tolerate a church that in both black and white congregations not only tolerates but perpetuates America's national sin of racism." I am convinced that the reconciliation of black and white believers as well as Native American, Hispanic, and Asian is a co-extensive condition, if not a pre-condition, to the great move of God's hand and Spirit so desperately sought and so drastically needed across the face of our land. As the Lord prepares His Bride and Body for His Second Coming, He yearns to purge her from spot, wrinkle, or any such thing (Eph. 5:27).

We have engaged in corporate reconciliation. We have traversed the nation and the world in identificational repentance for slavery and racial wrongs. We have sought power, but spurned purity. We have promoted our heritage, but spurned healing. We have prayed for righteousness, but rejected relationship.

There are no shortcuts to simple relationships. Jesus calls us to simply follow His simple example. He calls to you and me as He did to the Twelve after His resurrection, "Come and dine" (John 21:12). He calls us to come to one another with *The POWER of Hospitality* and break bread together. Perhaps some will have to follow the words of the old Negro spiritual of America's past, "Let us break bread together on our knees." It's not about rights, but about relationship. It's not about heritage, but about healing. It's not about culture, but about Christ and being crucified with Him.

The third time Jesus showed Himself to His disciples after the Resurrection, John records, "Jesus then cometh, and taketh bread, and giveth them..." (John 21:13). "So when they had dined, Jesus saith to Simon Peter...lovest thou me...?" (John 21:15–17). Jesus is asking you and me the same question. Do we really love Him? Do we love Him enough to break bread with brothers made in His image that we might be truly reconciled? This is God's "affirmative action" program. It is done individually and relationally, not corporately and organizationally.

Peter, seeing the beloved disciple John, then asked Jesus, "Lord, and what shall this man do? Jesus saith unto him, what is that to thee? Follow thou me" (John 21:21-22). Regardless of our color, we cannot wait for *the other guy*—whether black, white, Hispanic, Asian, or Native American—to make the first move. Jesus said, "You follow me."

Jesus said, "I am the bread of life." As they were eating, Jesus "took bread, and gave thanks and broke it, and said, This is my body which is given for you: this do in remembrance of me" (Luke 22:10). God does not seek a ritual, but a relationship. If we would break bread together, we will break racial barriers together.

Breaking Status Barriers

If we were all of one color, we would find some other basis upon which to set ourselves apart from one another. In fact, we do just that, don't we? Human nature is adept at finding ways to elevate one person or group over another. Financial status, the car we drive, the house in which we live , our occupation, the people we know, the church we pastor, or whether our name carries a pedigree are all familiar dividing lines creating barriers to relationship. The James River divides metropolitan Richmond, Virginia, where my family resides, and the river has historically divided relationships even among professing Christians. A bumper sticker reads, "South Side— by invitation only." You could most likely point out similar barriers in your city, or even out in rural areas.

The Scriptures call us to humble ourselves, but our flesh screams to be exalted. Self-exaltation, group exaltation, or any dividing lines, whether real or artificial, create difficult and seemingly impossible barriers. But remember, "With God, nothing shall be impossible" (Luke 1:37). **Breaking bread together with a heart of holy hospitality is God's ordained plan to span almost any relational chasm.** We all eat, whether rich or poor, wherever we live, whatever our pedigree or lack thereof. Just as the "communion" meal corporately shared in congregational worship brings us commonly to the foot of the cross for a brief moment before we again give place to the carnal nature, so the common sharing of a meal, a cup of coffee, or a spot of tea places us in a position of commonality, enabling us for that brief window of time to bridge barriers, making those barriers relatively irrelevant.

Breaking bread is nutritional therapy for the cancer of carnality that creates barriers frustrating genuine relationship. The more frequently persons separated by any such barriers intentionalize coming together over a meal, the less the barrier looms as a wall or chasm. Conversation is facilitated and becomes increasingly transparent. Secular folk ask, "Will you have a drink?" Jesus' folks ask, "Will you come and dine?"

While the breaking of bread together is effective regardless of our spiritual state because God created us as relational creatures in His image, the efficacy of a common meal is multiplied many fold by a holy heart of hospitality. There is no substitute for breaking status barriers or any other barrier, including denominational and ministry barriers.

Breaking Ministry Barriers

Regardless of whether we care to admit it, denominations are birthed in and perpetuated by division. The division occurs over practice or principle, over deeds or doctrine. We always have good reasons, usually to keep either our practices or our doctrines pure. There are more than twenty thousand denominations worldwide and far more than two thousand in the United States.

These denominational divisions reveal both the pervasive presence of the carnal nature among the professing Body of Christ and a pervasive corruption of true doctrine among those of us who profess to obey, serve, and worship the Anointed One who declared Himself, THE TRUTH. Added to denominations are independents, associations and movements, all founded around either doctrine, practice, geography or some combination thereof. It should be humbling to realize that if there is only one TRUTH, we cannot **all** be right. It should also assault our individual and collective pride to realize there is only one TRUTH.

This is truly a challenging dilemma if we truly believe we are on the near edge of the Second Coming. Scripture indicates Christ will return only "for a glorious church, not having spot, or wrinkle, or any such thing; but that it should be holy and without blemish" (Eph. 5:27). Jesus' prayer will echo to the culmination of history, "That they all may be one; as thou, Father, art in me, and I in thee, that they also may be one in us; that the world may believe that thou hast sent me" (John 17:21).

We cannot sanctify and anoint our differences as if they are God-ordained. That is impossible, since there is only one Truth. That is the problem with the current unity movement even among evangelicals; it borders on idolatry. Neither can we pretend our differences do not matter and drift to embrace many truths. That is the historical nemesis of the ecumenical movement.

What, then, should we do? We must break bread together. Consciously! Intentionally! Personally! This is not the stuff of organizational meetings, political maneuvering, or ecclesiastical assemblies. This calls for pure and undefiled relationship with another pastor or parishioner who is not of my historical stripe. It calls for reaching to virtual strangers whom I claim to be "my brother in Christ." If we will purpose to break bread together, we will break many seemingly impassable barriers together. We will give entré to the Holy Spirit to accomplish in the heart of faith what we have begun in the mind through fellowship. The Holy Spirit is just waiting to reveal truth to us.

Pastor-To-Pastor

Several years ago when God called us to relocate from Southern California to Richmond, we were baffled by the complex overlap of historical division that plagued the city, in both the secular and spiritual realms. For more than twenty years, numerous efforts had been made to bring unity to the city through gatherings of pastors for challenge, prayer, or ministry projects. Despite sincerity, the efforts had largely failed, and discouragement was palpable. The challenge seemed nearly insurmountable. Even industry determined Richmond to be a profoundly difficult testing ground for virtually anything, declaring, "If it will work in Richmond, it will work anywhere." Have you noticed that God takes personal pleasure in such challenges?

God had planted the message of hospitality in our hearts ten years earlier. We had seen it live in the more open and transient society of Southern California. But what were we to do as transplants in the former capital of the Confederacy, a city steeped in both social and religious tradition, where pedigree is the recognized ticket to relationships? How do you reach to pastors and help them reach to one another? How does one breed relationships among spiritual leaders who will not cross a river or even a street to talk to a fellow pastor in heart-felt relationship?

It would require time. It would require intentionality. It would require consistency. It would require breaking bread. If you can't get in the front door, how about the back door? And the Lord birthed the simple concept of Pastor-to-Pastor. We invited four pastors and their wives to join us for dinner at our home. There were a few simple rules: no coats or ties, no clerical collars, and no ministry "puffing."

At our first gathering, we chatted freely over a great meal and got to know a bit about each other and our families. We shared what God was doing in our lives. We prayed together, laying hands on some for very personal needs. The women were ecstatic! None even wanted to leave the dining room. One pastor leaned out over the table and said, "If we had all preached our best sermon tonight, it wouldn't have begun to have the impact this evening has had!"

We met once a month for a year with that group of pastors and their wives, breaking bread from house to house, so ownership was shared. One of those pastors started a new group. Kathie and I started another, and then another. Over three years, we facilitated six such groups, and two of them "multiplied" because the vision took hold. But it required persistence in relationship, seeing the "recompense of reward" afar off.

A Southern Baptist pastor's wife revealed, "I've never been with anyone outside my denomination." A Korean Presbyterian pastor begged us not to divide a group after one year because it had become an "anchor" for them in ministry difficulties. Charismatic, denominational, independent, Word of Faith, cell ministry—all have broken bread and broken barriers together. Many barriers just fall off naturally, permitting healthy respect, while allowing us together to "come in the unity of the faith, and of the knowledge of the Son of God, unto a perfect man, unto the measure of the stature of the fulness of Christ. But speaking the truth in love, may grow up into him in all things, which is the head, even Christ" (Eph. 4:13–15).

WITHNESS DEVELOPS WITNESS

Hospitality is reaching to strangers—even pastors. It will take your time. That is all we really have to give. A nation and a world is waiting to see if the Father really sent Jesus by looking at how those who claim His name reveal the Father's own heart of hospitality. Jesus, the Good Shepherd, broke barriers by breaking bread, and so must His under-shepherds. *Withness* **breeds authentic** *witness.*

Out of an organizational mind and heart-set, many pastors are convinced they must remain separated from the flock to preserve power, position, and authority. This view is diametrically opposed to our Lord's example. We are specifically told that Jesus "ordained twelve that they should be *with* Him" (Mark 3:14). We must recover *withness* if we would see the ministry of Christ unfold through our lives. Recovering *withness* will require the humble act of breaking bread together with the flock, not in organizational settings but in relational settings—in our homes and in theirs. **The** *organizational* **mind of the church must die for her** *organismal* **heart to live.** True discipleship demands that we follow the Jesus design—breaking bread together.

A proven model for developing pastor-to-pastor relationships within a metropolitan region is provided in the Appendix of this book.

Breaking Belief Barriers

As America "Searches for the Sacred," many are willing to believe almost anything, while many others believe nothing. Skepticism, doubt, disbelief, and unbelief abound, while pursuit of things spiritual has caught the fancy of the national soul. How can belief barriers be breached and credible faith be presented, breathing life into the often sterile creeds of much of westernized Christianity?

Relationship is again the key. The written Word must again be made flesh. Just as Jesus became the "living Word," so must we who profess His name, claiming to be Christ-ones. Jesus "fleshed-out" the Word of God in a society both profoundly religious and profoundly secular. His very name, "Emmanuel," meant "God with us." One powerful way Christ's disciples today can reveal the Word in their flesh is in the breaking of bread. Let's see how Jesus did it.

After Jesus' resurrection, He walked in relationship with two men along the road to Emmaus. The men were communing together, sad, having their hopes dashed over Jesus' crucifixion. Belief was shattered. Blindness prevailed. Darkness enshrouded their understanding to the point that they failed to recognize the very One for whom they mourned and sought. In hospitality, the men invited their unknown traveling partner to stay the night. The Scripture records that as Jesus sat down to eat with them, "He took bread, and blessed it, and brake, and gave to them." The results were astounding. "Their eyes were opened, and they knew Him" (Luke 24:30–31).

What will it take to open the eyes of unbelievers in this wicked and perverse generation? How can God use your life to provide a womb of faith to restore one whose belief has been crushed by circumstances or scandalized by the hypocritical lives of others who profess *faith* but present nothing but *flesh*? Perhaps your choosing to give yourself to hospitality in the breaking of bread will break belief barriers, allowing the Holy Spirit entré to do His redeeming, regenerating work.

The men on the road to Emmaus were ecstatic! They rose up "the same hour" that Jesus broke bread with them and returned to Jerusalem to spread the good news. Their belief barriers had been broken. They reported to the other disciples how Jesus "was known of them in the breaking of bread" (Luke 24:30–35). Breaking bread will often be the simple agency God will use in your life to break the belief barriers in another's life. But you must give yourself to *The POWER of Hospitality*. True hospitality has a mysterious power only the Creator fully comprehends.

Breaking Family Barriers

America's families are broken. The Church is no exception. Here are the disturbing facts which are distilled from the fact sheet entitled *The State of the Marital Union,* available on the Save America Ministries web site, *saveus.org.* These statistics have been gleaned from a variety of sources, including the Barna Research Group, a Hartford Seminary study, and the *State of Our Unions* report from Rutgers University.

- The divorce rate among "fundamentalist" Christians now exceeds the nation as a whole by seven percent.
- The divorce rate among "born-again" Christians now exceeds the nation as a whole by four percent.
- The divorce rate in the "Bible Belt" exceeds the nation as a whole by fifty percent.
- The divorce rate among pastors in ten denominations equals that of their parishioners.
- The divorce rate among pastors is the second highest of all professions.

America is now exporting this brand of dysfunctional Christianity that rhetorically exalts the family but in reality exalts *self*-ish feelings, around the world. The February 4, 2000, issue of the *Jerusalem Post* reports a thirty percent divorce rate among Israeli marriages. Rabbi Ben-Dahan "voiced regret that families in Israel are becoming similarly dysfunctional to those of the U.S." How did this happen? How does this relate to the subject of hospitality?

Without wanting to become overly simplistic, the simple truth is that professing Christian husbands and wives have become strangers to both one another and to their children as well. Much strangerhood has occurred in the name of ministry, but much more has developed in the pursuit of McWorld. Our strangerhood has been clothed in religious rhetoric and our divorces justified in perverse religious jargon. God says, "Be ye holy," but we have cried from pulpit to pew, "Be ye happy." Now we are neither happy nor holy.

Here is a simple start to establish an environment that both reaches to our covenant partners, who have become virtual strangers, and helps to insulate against strangerhood. We must break bread together daily. That will require the elusive commodity we call "time," which is an extension of our *self*, the investment of which reflects what we truly value. There is no substitute for breaking bread together.

We must redevelop a heart of hospitality, even for our spouses. Remember, hospitality means to reach to strangers. If we would avoid broken hearts and broken homes, we must intentionalize breaking bread together around the family table. Men, if we want Christ to break bread with us at the "wedding supper of the Lamb," then we must break bread with our bride here on earth to fulfill the "great mystery" of Christ and His Church (Eph. 5:25–32).

Breaking Relational Barriers

SONS AND DAUGHTERS

As our three daughters were growing up, I regularly took them on a date. We always "broke bread." Now that each of my daughters has reached adulthood, I continue to periodically break bread with them alone over a meal. It tells them that I care. It speaks to them that my heart is open to them. It facilitates conversation. And, it facilitates reconciliation when needed. Our sons and daughters, and our grandchildren, are yearning for moms and dads with open hearts of hospitality who will reach to them that they not become strangers. Strangerhood is epidemic among America's youth. Don't let it happen in your family. Break bread together daily around the family table, not around the television. Break bread individually to open the deep recesses of the heart.

IN-LAWS

In-law relationships are often a challenge for families. It is possible to preempt potential problems, however, by purposing to break bread over a common meal as the underlying relationships of sons and daughters of the families begin to blossom and appear serious. It requires that at least one couple reaches to the other to initiate breaking the strangerhood between you. Do it more than once. Remember, hospitality requires that I *reach*. Reaching always requires risk for the sake of relationship. Turn a mutual burden into a mutual blessing.

I was inspired to gather our sons-in-law together to break bread and to build relationships with both God and one another. It became a delicious time of discipleship. For men only. We get together for a meal and to massage what God is doing in our lives and families. I am purposed that there be no strangers to God or one another in our expanding family. Kathie shares a meal or coffee with each of our daughters almost weekly as well. The joy of fellowship and friendship nurtured and nourished by breaking of bread is a beauty to behold.

NEIGHBORS

There is nothing like breaking bread to break barriers with neighbors. Strangerhood breeds suspicion and fosters unwanted speculations. Thirty years ago, we heard Ann Kimmel speak of her "cookie" ministry to neighbors. That message hooked us on hospitality to neighbors.

The heart of neighborly hospitality is the breaking of bread—a cup of coffee and a cookie, a spot of tea. A cookout for one or more families is simple but states, "my heart is open to you." Twenty-five years ago, a few months after moving into an upper-middle class neighborhood, Kathie and I personally served a "Subpoena" on all of our neighbors on a Sunday afternoon, inviting them to a Christmas open house with goodies. Fifty people showed up, all strangers to us, from a two-block street. They loved it! Two couples remarked that they had lived across from each other for seventeen years and had never met.

Hospitality means to reach to strangers. In our world, strangerhood abounds. This is the simplest and most foundational of all expressions of the heart of God. Just as God reached to you, we must purpose to reach to our neighbors. It will revolutionize your life! And *The POWER of Hospitality* might just change their lives as well.

BUSINESS RELATIONSHIPS

Doesn't it strike you that business lunches are so common? It has been said that some of the most important business transactions have been written on napkins. Why is this? Breaking bread breaks barriers. It lubricates life. It is an expression of hospitality, of openness. We will break bread when we are serious about breaking barriers. We will invest our time, talent and treasure in that which we deem important. Are those whom God has placed in your sphere of life as important to you as they are to God? Are they as important to you as doing your next business deal?

BROKEN RELATIONSHIPS

There is no broken relationship for which the breaking of bread cannot assist in nurturing reconciliation. If the leaders of nations at odds with one another break bread to break barriers, why not you? The purer the motive, the more profound the message of the meal. The heart of the matter is the heart.

Are there broken relationships in your life? Perhaps you are estranged in some way or to some degree with a ministry colleague, a relative, a neighbor, a friend, a business associate—even with the Lord. Over the "communion cup," Paul exhorts, "Let a man examine himself, and so let him eat of that bread, and drink of that cup" (I Cor. 11:28).

The Blessedness of Eternal Bread

From the time God led His people out of Egypt, out of the house of bondage, into the Promised Land, He revealed Himself and His reconciling purposes in the breaking of bread. He began with unleavened bread.

The night before they were freed to pursue their relationship with God, on the way to Canaan, God instructed Moses to lead the people in a memorial feast. For seven days, the people were to break "unleavened bread," representing the need to be freed of sin that creates a barrier in our relationship with our heavenly Father (Ex. 12:14–20). Even the stranger who would be saved and blessed with Israel was required to break unleavened bread (Ex. 12:19). On the first day, they were to observe the memorial feast with the strangers who would join them. That feast, known as the "Feast of Unleavened Bread," was to be observed "forever" and throughout the generations until the final feast of reconciliation (Ex. 12:17–20).

We began this chapter with "the Lord's Supper." But that was not the final supper. Jesus, who had identified himself as "the bread of life" during his life, now, on the eve of His crucifixion, declared as He took the bread, "this is my body which is broken for you" (Luke 22:19). He instructed His disciples, "Take, eat." He then said we were to remember Him in the breaking of bread together, evidencing our reconciliation through Christ to God as a result of the Father's heart of hospitality, not willing that any should be excluded from His eternal table. All that was necessary for reconciliation and restoration to God's favor was to "eat" of Christ, to become "broken bread" with Him in reconciling the world, and to live a life of righteousness (unleavened bread), hating the sin that separates us from God.

But the best is yet to come! Just as the memorial Feast of Unleavened Bread was to conclude on the **seventh** day, after six days of man's obedience to rid the sin that separates from God and those created in His image (represented by leaven), even so, on the "seventh day" of creation, after six thousand years of God's redemptive work among men on earth, God the Father will hold a final and fulfilling supper for all of His ministers of reconciliation. It is called "The Marriage Supper of the Lamb." The "Lamb" is both the "lamb without blemish" and the "unleavened bread" of the great memorial feast for He declared himself to be "the Bread of Life" (John 6:35).

The "Bread of Life" now, in holy hospitality, bids all who will "eat of Him" to that great Wedding Supper. Will you join Him? To do so, you must, with Him, become "broken bread." The ultimate breaking of bread brings the ultimate blessing of breaking the ultimate barrier—eternal separation from the Father's home. Will you break bread with and be broken bread for others that they might be eternally blessed with God's amazing hospitality? It will require you to embrace, with God Himself, *The Power of Hospitality*. As it is written by our Lord Himself, "Blessed is he that shall eat bread in the Kingdom of God" (Luke 14:15).

If we would break bread together, we will break barriers together.

Heart-Opening Questions
for Personal and Group Reflection

Chapter 6

1. Why might it be said that "until we break bread together, we are virtual strangers?"

2. In what ways are we all strangers without Christ's hospitality?

3. Why do you think the Bible places such focus on Jesus breaking bread with people? On the surface, doesn't that seem somewhat mundane or even irrelevant?

4. In what way is "Communion" an expression of hospitality?

5. Do you see any ways in which the Church's practice of communion has been incomplete in either actual practice or understanding? How was communion intended to be an avenue for breaking barriers among Christians?

6. Why does breaking bread together break barriers? Do you have any such examples in your own life?

7. Do you believe breaking bread together can be an effective tool in breaking down racial barriers? Are you willing to give it a try? If not you, then who?

8. Can you see how our increased failure to break bread together as families has contributed to the estrangement of both spouses and children over the past generation? Has this happened in your family?

9. Why is "withness" so important for true and lasting ministry?

10. Can you see how breaking bread can be a powerful tool to pave the way in reaching people for Christ? What happens when we break bread with someone else?

Chapter 7

Hospitality Is Ministry

Take time to build significant

relationships so God can use

your life as a highway for

Himself to others.

HOSPITALITY IS THE HEART OF MINISTRY. Hospitality may well be one of the most misunderstood and most ignored essentials of Christian life. Hospitality is perhaps the quintessential requirement for all legitimate ministry outside empowerment by the Holy Spirit. It is so essential that the Apostle Paul twice declared that anyone aspiring to any level of oversight in the Body must be "given to" hospitality and be a "lover of hospitality." This chapter expands on hospitality as the heart of and the "grease that lubricates" all legitimate ministry to the unbeliever, the poor, the homeless, the oppressed, the single, the outcast, the divorced, the unwanted child, and even the immigrant.

Legitimate Ministry

Not all *ministry* that passes in the name of the Master is legitimate. This may seem to be a strong and all-encompassing statement, but we are increasingly convinced of its truth. Jesus declared in concluding His Sermon on the Mount, "Not everyone who saith unto Me, Lord, Lord, shall enter into the Kingdom of Heaven; but He that *doeth the will of My Father* which is in Heaven" (Matt. 7:21).

The Lord of the Church, then, became more explicit, stating: "Many will say to me in that day, Lord, Lord, have we not prophesied in thy name? And in thy name cast out devils? And in thy name done many wonderful works? And then I will profess unto them, I never knew you: depart from me, ye that work iniquity." Therefore whosoever heareth these sayings of mine, *and doeth them*, I will liken him unto a wise man...(Matt. 7:22–24).

When Jesus was asked by His disciples to give His prophetic summation of the end of the age, He chose to conclude His wooing and warning with words of hospitality, expressing His viewpoint of the heart of the Father as to the heart of legitimate ministry. Since Jesus declared He neither said anything He did not hear the Father say, nor did anything He did not see the Father do (John 5:19-30), His words given just a couple of days before His crucifixion should have particular significance. Here they are:

> I was an hungered, and ye gave me meat: I was thirsty, and ye gave me drink: I was a stranger, and ye took me in: Naked, and ye clothed me: I was sick, and ye visited me: I was in prison, and ye came unto me (Matt. 25:35–36).

Then those professing Christians and ministers on His left hand will say, "Lord, when saw we an hungered, or athirst, or a stranger, or naked, or sick, or in prison, and *did not minister unto thee?*" (Matt. 25:44). The Scripture then records Jesus' troubling words:

Inasmuch as ye *did it not* unto the least of these, ye *did it not* to me. These shall go away unto everlasting punishment, but the righteous into life eternal (Matt. 25:45-46).

The Apostle James, the brother of our Lord, seemed to grasp the essence of Jesus life, ministry, and view of legitimate ministry, declaring bluntly,

Pure religion and undefiled before God and the Father is this, To visit the fatherless and widows in their affliction, and to keep himself unspotted by the world.

Be ye doers of the word, and not hearers only, deceiving your own selves" (James 1:27, 22).

The heart of the Gospel seems to require a visceral connection with a man's or woman's heart that reveals itself in outward ministry connecting tangibly with the heart and life of others. It is not a mantra of religious facts but a message of relational fellowship. A restored relationship with God will necessarily reveal itself in restored relationships with others, except when the Lord is rejected and rebellion against God is transferred to His messenger.

Creeds are religious scripts that attempt to distill essential "gospel" facts. They are important to keep nomadic Christians on mental track. But they are almost always inadequate to express the heart of a reborn relationship with God that manifests itself in hospitality from the heart. A creedal faith is not a credible faith, either with God or with a skeptical and unbelieving world. Both Jesus and James made this fact abundantly clear. While we are not saved by works but by faith (Eph. 2:8–9), neither is there legitimate faith without works (James 2:14–26). God is not impressed with the ritualistic works of a ritualistic faith rooted in intellectualized creeds however well intended; neither is a numbed and desensitized world starving for legitimate relationship with a legitimate God. The world must see sons and daughters who legitimately represent God their Father with works of righteousness that reveal true inward regeneration. The gospel will again become good news when it both leads us in reconciliation to Father God through repentance of sin AND leads us to reconcile and be reconciled with others through a heart of holy hospitality.

Lifelessness and emptiness characterizes much alleged ministry because it is creedally motivated rather than credibly motivated by hospitality from the heart. Capturing the difference will transform the ministry of most Christians and congregations. It will provide open vision for restoring the city-wide church and open new doors to the healing of our cities. It will transform our homes. It will remove a veil from our eyes, opening entirely new and refreshing perspectives on "reaching people for Christ." It will provide a tangible handle to agape love, enabling us to truly "speak the truth in love." It will restore credibility to our creeds and righteousness to our religion and relationships.

Transmitting and Translating Good News

The good news of the Gospel is *transmitted* by the lips, but *translated* by the life. "Actions speak louder than words," we are told. We believe this as a truism, but seldom practice it in truth.

The statistical revelations from secular and spiritual sources alike confirm that there is little behavioral difference between the professing Christian and the unbeliever in our modern, compartmentalized world where faith flies on Sunday and the fun flies on Monday. Pollsters George Gallup and George Barna report a growing religious spirit betrayed by increasingly unrighteous lives from the Church House to the White House. Religious pluralism rules in a land where individualism reigns. The inexorable march of democracy long ago supplanted the inviolable Word of God. And the Gospel of "Constitutional Conservatism" waging culture wars has overshadowed the Gospel of crucifixion with Christ in spiritual and eternal wars. In such an environment, how does one, or a congregation, effectively and credibly transmit and translate truth?

The Master's Message and Method

Jesus had just been baptized in water and by the Holy Spirit. He returned from the Jordan River and was immediately confronted by forty days of temptation in the wilderness. Luke records, "Jesus returned in the power of the Spirit," "full of the Holy Ghost" (Luke 4:1, 14); began fleshing out the faith of God; and declared a mission statement encapsulating his life message:

> The Spirit of the Lord is upon me, because he hath anointed me to preach the gospel to the poor; he hath sent me to heal the brokenhearted, to preach deliverance to the captives, and recovering of sight to the blind, to set at liberty them that are bruised, to preach the acceptable year of the Lord (Luke 4:18-19).

Did you notice that five of the six items Jesus expressly mentioned that defined his ministry required relationship with people estranged from the prevailing society, either by practice or by perception? They were seen to be estranged from both God and those created in God's image—strangers. From God the Father's perspective, we all fit that description regardless of pride, power, prosperity, or position for "all have sinned, and come short of the glory of God" (Rom. 3:23). The words framing Jesus' message are critical to understanding how the message had to be communicated. The message required relationship to reveal its truth. It had to be both transmitted and translated. It had to be *fleshed out*. For this reason, the Apostle John described Christ's ministry in these beautiful and simple relational words:

> *The Word was made flesh, and dwelt among us*, and we beheld his glory, the glory as of the only begotten of the Father, full of grace and truth (John 1:14).

Jesus' *method* to deliver the Father's *message* of restoration, reconciliation, and regeneration was to *flesh it out*, to live it out, to translate the "Word" in behavioral and relational form. God could have sent a flying scroll; but instead, He sent a suffering servant who could be "touched with the feeling of our infirmities," be "in all points tempted like as we are," yet be "without sin" (Heb. 4:15). The Gospel is a relational Gospel and must be communicated relationally. It was the Father's heart of hospitality that opened His hand to send forth His only begotten Son in the fulness of time to men estranged from Him in an unpleasant and ungodly planet that we might be invited to join Him in His home. As Jesus declared,

> In my Father's house are many mansions [rooms]. I go
> to prepare a place for you. And I will come again and
> receive you...that where I am, there ye may be also
> (John 14:2–3).

Until the sons and daughters capture the heart of the Father's hospitality, we will remain woefully inadequate in communicating His heart to others. The message of salvation has little to do with the quoting of a creed, but it has everything to do with a heart connection that fleshes out the Truth. Henry Blackaby put it thus: "Take time to build significant relationships so God can use your life as a highway for Himself to others."

The heart of the Gospel is the Father's heart of hospitality, revealed in the life of His only begotten Son and to be fleshed out in adopted sons who profess His name. This does not call for a touchy-feely faith or abandonment of truth but for fulfillment of rhetorical truth in relational reality. It must become a reality before the Father can receive us into His home. The Father's heart of hospitality must be manifest in our "reaching people for Christ" before Christ can return for His Church. The Bride must become like Him, revealing the Father's heart of hospitality. We will then fully see *The POWER of Hospitality* and its fruit.

Marketing vs. The Master's Method

Hospitality is God's revealed method for communicating His heart. But the American church has substituted *marketing* for God's ordained *method* of reaching the lost. We have become adept at substitutionary ministry, finding modern alternatives to the Divine mandate.

Marketing, by its very nature, always modifies the message, tweaking and twisting truth to conform to the marketer's perception of what the broadest spectrum of the public will "buy." The edges of hard truth are cut away as "unmarketable." The message of the Cross, of being crucified with Christ and of forsaking all, are not perceived by evangelistic marketers as palatable or salable to the fickle feelings of the masses whom we have fed with a steady diet of "gos-pills" rather than the gospel. Modern church marketing has largely inoculated the nation to the truth and heart of the gospel message.

There are several underlying reasons why marketing undermines God's ordained method. Consider how marketing is clearly contrasted with the ministry of hospitality.

1. Marketing offers a *message*; Hospitality offers a *person* and a relationship.
2. Marketing reports a *version* of truth; Hospitality reveals through relationship a *vision* of truth.
3. Marketing proceeds from the *head*; Hospitality proceeds from the *heart*.
4. Marketing is *manipulative*; Hospitality is truth *massaged* in and through relationship.
5. Marketing is *heresay witness,* lacking credibility; Hospitality is *percipient* witness, lovingly credible.
6. Marketing begins with "*hype*" leading to *hyp-ocrisy*; Hospitality is holy, leading to *holistic* living.
7. Marketing is premised on a *lure*; Hospitality is premised in *love*.
8. Marketing offers a *form* of faith; Hospitality *fleshes out* the faith.

9. Marketing is rooted in *insincerity* and twisting the truth; Hospitality is rooted in *sincerity* and in truth.
10. Marketing is directed to the *masses*; Hospitality is directed to a *man* and his family.

If we would restore the Master's method, we would more closely approximate the Master's results. Virtually all of Jesus' "outreach" was directed to individuals through relationship. He invited Himself to abide at sinner Zaccheus' house, to which the despised tax collector responded in repentance, "the half of my goods I give to the poor." Jesus declared, "This day is salvation come to this house" (Luke 19:1–10). Jesus touched the lives of men and women one-on-one, not for public consumption or display. We so often attempt to touch people *publicly* and hope it will take effect *privately*. Ours is often a spiritually reversed method that does not bring the desired or lasting spiritual results. We really don't trust the Master's method.

Although Jesus ministered *privately* in holy hospitality, His converts proclaimed the message through their lives *publically*. Jesus tried to keep them quiet, but they hollered the louder. We try to make our converts holler, but they are largely quiet. Hospitality is the heart of legitimate ministry and will reveal its legitimate fruit. Dare the American mind trust the Master's method in an age when we have convinced ourselves that bigger is better and that ministry to the masses is the preferred method? As it is written, "By their fruits ye shall know them" (Matt. 7:20).

Homogeneous Groupings vs. Hospitable Gospel

Have you noticed how we try to bring people to Christ by dividing them, and then after they make a confession of faith, we divide them again? While referred to as "homogeneous grouping," this unbiblical model passes under many euphemisms and rationales, but is motivated fundamentally by a lack of hospitality. We have "sold it" on the basis that "it works" or is "more convenient," but there is no

New Testament support for such division in the name of Christ. Our aphorism says "Birds of a feather flock together," but why is that? Could it be largely because the hearts of others are perceived to be closed rather than open? This matter of hospitality has vast ramifications for the way we "do church" and the way we think about ministry.

THE SINGLE PERSON

We have established singles ministries to lure people to Christ and to keep them "in the body" once they have professed faith in Christ. But why do we do that? The *why's* of ministry and our lives are every bit as important as, and perhaps more so, than the *what's* or the *how's*.

It is said that singles feel uncomfortable around married couples and married couples feel uncomfortable with singles. But why? We can and do compile a raft of reasons from a psychological or sociological viewpoint why singles should be separate, but seldom, if ever, will one hear a truly spiritual or biblical justification other than "it works" to help us evangelize. This, however, is the argument of pragmatism rather than principle.

Why does single separation seem to "work" to accomplish our particular ministry objective? Is it not because our hearts are really not open to one another in genuine hospitality? Singles feel like "strangers" in the Body because married folk do not reach to them. Married folk feel like strangers with singles, because they perceive singles as being estranged from the folksy flow of fellowship. Singles, then, are separated into singles enclaves within the broader Body or congregation to protect and preserve the fleshly comfort of both singles and couples. This segregation only reinforces the underlying spiritual "dysfunction" that divided them in the first place. It appears to "work" only because it provides a measure of temporal comfort, yet it ignores and forever frustrates the eternal purpose of holy hospitality that would bring the Body into oneness.

Furthermore, singles separateness fosters and exacerbates the spiritual and relational challenges that singles face and deprives couples of the spiritual opportunity to reach in genuine love and hospitality to open heart and home to unmarried members of the Body. It is a travesty perpetuated by pragmatism in the name of "The Truth" that actually perverts the truth while enabling all of us to hide from God's mandate to give ourselves to hospitality. "House-to-house" ministry, book-of-Acts style, is the New Testament model for folding the entire Body into effective and fully-functioning fellowship where everyone is needed, wanted, and built up in relationship with one another and in Christ, our mutual Head. Anything other than following the biblical model, regardless of rationale, must be seriously questioned as counterfeit.

OUR CHILDREN

The United States Congress decreed 1979 to be "The Year of the Child." One wonders if it was not an "In Memorium." Since then, children have increasingly ruled and reigned while parents have reneged. Lip service has replaced life involvement. Pop football, T-ball, soccer and ballet have replaced family fellowship.

The same patterns have infiltrated ministry models. Of course, good rationales always exist, but most of them are born of pragmatism rather than principle. Seldom do we stop to evaluate either the long-range consequences to family and faith or the fundamental heart thoughts and conditions that motivate or provide the environment in which we can so easily isolate our children from the most essential elements and relationships comprising what we euphemistically refer to as "the work of the church" or "the fellowship of believers."

Why do we banish our children into homogeneous ghettos, relegating their development of spiritual vision to child models? Is it for their benefit, or for ours? Is it because they somehow defile our desire for personal peace? Is it because we don't want to invest ourselves in them sufficiently to train them in self-discipline and respect so that they can listen attentively in an adult world? Is it because we do not really believe they should occupy valuable seats that could be provided to adults who "are really the focus of our ministry" and who may put more in the collection plate? Do we believe our children are a valuable and viable part of "the Church of TODAY," or do we promise them a place only in "the Church of TOMORROW"? The chosen

Twelve, Jesus' own disciples, were plagued with this problem of a closed heart toward the "heritage of the Lord," our children. The children were troubling to them. They got in the way of what the disciples perceived to be real ministry, and "when Jesus saw it, He was much displeased" (Mark 10:13–14).

Jesus responded with a simply profound and profoundly simple observation on the Kingdom of God from God's viewpoint. We would do well to consider its profound implications.

> Suffer the little children to come unto me [in the midst of adult ministry] and forbid them not: for of such is the Kingdom of God. Whosoever shall not receive the Kingdom of God as a little child, he shall not enter therein (Mark 10:14–15).

At root, these are heart questions. Could it be that our hearts are really not as open to our children as we like to believe? Could it be that much of our practice and philosophy of both life and ministry has increasingly relegated our beloved children to roles of virtual strangerhood? Having removed their real-life exposure from the reality of normal adult life where dads and disciples become heros of holiness, we cast them into the playpen with their peers, where they embrace either peers or prominent sports or music celebrities as their prophets. Perhaps one of the most healing things that pastors and parents could do in our generation is to sincerely pray for a renewed heart of hospitality for our children. We must not pander to them, but prepare them. If we would revise our plans, practices and philosophies to truly fold them into our lives collectively and individually today, we might not have to reach to them tomorrow as strangers in drug dens, abortion clinics, homosexual clubs, and prisons as they tumble toward the eternal abyss.

THE GOSPEL—MAKING OUTSIDERS INSIDERS

There are undoubtedly few glitches in our Gospel greater than that of making outsiders into Kingdom insiders. Making *outsiders* into *insiders* is an assault against a human nature that craves to be comfortable. Yet Jesus framed the essence of His "gospel" ministry around that very purpose. "The Spirit of the Lord God is upon me," He said, "because he hath anointed me

>...to preach the gospel to the poor;
>...to heal the brokenhearted,
>...to preach deliverance to the captives, and recovering of sight to the blind,
>...to set at liberty them that are bruised,
>...to preach the acceptable year of the Lord" (Luke 4:18–19).

How does Jesus' call as the "only begotten son" connect with our call as sons and daughters to fold outsiders into the family of faith? If we have the *mind* of Christ, do we also have the *heart* of Christ? Am I reaching with open heart, open hand, and open home to those whom my Lord embraced as the central focus of His ministry?

The Immigrant

The immigrant is usually a social outcast, a societal misfit, received by government (if legal) but rejected by the good people of the land. As a people, we revel in Emma Lazarus' words engraved on the Statue of Liberty: "Give me your tired, your weary, your huddled masses yearning to breathe free," but the promised "lamp beside the open door" can usually be found only by those bold enough to break down the door. Our "open-door" policy is more frequently a closed-heart polity. This compels the ostracized to become ghetto-ized as "birds of a feather" once again flock together to bear one another's burdens in a world of rejection. What would Jesus do? What is God's heart for the immigrant? Is this a place for hospitality from the heart by those whose hearts are reborn in Christ? Three thousand years of Jewish history reveal a just answer. Hospitality is reaching to strangers. When God delivered Israel from Egypt, He commanded them to deal well with the stranger in their midst—those who were not Hebrew or Jewish, who were not the sons of Abraham by blood.

The stranger in Israel in those days was akin to the immigrant in our day. America is a nation of immigrants. The early immigrants, in large measure, shared a common spiritual vision and worshiped a common Lord. They birthed what has been called the "American Vision" that produced what we now extol as the "American Dream." Now, despite flag-waving rhetoric proclaiming the indestructible dream, a decade of statistics reveal that the dream is unraveling. How did it happen? The dream was built on a vision, and the "American Vision" has all but vanished.

A vacuum of holy hospitality has had a profound impact in precipitating and promoting the vanishing vision. The insidious growth of the spirit of individualism noted by French political and social observer, Alexis de Tocqueville, relegated immigrants to fend for themselves, to create their own culture, to band together to build their own identity, to serve their own gods, and to create their own vision. As a nation, we offered them citizenship to benefit from their time, talent and treasure, but we did not impart the vision. The Church did not have a vision of holy hospitality to reach to the stranger as the hand of Christ extended. The cry of culture has now replaced the call of Christ, and *TIME* reports, "In so many gods we trust."

At the close of the Old Testament, the prophet Malachi gives the warning of God's attitude and response toward those who do not embrace the stranger...

> I will come near to you in judgment; and I will be a swift
> witness against...those...that turn aside the stranger from
> his right and fear not me, saith the Lord. I am the Lord, I
> change not. Return unto Me and I will return unto you
> (Malachi 3:5–7).

Could it be that turning our hearts as God's heart toward the immigrant might have a catalytic effect of turning God's heart toward the healing of our land? Imagine what the affects might be for turning the hearts of immigrants toward "the God who hath made and preserved us a nation."

THE POOR

It is inescapable that Christ declared His first calling of ministry was to the poor (Luke 4:18). It is not that Jesus' heart was not open to the rich, the middle class, or the "beautiful people," for we have record of His personal encounters with the "rich young ruler," Nicodemus the lawyer, and Zacchaeus the tax collector. But the poor were prominent in the Lord's eyes. Why is that?

1. The Stranger Issue
   God abhors strangerhood. It is the Creator's intent and desire that none of His creation be estranged from Him or from one another. He created us for fellowship with the Father and with our fellows. It is not the Creator but our carnal nature that countenances class consciousness.

2. The Image Issue
   In the beginning, "God created man in His own image," and after His own "likeness" (Gen. 1:26–27). Class distinction displayed either in action or attitude destroys God's creative design and deprecates His creative intent. When we reach to the poor, we most closely approximate the heart of the Father, for "Inasmuch as you have done it unto the least of these my brethren, you have done it unto me" (Matt. 25:40). This is the true ministry of "inclusion." James, our Lord's brother, derided those who gave preferential treatment to the prominent while pushing aside the poor. "If ye have respect of persons," he warned, "ye commit sin, and are convinced of the law as transgressors" (James 2:1–9).

3. The Openness Issue
   The prominent are characteristically prevented by pride, power, and position from receiving a message of salvation requiring that one come humbly "as a little child" (Mark 10:13–16). Jesus' own disciples were specifically rebuked for their partiality, and

"when Jesus saw it, He was much displeased" (Mark 10:14). The poor, by contrast, have nothing of power or prominence to lose and can more readily perceive their need of redeeming love and forgiveness.

When God retained His prophets to decree His righteous cause to the covenant people who had forsaken His ways, they measured the extent to which the people individually and collectively displayed God's truth in these primary areas of life. The defining questions were as follows:

How do you treat My Sabbath?
How do you treat your spouse?
How do you treat the poor?

So, how do you measure up? How does your congregation line up with God's plumb line? What would the Father require of you?

THE UNBELIEVER

The unbeliever is estranged from God and His "household of faith." If the unbeliever would embrace life in our Lord, he must first see God's heart of hospitality revealed in the living witness or example of His servants. While it is wonderful to display welcoming greeters at our church doors as a gesture of organizational hospitality, God is more interested that we display His heart of hospitality all week long at the door of our own hearts and homes. This will almost always be reflected in what we do with our hands—the practical, tangible touching of people's lives that makes credible our creeds.

THE FAMILY FIASCO

The American family is desperately estranged. Husbands and wives are estranged. Parents are estranged from their children. What is driving this epidemic of estrangement? We could point to many contributors and causes, but when all has been said, the American family portrait reveals hyper-individualism bent on self and self-fulfillment.

We have sold ourselves to SELF-ishness, and our hearts are not even open to our own flesh. Selfishness is not a problem primarily resident among unbelievers. Professing Christians now display selfishness as a veritable art form wrapped in a religious cloak. Consider again that the divorce rate among "born-again" Christians exceeds the national average by four percent. And the rate at which men and women divorce their spouses in America's "Bible Belt" exceeds that of the nation by FIFTY percent (per the *Barna Report* and Rutgers University report, *The State of Our Unions*).

These statistics are so staggering that most pastors and their people have chosen to either ignore or deny them. Clearly, the "Christian" heart in America has become calcified. Certainly it has not been crucified with Christ. Godly hospitality cannot flow to and through our families when the spiritual pipelines are occluded by the sludge of selfishness. The flow of holy hospitality is so impaired that the collective heart of the American family is suffering a massive coronary infarction threatening the very existence of what we euphemistically call "the basic building block of society." We are hiding ourselves from our own flesh even as we increasingly "walk in the flesh."

Abortion, nearly as prevalent among Evangelicals as in the outside world, is a reflection of not only promiscuity but of our flagrant rejection of our own flesh to preserve personal happiness. Growing homosexuality and lesbianism likewise is largely a consequence of men and women rejecting their sons and daughters, either in attitude and daily practice or through divorce. As it is written, " the curse causeless shall not come" (Proverbs 26:2).

These heart-rending realities reveal our most essential ministry calling for *The POWER of Hospitality*. Hospitality must begin at home. I must open my heart, my hand, and my home to my spouse, to my children (born and unborn), and to my grandchildren. This is ministry that matters. It matters so much that Creator God, the one whom we declare as our Father, declares that the very destiny of the nation will be determined by our decision to open our hearts in holy hospitality.

Destiny and Divine Hospitality

God is speaking. He spoke to Israel through Isaiah, and so He speaks also to the Church in America, those who claim His covenant. "Cry aloud, spare not, lift up thy voice like a trumpet, and show My people their transgressions...."

Here is God's viewpoint of the "covenant people." "They seek Me daily." It's as if they "delight to know My ways, as a nation that *did* righteousness." "They ask of Me." Yes and "they take delight in approaching to God." They even fast, yet they say of Me "thou seest not" and "thou took no knowledge" (Isaiah 58:1–3). This is our precise condition among professing Christians in America, having cried out to the Lord of Nations for spiritual revival since our nation's bicentennial. What is God's remedy? It is to restore the foundational ministry of hospitality. Listen to the Father's own words:

> Is this not the fast that I have chosen?
> 1. To loose the bands of wickedness.
> 2. To undo heavy burdens.
> 3. To let the oppressed go free.
> 4. To break every yoke.
> 5. *To deal your bread to the hungry.*
> 6. *To bring the poor to your house.*
> 7. *To cover and clothe the naked.*
> 8. *To "hide not yourselves from your own flesh"* (Is. 58:6–7).

Now, here is what God says will happen if an individual, family, congregation, or nation will agree with Him and practice the ministry of holy hospitality. It is one of the most beautiful and bountiful promises of all Scripture. "If thou draw out thy soul to the hungry, and satisfy the afflicted soul...

"THEN...

There will be changes in your circumstances.
- Your light shall rise from obscurity.
- Your darkness shall be as noonday.
- You shall call, and the Lord shall answer.

There will be changes in your life.
- The Lord will guide you continually.
- The Lord will satisfy you in drought.
- The Lord will make you like a watered garden.
- The Lord will make your life a spring of water.

There will be changes in your ministry effectiveness.
- You shall build the old waste places.
- You shall raise up the foundations of many generations.
- You shall be called a repairer of the breach.
- You shall be a restorer of paths to dwell in.

Promises do not come much better than these to individuals, families, congregations, or nations. Here is real hope rooted in holy hospitality. Are you beginning to catch God's vision for hospitality? Now we can begin to understand why the Apostle Paul decreed the most essential requirement for anyone in ministry leadership is to be "given to hospitality" (I Tim. 3:2). Salvation may be our fundamental *message*, but hospitality is our foundational *method*.

Our families, congregations, and entire nation are yearning to see a divine display of holy hospitality. Destiny rides in the balance. Let's prepare the way of the Lord for the Second Coming by displaying *The POWER of Hospitality* revealed through His first coming. Hospitality is ministry.

Heart-Opening Questions
for Personal and Group Reflection

Chapter 7

1. Can you see how and why "hospitality is the heart of ministry?" Take a moment to describe why this is true.

2. If that which purports to be "ministry" is missing the very "heart," is it truly legitimate? Or does it become somewhat artificial, at best seriously lacking, and at worst, counterfeit? Consider a body without its heart, consider the Church without its Head (Christ), and consider ministry without Christ's heart of hospitality.

3. How did Jesus' method of reaching the lost compare with our most common methods? In what ways does John 1:14 reveal God's method of hospitality in reaching a world estranged by sin?

4. In what ways does *marketing* become an artificial substitute for the Master's *method?*

5. In what ways have ministry methods, policies, and programs been affected or determined by a lack of vision for and practice of hospitality?

6. How does the Gospel turn *outsiders* into *insiders?*

7. Why are we not more motivated to minister to the poor in our own country?

8. How is the divorce rate significantly driven by lack of *The POWER of Hospitality* among professing Christians?

9. How is the ministry of hospitality connected to being a doer of righteousness?

10. What does God promise will happen in your life if you actively practice hospitality?

Open Heart, Open Hand, Open Home

Use hospitality

one to another

without grudging.

(I Peter 4:9)

AN OPEN HAND REFLECTS AN OPEN HEART. Show me a man with a closed hand, and I will show you a man with a closed heart. It is indeed a strange phenomena that the hand is morally and spiritually connected to the heart. For this reason, Jesus warned, "Where your treasure is, there will your heart be also" (Matt. 6:21).

Hospitality is practical. It allows our faith to find a tangible connection with people in ways that allow our lives to be an earthly connecting link to the very heart of God. Because hospitality provides this "tangible" connection in the life of others, it usually requires a tangible expression from our own life resources. These resources include our time, our talents and our treasure.

Hospitality Is To Be Used

Peter, James and John seemed to enjoy a more intimate relationship with Christ than the other disciples. Jesus chose to confide in them and reveal Himself to them in greater measure than to the others. Peter gives us a measure of insight into the role of hospitality not otherwise expressed in the Scriptures. Consider his words:

> Forasmuch as Christ hath suffered for us in the flesh, arm yourselves therefore with the same mind: That he no longer should live the rest of his time in the flesh to the lusts of men, but to the will of God.

> The end of all things is at hand: Above all things have fervent charity among yourselves: **use hospitality one to another without grudging** (I Peter 4:1,2,7–9).

Did you notice Peter's use of the word *use?* The word *use*, a verb in this passage, is perhaps one of the most practical, down-to-earth expressions in the Bible. It seems to convey an understanding that hospitality is important not only as a heart expression but also because it is a kingdom tool God has given to us to assist in accomplishing other Kingdom purposes. Some of those purposes we have already discussed, and others remain for our review. Because it flows from the heart, hospitality (as a tool) is not manipulative but is a practical manifestation of both God's work in a person's heart and of His desire and intent to use us as practical expressions of His heart in interactions with those who are made in His image.

Since hospitality flows from the heart of God to His creatures who have been converted to the mind of Christ and are walking according to His Spirit, if you and I are to **use** hospitality, it will necessarily require that the time, talents, and treasure God has entrusted to us be employed and marshaled for the task of hospitality. Therefore, for hospitality to be fully operational, requires conversion of mind, conviction of heart, and spiritual conscription of material resources for accomplishing Kingdom purposes.

When Peter prefaces his call to *use* hospitality with the statement "the end of all things is at hand," it seems clear that he envisioned the practical use of our time, talent, and treasure through hospitality as an essential part of the end-time mission of the end-time Church. Let's explore, then, considerations related to these 3T's so essential to our using or doing hospitality. To do so, we must first look at the matter of *ownership*.

Open-Hearted Stewardship

Who owns your home? To whom are you accountable for your time? What rights do you claim to your bank account or to the fruit of your labors at the shop, the law office, or with the congregation? The easy answer is that "God owns everything." But does He? Would God's heavenly accountancy firm, auditing your time, talent and treasure, determine your use of resources, which you attest belong to God, were actually used for Kingdom purposes? How much is devoted to holy hospitality, without which no man or woman can rightfully claim any level of oversight or leadership in the Body?

Hospitality has not been seen as a heavenly mandate and has therefore received little of heaven's resources. Yet hospitality is foundational to all legitimate ministry. Hospitality is not *only* a matter of the *heart* but is also a matter of the *hand* and the *home*. The good intentions of the heart will never materialize into meaningful ministry without marshaling the resources entrusted to us. This marshaling of resources is called *stewardship*.

A steward is one who marshals the resources of someone else for the purposes for which the resources have been entrusted by the true owner. Since we have already admitted that God is the true owner, we actually own nothing. The more modern term for *steward* is *trustee*. For those who are born again by the Spirit of God, we are crucified with Christ (Gal. 2:20), we are dead (Col. 3:3), and dead men own nothing. "I count all things but loss for the excellency of the knowledge of Christ." (Phil. 3:7–8). I am but a steward or trustee of God's Kingdom resources entrusted to me. And "it is required in stewards that a man be found faithful" (I Cor. 4:2).

This matter of stewardship is of substantial end-time significance. Jesus chose three parables to present the Kingdom concept of how we are to see the resources entrusted to us to be used in anticipation of His Second Coming. He shared those with His disciples from the Mount of Olives a couple of days before His crucifixion. Each of these is an application of Kingdom stewardship defining readiness for Christ's return. You can find them in Matthew 25.

Some scholars refer to the middle parable, verses 14 through 30, as the *Parable of the Talents*. In reality, it is a parable or story illustrating stewardship. Jesus begins,

> The Kingdom of Heaven is as a man traveling into a far country, who called his own servants, and **delivered unto them his goods** (Matt. 25:14).

The rest of the parable reveals God's expectations of you and me with regard to the time, talent, and treasure He has entrusted to us for the advancement of His Kingdom. Jesus concludes, after complimenting and rewarding those who faithfully used the trusted resources, by severely castigating the one who kept the resources to himself, consigning that "unprofitable servant into outer darkness," where there is "weeping and gnashing of teeth" (Matt. 25:30).

Stewardship is serious end-time business. Although hospitality begins in my heart, it must be manifested through my hand and my home. That requires that I reassess how I use the resources God has entrusted to me, be they great or small. "Unto whom much is given, of him much shall be required" (Luke 12:48). This truth demands open-hearted stewardship.

What are the resources God has entrusted to you? They fall into three broad categories: time, talent and treasure.

Time needs little explanation. Talents are my unique strengths and abilities, whether natural or developed. My treasure consists of all that is of a material nature under my hand and governance, including my home, furniture, automobiles, income and bank accounts. The little word *MY* has enormous import for whether we will *be* hospitable and, if so, to what extent that hospitality will reach.

Does My Viewpoint Agree With God's?

The Scriptures make clear that from God's viewpoint He owns everything. The question becomes, "Does my viewpoint agree with God's viewpoint?"

Few Christians would publically disagree in principle with God's claim that He owns everything, yet in private, our practices reveal profound disagreement. Perhaps no greater proof of this practical disagreement exists than in the area of Christian *"giving."* God called His covenant people to present the *first fruits* of their labors to Him and His service as a tithe. The tithe consisted of ten percent of their total produce or earnings. Israel disagreed in practice. They disagreed with God's claim to ten percent primarily because they, in their hearts, did not really believe God owned it all. So God warned them in the closing chapters of the Old Covenant,

> Will a man rob God? Yet ye have robbed me. But ye say, Wherein have we robbed thee? In tithes and offerings. Ye are cursed with a curse: for ye have robbed me, even this whole nation. Return unto me, and I will return unto you (Malachi 3:7-9).

Some contend that the tithe was abolished under the New Covenant and was replaced by the higher standard, "that God owns it all." Although no scriptural statement clearly authenticates such a change, it *is* clear that God ALWAYS owned it all, from His viewpoint. What is also clear is that the greater our prosperity, the less our collective conviction that God owns anything. Proof of this disconnect between principle and practice is that, in this moment of unprecedented prosperity, total giving by American Christians now hovers around 2-3 percent of gross income. Only seven percent of American Christians tithed in 2003. If God owns it all, one would never know it as demonstrated by the life practice of the majority of those who profess His name.

This very real revelation of reality has profound and practical application for our hospitality, as we shall see. But before we touch on that, let's allow God to remind us of His perspective.

THE OWNERSHIP PRINCIPLE

Principle #1 **God is owner of ALL (Ps. 50:10–12).**
Principle #2 **The earth is the Lord's (Ps. 24:1).**
   • No earthly power has valid claim (Ex. 9:29).
   • **ALL** the earth is God's (Ex. 19:5).
   • The land belongs to God. We are mere strangers and sojourners (Lev. 25:23).
   • All animals and livestock are God's (Ps. 50:10; 60:7; 89:11).
   • All gold and silver are God's (Hag. 2:8).
Principle #3 **The souls of all men are the Lord's (Ezek. 18:4).**
Principle #4 **The souls of the saints are the Lord's (I Cor. 6:19).**
Principle #5 **The Lord owns all; His followers cannot claim any (Luke 14:33).**

THE STEWARDSHIP PRINCIPLE

Principle #1 **The Kingdom is a trusteeship (Matt. 25:14–15).**
   • Body and spirit are held in trust (I Cor. 6:20).
   • Truth is held in trust (I Tim. 6:20).
   • Gifts and talents are held in trust (I Pet. 4:10).
   • Words are held in trust (Matt. 12:36).
   • Material wealth is held in trust (Luke 19:15).
Principle #2 **A steward (or trustee) must be found faithful (I Cor. 4:2).**
Principle #3 **All will give account to God (Rom. 14:12).**

Note the pattern. The Old and New Covenants are consistent. The Torah, Wisdom Literature, Prophets, Gospels and Epistles all confirm not only that God owns everything in the "Church Age" but also that He has *always* owned everything. The New Covenant has changed nothing, except to increase responsibility to give beyond the tithe. The Old Testament confirms God's ownership of all. The New Testament, building upon that ownership, reveals more clearly and explicitly the profound responsibility of caring for and disbursing freely from the heart the assets belonging to God for Kingdom purposes.

Hospitality Is For Grownups

The tithe is only a test. It is a test of our trust. It is a test to determine whether we see ourselves as *owners* or as *trustees*. Do you pass the test? Tithing does not make you mature. It is merely a threshold test to see if you might be trusted with more. A legalistic tither who does not truly function as if all he has belongs to God is consigned to perpetual spiritual childhood. Tithing is a mere "right of passage" into trustee-hood.

A trustee is one who holds money or property that belongs to someone else to be used for the express purposes the other person (the owner) has designated. The Bible uses the term *steward* to describe this relationship. All that is under your dominion and control—your time, your talents, and your treasure—belongs to God. In reality, it is not *mine*, but His.

Understanding and practicing this principle moves a man or woman from the realm of immaturity to spiritual maturity. Two words are characteristic of every infant: *No* and *Mine*. These two words also describe the operational lifestyle of the majority of professing Christians in America today. We say "No" by disagreeing with our Heavenly Father on most points where His Word confronts our lives and culture, and we claim our rights to time, talents, and treasure, jealously grasping them as "Mine!" It's time for us to grow up. Hospitality is for grownups.

Kingdom Conduits

Hospitality will require you to gradually release what is *mine* and declare it, in practical ways, to be *thine*. Holy hospitality will be revealed in an open heart, an open hand and an open home. You will become a Kingdom conduit. You will become an unobstructed channel of God's blessing. Abraham, Father of the faithful, was blessed that he might be a blessing. And that is why God desires to bless you. Will you let Him? Will you become a Kingdom conduit? It will require release of your time, talents and treasure, holding them in trust for the Master's use. And you can be sure He will use them.

Time for Hospitality

Time is our most precious commodity. Without time, our talents and treasures become irrelevant. Time becomes more and more relevant and precious as we run out of it. And we are running out of time. The Apostle Peter reminds us, "the end of all things is at hand" (I Pet. 4:7). It is precisely because time is running out on history that hospitality finds its most holy mandate (I Pet. 4:9).

As time is running out on history, our own supply of time seems to be in increasingly short supply. Busyness has become a blight, and the constant cry is, "I don't have enough time." As a bumper sticker so aptly stated, "The hurrier I go, the behinder I get." So how do I release *my* time to become God's time when I seem to have no time?

A little perspective will help. Generally speaking, we all are given the same amount of time. Those created in God's image are given three score and ten years to fulfill His calling on our lives. Each of us is given seven days in each week, twenty-four hours in each day, and twelve months in each year. So the real issue is not whether I *have* time, but *what I do with the time I have*. If business men and women can make time count, how can I make my time count for the Kingdom?

"To every thing there is a season," writes the preacher, "and a time to every purpose under the heaven" (Eccl. 3:1). There is time for every work God has ordained for you and me to do. The reason it does not seem so is that we have co-opted *His* time as *our* time, doing things that are irrelevant and often even contrary to God's purposes. For this reason, Paul exhorts us to "walk circumspectly, not as fools but as wise,

> Redeeming the time, because the days are evil. Wherefore
> be ye not unwise but understanding what the will of the
> Lord is" (Eph. 5:15–17).

Just as time is our universal commodity, hospitality is our universal ministry. Both pastor and people alike are exhorted—yes, commanded—to give ourselves to hospitality. From this clear and foundational expression of God's will and eternal plan there is no escape. We must therefore readjust *our* time, because it is really *his* time, so that we might embrace and do His will in these final days of history.

Time is the greatest gift I can give, other than life itself. Most of us see our time as the very extension of ourselves. We are willing to sacrifice money to *save* time. In fact, many professing Christians and entire congregations would rather give money than time. Time means life involvement, and the unfortunate commentary on American life is that the spirit of individualism has caused us to become isolated from one another, depriving us of time with one another and our neighbor.

Time is an investment of myself. It reveals who and what is of true value. Do I value projects and programs, or the people they purport to serve? Do I value personal peace over the people in my family or congregation? Do I value professional pride, power, or position over the people in my life? I will invest my time in that which I truly value, and I will reap accordingly.

Jesus, the Lord of the Church, revealed what God the Father valued in His ministry method and model. He spent, by far, the majority of His limited ministry time on earth (only three-and-a-half years) with twelve chosen disciples. He chose twelve "that they should be *with* Him" (Mark 3:14). He did not cultivate crowds, but individuals. He was not concerned about public rejection, but about private relationships that would produce eternal Kingdom returns. Time was of the essence, and with a holy heart of divine hospitality, He invested His time accordingly. This is our model. There is no true hospitality without an open heart that extends the hand with the gift of time. The applications are endless.

OUR FAMILIES

1. Marital Relationships

Closed hearts that claim ownership to time have cost us dearly at the family level, particularly in our marriages. Husbands' hearts have not been open to wives, depriving them of relational time that is the very lifeblood of marital relationship. Women shrivel with the meager allocation of time eked out by husbands who claim ownership of their time. Husbands also suffer brokenness and deprivation as a result of wives who, pressing into the modern world, claim ownership of time to pursue their *place in the sun.*

Marriages topple without the lifeblood of time. Spouses become virtual strangers for lack of hospitality. With a divorce rate in the Church now exceeding that of the nation as a whole, our hearts clearly are not open. Neither are our hands and homes.

2. Parent-Child Relationships

As we advance closer to the end of the age, selfish claims of parents to ownership of time reveal hearts closed to children whom God ordained to rise up and call their parents "blessed." Instead of blessing came a curse. Precisely for this reason, God promised a prophetic voice in the Spirit of Elijah to rise up in these last days to "turn the hearts of the fathers to the children" (Mal. 4:5–6, Matt. 17:11). The Father is calling the fathers to reopen their hearts in holy hospitality to their sons and daughters, extending to them the gift of God's truth and their time.

3. Grandparent-Grandchild Relationships

Our children and grandchildren yearn for the quality and quantity time of Christian moms and dads, papas and nanas, who will invest themselves in them—"living messages" we will send into a world we ourselves will never see. Even secular prophets now decry through otherwise liberal media the tragic myth of *quality* time versus *quantity* time.

Grandparents have a grand opportunity to tender their time to grandchildren. Many, however, choose to forfeit this irreplaceable relational opportunity promising eternal returns with their grandchildren, choosing rather to squander precious time in pursuit of personal pleasure, chasing elusive peace in perpetual travel and tracking little white balls on golf greens. The artery that supplies the lifeblood of holy hospitality is occluded by the spirit of selfishness that is suffocating tender tots who yearn for grandpa's tender touch.

A heart of hospitality releasing true time from America's moms, dads, and grandparents to our children, in Jesus' name and for His Kingdom, could alone revolutionize the "land of the free" that is increasingly becoming only the "home of the brave." Until then, virtual strangerhood will continue to plague our sons and daughters. Consider prayerfully! If the "sins of the fathers" are indeed visited on the next generation, what is the hope for the next generation without a refreshing outpouring of holy hospitality in our generation? The hellish prospects should compel us in horror to open our hearts in hope. Will you be the first?

OUR NEIGHBORS

The pace of life seems to be accelerating. Privacy is an increasing priority. Wives and mothers who once chattered over backyard clothes lines now race in vans with rolled-up windows to get kids to ballet lessons and soccer matches. Garage doors close instantly behind vehicles driven by men panting for the privacy of their "castle." Never has the question "Who is my neighbor?" been more difficult to answer (Luke 10:29). Yet neighbors, starved for relationship with God and man, scream silently for someone who cares to break through the bondage of their treadmill existence with living water poured out of real relationship.

The neighborhood that was once the cultural cradle for common caring has increasingly become the incarnation of hyper-individualism. It is the place where the stressed out and burned out are now shut out from one another's lives. Is there an answer to this modern dilemma?

Perhaps the best hope for healing and restoration of relationship in such an environment is holy hospitality. It requires an open heart that opens both hand and home to people living around us who are, in reality, virtual strangers. But good intentions will not translate into the truth of tangible hospitality. Only our time will tell the tale of true intention. Your time will testify to the true condition of your heart. That's tough talk for these troubled times, isn't it? How would the God who gave us the Gospel as an expression of His heart of hospitality have us use our time to reach to neighbors who are estranged from Him? Your gift of time may turn the course of eternity for a neighbor.

Our Business and Ministry Colleagues

Rushing and relationships do not peacefully coexist. Technology seems not to create time but to crunch it. With cell phones glued to ears as we walk between offices and appointments, we barely have time to think, let alone talk. Heart-to-heart communication has been replaced by fax-to-fax or email-to-email. Even pastors substitute mechanics and methods for investment of time as we collectively hurtle past hurting hearts and fellow ministers hungry for relationship. Hope collapses over the cacophony of cell phones.

Email now threatens to destroy the last vestiges of relationship in our frantic frenzy to save time. Like anything else, email can be a legitimate servant or become a tyrannical master. Strapped into seats compelling us to time together, I shared conversation with a seat partner on a recent cross-country flight. The man identified himself as a neuro-chemist. I asked him how he communicated in such a world of hyper-specialization. He said it was tough but made tougher by technology.

His company was experiencing a severe breakdown in relationships. Tensions were mounting. The working atmosphere was stifling, and anger was flaring. They hired a consultant to study and advise. Ten thousand dollars and two days later, the consultant delivered a memo to corporate headquarters, "Get rid of intraoffice email." They did, and instantly relationships began again to flourish. Email is great for facts, but is a potentially destructive substitute for conversation. By extracting time, it often replaces the *heart* with pure *head*. Time and expense may be saved, but the cost may be destroyed relationships.

What do these things reveal? A loss of heart. The heart of the matter is still the heart. And hospitality begins with the heart. It allows me to consider people as made in God's image and not as objects to accomplish or further an agenda. Even pastors and parachurch leaders desperately need to give and receive the regular investment of relational time for other than organizational purposes. Time is not just to be saved but to be spent, not on projects but with people.

Jesus took time for tea. In the press of people, He chose to invest precious hours out of just three years of total available ministry time with a tax collector, a business man who evidenced a desire to be with Him. What would you have done? Salvation came to Zaccheus' house that day because of holy hospitality (Luke 19:1–9).

There is no substitute for time! Our time will tell the truth about the reality of our relationship with our God. Once a heart of hospitality grips you, entire new vistas of life investment and involvement will open before you. You will notice it first in the way you see people and in the way you spend "your" time.

Your Talents—A Holy Trust

My talents or unique abilities will often define or direct the manner in which I display hospitality. Talents are not "spiritual gifts" as defined in Scripture, whether motivational, ministry or manifestation gifts, although these could and may well play a part at times as we live out hospitality in its many applications. Rather, our talents are unique abilities that may be learned or acquired, or may be seemingly inherited or part of our natural makeup. They may be God-given or God-permitted, but they are, like everything in our lives, to be employed for Kingdom purposes.

Talents, like time, are a Kingdom trust. Use them, or you may lose them. But if you use them appropriately, expect that God will prosper them and cause your life to become progressively useful in His Kingdom. "A man's gift maketh room for him, and bringeth him before great men" (Prov. 18:16).

Jesus gave three end-time parables just before His crucifixion. One is referred to as "The Parable of the Talents" (Matt. 25:14–30). Jesus told this story to cement in our hearts for all time the seriousness of God's expectation that all that He has placed at our disposal is to be used to our best ability to advance His Kingdom purposes. Although the word *talent* in that parable is actually referring to money, the principle is universally applicable beyond money to our time and our abilities. From this parable we recall those wonderful words the Master gave to His faithful steward, "Well done, thou good and faithful servant" (Matt. 25:21).

What talents or unique abilities might you have to apply to the ministry of hospitality? Consider the following short list of examples applicable for men and women:

- A talent for interior decorating that makes people feel at home and welcome.
- A talent for landscaping that creates a restful and welcoming outdoor environment.
- A talent for telling stories that helps build relationships.
- A talent for cooking that makes people feel special, revealing that you care.
- A talent for yard maintenance that shows people you care for and respect them enough to provide a clean outdoor welcome without distractions.

- A talent for diagnosing and repairing vehicles that allows you to help your neighbor in a time of need to facilitate relationship.
- A talent for diagnosing and correcting computer problems that can help a neighbor as a means of building relationship.

Hospitality does not require any unique talent or ability. It is a matter of the heart. But any unique talent or ability you may have can meaningfully and sometimes dramatically increase the impact of your time and efforts.

Remember, your talents and abilities belong to God, not to you. Do not display them in pride but in humble service. It is not your talent that is on display but your heart, your heart of hospitality. Our homes, our yards, our church facilities are not for show but for service. People must feel welcome, but not overcome.

Use your talents and abilities as a Kingdom investment. Let God bring a return on that investment in due time. If you have talent "in the raw," develop it. To deny your talent is false humility and a rebuke of your Creator. Use it, or lose it. When you begin to allow your special abilities to be used in holy hospitality, it will have a transforming effect on your entire life. Begin today.

My Treasure—My Heart's Measure

All of us have treasure in some measure. Even the poorest American is rich in contrast to the vast majority of people worldwide. And God calls all, rich and poor, to holy hospitality.

Since hospitality is a matter of the heart, it does not depend on material things. Our treasure, however, can help translate hospitality in tangible ways that increase with the increasing measure of material resources. To whom much is given shall much be required (Luke 12:48).

Since hospitality is a matter of the heart, it will require a heart willingness to invest in other people a portion of the resources God has entrusted to me. It was truly liberating to begin to see how the resources in our hands could be used to bless others. It was not always so in my life, as head of the home. For the first ten years of our marriage, I saw myself and our family as a Kingdom reservoir. We gathered unto ourselves with little vision for others.

As God began to break through the closed door of my heart as husband and father, opening my eyes to others to unite with my wife's long-standing hope for hospitality, our life and family began to change. We discovered indeed that "happiness is a door opening outward." Our thinking began to change. A new vision opened to a whole new world and vista. We were shifting from the stagnant world of Kingdom reservoirs to the fresh water and flow of a Kingdom conduit. That is where power is generated.

We began to acquire resources with which we could bless others and facilitate hospitality in groups, both large and small. We redesigned our yard, both front and back, to create an atmosphere of peace and welcome. We invested in constructing a beautiful pavilion with an outdoor fireplace under which we could gather forty people to break bread with us. We decorated our home to offer a peaceful retreat and gathering place for people.

A local rental agency was selling out much of its stock, so we, as husband and wife together, invested in used china to serve fifty, purchased ten round tables and fifty white folding chairs. We gathered a variety of colored and white tablecloths, purchased outdoor lighting, gathered a plethora of decor items for ambiance, and, at every opportunity, invited people to gather both for relationship and ministry. It was exciting!

Our storage needs grew exponentially, but we rejoiced that others were blessed. Our time, talents, and treasure were being channeled in holy hospitality. I recently gave my wife two large chafing dishes for Christmas which I found at a substantially reduced price, enabling her to more efficiently provide warm meals to many. She was thrilled!

You will be thrilled, too, as you channel your time, talents and treasure into holy hospitality. But it begins with a seed sown in your heart. **Use of your treasure will be the truest reflection of your heart.** "For where your treasure is, there will your heart be also" (Matt. 6:21). "A good man out of the good treasure of the heart bringeth forth good things" (Matt. 12:35).

Begin small. Use what you have. Give of yourself. Let God unfold your own unique expression of His heart of hospitality. Let your home or apartment become known as a haven of hospitality. "There is a sore evil under the sun, namely, riches kept for the owners thereof to their hurt" (Eccl. 5:13). Become a Kingdom conduit, not a reservoir. Let God's power flow.

Without Grudging

Remember! If we truly belong to Christ and are crucified with Him, He owns it all. We are mere trustees, conduits of His blessing and provision flowing from a holy heart of divine hospitality. Therefore, hospitality must be given without grudging.

Why would we do hospitality grudgingly? Perhaps you have personal experience to recall here. I do. For years, as my wife periodically expressed her heart desire that we open our home in hospitality, I could only count the cost—lost valuable time, squandered talent, and wasted treasure—and to what purpose? Besides, I was quite content to preserve the peace of my place and did not need others invading my privacy. Furthermore, and quite frankly, I could not give of myself to others in this way. My heart was not open, so my hand and home were closed. Whenever I found myself pressured into such a position, I begrudged the hours, the dollars, and the energy expended. *I have more important ways to use my resources*, I thought.

Peter understood that this problem would paralyze the heart of hospitality. He knew selfishness and greed would explode exponentially the closer we would come to the end of the age. In fact, Peter's command to "use hospitality" follows directly his observation, "the end of all things is at hand" (I Pet. 4:7). The Apostle Paul, who told Timothy that anyone desiring leadership in the Church was to be "given to hospitality" (I Tim. 3:1–2), described to Timothy the perilous times of the last days in which "men shall be lovers of their own selves, covetous, lovers of pleasures more than lovers of God; having a form of godliness..." (II Tim. 3:1–5).

We are in those *last days*, and God is calling us to "hospitality **without grudging**" (I Pet. 4:9). He calls us to open hearts revealed in open hands and open homes that lead others to His open hand and open home. It will require new vision, understanding, and application of Kingdom stewardship.

The great Apostle Paul revealed God's Kingdom thinking about giving of ourselves, our time, our talents, and our treasure: "He which soweth sparingly shall reap also sparingly; and he which soweth bountifully shall reap also bountifully.

> Every man, according as he purposeth in his heart, so let
> him give; **not grudgingly, or of necessity**: for God loveth a
> cheerful giver" (II Cor. 9:6–7).

Giving is not a debt I owe; giving is a seed I sow. Hoarding is not holy. Hospitality is the heart of God. Let it be your heart as well. "And God is able to make all grace abound toward you; that ye, always having all sufficiency in all things, may abound to every good work" (II Cor. 9:8).

We began this chapter with Peter's exhortation to us, and we will conclude with the same words: **"Use hospitality one to another without grudging"** (I Pet. 4:9). Why are we to do this? It is an expression of fervent charity required of our Lord and as an expression of His heart because **"the end of all things is at hand"** (I Pet. 4:7).

Heart-Opening Questions
for Personal and Group Reflection

Chapter 8

1. How does an open hand reflect an open heart? Can your heart be truly open to others if your hand is not open to them?

2. Does it seem strange to think in terms of "using" hospitality?

3. Why do you think Peter speaks of "using" hospitality in the context of preparing for the end times?

4. Who owns your home, your car, your furniture, your money, your time? If a legal accounting of your use of these items was made by an independent auditor, would the auditor agree with your own assessment? Would God?

5. On a continuum of 1 to 10, with 1 being the least used and 10 being the most used for Kingdom purposes, rate yourself collectively on use of your home, car, furniture, money, talents and time as revealing God's ownership of these items.

6. For many, time has become their most precious commodity. How does the way you use your time reflect on whether you truly have a heart of hospitality?

7. Can you think of ways you might use your time to improve, heal and restore relationships in your family, neighborhood and place of employment?

8. What talents or abilities do you have that could be honed to be used effectively in the ministry of hospitality?

9. Why is the use of our treasure the truest reflection of our heart?

10. Many increasingly are convinced we are in the last days. Are you willing, as Peter exhorts, to use your time, talents and treasure to fulfill God's call to "hospitality without grudging" (I Pet. 4:9)?

Chapter 9

Think Hospitality

As a man thinketh

in his heart, so is he.

(Prov. 23:7)

HOSPITALITY MUST ENGAGE YOUR MIND after it issues from your heart. A few years ago, as I was being seated for lunch with a businessman at a restaurant on the East Coast, part of a national chain, my attention was arrested by a button worn by the hostess and all of the waiters and waitresses. It contained a single word, *Hospitaliano*. More recently another national chain of restaurants displayed the sign "I AM HOSPITALITY." The message was clear. These folks had *hospitality* on their mind. What was on their mind was displayed in their service.

A few years ago, I was drawn to a sign in the window of an auto parts store on the West Coast that read, "We SPEAK and STOCK

129

foreign car parts." I thought, *These people are serious about what they're doing. They not only "stock" parts; they "think" them and "speak" them.* The classic, however, was the name boldly lettered on the facade of a store renting party equipment and supplies: "Hospitality Inc." *What a name!* I thought *If only God's people could think like that. "Hospitality (Inc.)—in the name of Christ."* If we would be doers of hospitality, we must have hospitality on our minds.

Noah's Nuisance

Mr. and Mrs. Noah were engaged in business as usual. Life lurched on in the midst of a culture engulfed in wickedness and violence. People were eating and drinking, marrying and giving their children in marriage. Noah alone was righteous in his generation, and Jesus warned that as it was in the days of Noah, so will it be at the moment of His Second Coming (Matt. 24:37).

God put a thought in Noah's mind and heart. God said to Noah, "The end of all flesh is come…make thee an ark…" (Gen. 6:13–14). The ark was for people. It was to be a safe haven from the coming flood that would sweep everything in its path to eternal destruction.

Now Noah had never seen a flood. He may never have even seen rain. He was a family man, doing his best to live a godly life in the midst of a morally decaying world, focusing on his wife and family. But God expanded his vision with a single thought, a command: "Make thee an ark."

What a nuisance! Here was a totally disrupting enterprise to Noah's personal peace and family-focused tranquility. Can you imagine Noah's first reaction? *What a pain! Why do I have to put all this time and effort into building this monstrosity of a boat? This is way beyond what I need for my family!*

Apparently, God intended for all those who were righteous or who would repent of their wicked ways to find a safe haven of hospitality in the end, for the Apostle Peter notes that God saved Noah, "a preacher of righteousness" (II Pet. 2:5). Why would Noah preach righteousness during the many years it took him to build the ark if God's heart was not to receive others into the ark? Yet no one responded. So God, Himself, "shut him in" (Gen. 7:16). But it took years of preparation before that day, cutting and hauling timber, preparing pitch, and gathering provisions.

Noah most likely would never have been able to build an ark if he had not come to "think hospitality," for God looks on the heart. Jesus would never have built an "ark" of His flesh, suffering obedience to death on the cross, if He had not come to "think hospitality," for He declared, "I go to prepare a place for you"(John 14:2). Without the first ark, no flesh would have survived; without the second ark, no soul would be saved. There must be preparation. Preparation requires planning my MIND, my HEART, and my HOME, out of which I ultimately open my HAND. As I *think in my heart*, so will I do.

Planning for Hospitality

Most of us have heard the catchy phrase, "Plan your work; work your plan." But there is another similar phrase that cuts more closely: "Fail to plan; plan to fail."

Planning is not necessarily plotting. Planning is more akin to preparation. Planning requires an activated state of mind and heart that brings particular focus to the subject of our plans, resulting in corresponding action. I must *think* hospitality before I will *do* hospitality. Thinking issues out of the heart (Prov. 23:7); therefore, all planning and preparation for hospitality begins in my heart.

My Heart for Hospitality

If indeed hospitality is a priority with God, it must become a priority with me. The Scriptures encourage, "Apply thine heart unto instruction, and thine ears to the words of knowledge" (Prov. 23:12). We are also given insight as to how our hearts and minds are connected to our behavior—what we do—for as a man "thinketh in his heart, so is he" (Prov. 23:7). Jesus then tells us, "Out of the abundance of the heart the mouth speaketh (Matt. 12:34).

If indeed hospitality will become a priority in my life as it is with my Creator, I must consider it first in my heart, I must agree with my mind, and I must affirm it and talk about it with my tongue. The more I think about it and talk about it so as to agree with God's priority on this seemingly "insignificant" matter of hospitality, the more I will come to see its significance from God's viewpoint, and God will reveal His plans and purposes for hospitality to me (John 14:21, 23). Faith will come by hearing, and hearing by the Word of God (Rom 10:17). And I will be able to walk in agreement with God and in tune with His heart (Amos 3:3).

I must give myself, my heart, and my mind to hospitality as part of my reasonable worship (Rom. 12:1, 13). The natural man's mind is not hospitable. It is carnal and conformed to this world in selfish pursuit. I must become transformed by the renewing of my mind to correspond to God's mind and heart of hospitality, that I may "prove what is that good, and acceptable, and perfect will of God (Rom. 12:2).

As my mind and heart become open and conformed to God's mind and heart of hospitality, I will begin to take active steps, making provision in my life space—allocation of my time, talents and treasure—for hospitality as an essential to my spiritual worship. I will pray that the Lord will open my mind and heart to people, enabling me to see others with an open heart as He sees them. That will lead me to prepare my home.

Preparing My Home For Hospitality

Most American Christians want to prepare their homes for hospitality before they prepare their hearts. We want the practical steps of action to *do* hospitality. But we cannot truly do hospitality unless we are first hospitable. Everything must flow from the heart. So now that your heart is hot for hospitality, how can you prepare your home?

The Spirit of God is renewing an emphasis on our homes as the Second Coming of Christ draws near. There is good reason. The early Church of the first century worshiped in the temple, breaking bread from house to house and praying together (Acts 2:42–46). "Home," we say, "is where the heart is." And God is calling His Church and the epicenter of ministry back to our homes before Christ comes again to take us to His home.

If home is where the heart is, what is the condition of your home? What does it reflect about your heart? Is it neat and orderly? Is it welcoming? Does it reflect your Kingdom priorities?

Jesus said, "In My Father's house are many mansions [rooms]. I go to prepare a place for you, that where I am, there ye may be also" (John 14:2–3). If you were ushered into your *mansion* and found it strewn with clutter, the yard overgrown, the carpet stained with food and animal excrement, and permeated with the foul odor of unwashed sheets and clothes, what would you think of your host? Would you think He had truly been preparing for you? Would you be drawn to the Father's love?

Why should we, then, expect others to be drawn to the heart of the Father if we do not display His heart in our homes? You may be thinking, *Well that's why I don't invite people to my house.* If I refuse to prepare my home to the best of my ability to receive those made in God's image, why should I expect my Creator to prepare His home appropriately to receive me? If I want others to embrace my God of love, how can I expect them to find Him in my house filled with anger, bitterness, complaining, and resentment? If I would welcome others to the Pearly Gates, they must feel welcome in my gates.

So let's get practical, since you surely want God's heart of hospitality to be revealed through your home. Here are a few ideas for starters.

General House Condition
- Do your best to keep your house orderly.
- Do your best to keep your house clean.
  Note: It may not be true that "Cleanliness is next to godliness," but filthiness cannot possibly reflect godliness.

- Do your best to keep your yard neat and orderly.
- Do your best to keep your home in good repair.

Gathering Space

- Do provide the largest possible space for gathering people, both inside and outside.
- Do provide basic seating and tables in your gathering space that are neat, clean, and inoffensive to the average person who might join you.
- Do provide adequate lighting in your gathering space.
- Do provide quietness in your gathering space without television interference.

Your Kitchen

- Do make every effort to keep your kitchen both neat and clean. Counters, floors, table and chairs should be free of crumbs and other food residue.
- Do ensure that dishes are properly washed and put away.
- Do ensure that your kitchen and home are free of flies, roaches, and other insects.

Your Guest Bathroom

- Do provide clean towels and wash cloths.
- Do provide a clean sink, toilet and shower or tub.
- Do provide other toiletry necessities.

Your Yard

- Do your best to design your yard to avoid hazzards and to facilitate comfortable relationship.
- Do provide a grill that is clean.
- Do provide lawn furniture that is clean.
- Do provide adequate lighting.
- Do provide means to eliminate, insofar as possible, insects.
- Do provide a means to restrict pets from guests.

A pleasing ambiance is one aspect of the environment you provide for your neighbors, friends and guests that God would bring your way. Your goal is to make them feel comfortable and welcome. Most of those things discussed to this point require relatively little money, only loving attention and time. But there are many other things you can do to maximize the joy and comfort of your guests based upon your financial ability and skill. Here is a mere sampling.

- Provide fresh flowers in the living room, kitchen, or bedroom.
- Provide aroma of cider or other spice heated on the stove.
- Provide a welcome basket in the bedroom with sparkling cider, fruit, crackers, etc.
- Provide fragrant candlelight in the bathroom.

Remember, your hand becomes God's hand extended. What does your hand reflect of God's heart toward those God brings your way? Would your love reflect His love? Would your generosity reveal His generosity?

Your Home an Ark

Let your home be an ark of hospitality. Who knows but what many might enter God's eternal ark of safety in Christ through your heart expression of hospitality.

Do you have the mind of Christ? He said He is going to prepare a place for you. He is thinking hospitality. Are you? Your home may be the last hope on earth for someone to experience eternal hospitality in God's house.

Noah planned, prepared, and presented his ark as a place of safety. Noah never shut the door; God shut the door. **Never shut the door of your heart or home on holy hospitality. Think hospitality!**

Heart-Opening Questions
for Personal and Group Reflection

Chapter 9

1. If a man or woman does not *think* "hospitality" as a basic pattern of life, is he or she likely to *do* hospitality?

2. Do you believe Noah would have been able to build the ark as a place of hospitality for all who would accept the invitation to enter if he had not placed the holy purpose as a priority in his mind?

3. Since Proverbs 23:7 reveals that what we think comes out of our heart, is the condition of your heart such as to produce and sustain hospitality in your thoughts?

4. How is hospitality part of our reasonable worship? How does worship connect to our minds and thoughts?

5. If the home was the epicenter of ministry for the early, first-century church, would you expect God to recover that focus in the twenty-first century if Christ is returning soon?

6. It is said, "Home is where the heart is." What does your home reveal about the condition of your heart? Is it a place of order, of peace, of welcome, of joy, of love?

7. Name at least three things needing change, that come immediately to your mind when considering your home as a place of hospitality. Are you willing to allow God to help you get these things in order? You make the choice. God will help you make the change.

8. Would your family, your neighbors…your Savior consider your home as a trustworthy "ark of safety" for these end times that are being ushered in rapidly?

9. Are you willing to put hospitality on your mind?

Hospitality Is for Men

If a man would

have the heart of God,

he must have a heart

of hospitality.

BEFORE NOAH SAW HOPE in the promise of God confirmed by a rainbow, he gave himself to a full century of hospitality as he faithfully planned and produced an ark of safety for all who would enter. Abraham, father of the faithful, demonstrated an open heart, open hand, and open home of hospitality, even in the desert. Jesus, without even a place to lay His head, driven by holy hospitality, gave His life, extending invitation to His Father's house.

Men must reclaim a vision for hospitality before the God-man, Jesus Christ, returns to receive us to His eternal home. Hospitality is for men!

Hospitality is Revolutionary

HOSPITALITY HAS REVOLUTIONIZED MY LIFE! It has been a revolution driven by a fresh revelation of relationships and how God uses them to perform His purposes in the earth. Yet it was not always so for me.

When Kathie and I were married in 1966, with a year left before graduation from college and professional hopes on the horizon, I had little heart for people. Mine was a world of principle rather than people. Kathie thought she had made the "catch" of a spiritual leader who would fulfill her dream of a home graced with hospitality for which she had yearned growing up. As the eldest child among five in a pastor's home with few of this world's resources, I had not experienced the brand of open heart, open hand, and open home my wife so desperately desired. Her frequent heart cries gradually diminished into disillusionment. For me, there seemed to be a missing translation. I heard with the ear but not with the heart.

For a number of years, I engaged in the often-isolating sport of mountaineering—peak climbing and rock climbing. It is a sport both taxing and rewarding. A climber will endure great trial and face fear, testing courage and endurance for the joy of accomplishment and a spectacular mountain-top vista. His manhood is magnified by the sense of fulfillment arising from experiences not otherwise realized or apparent to those trapped in the perpetual valleys of life.

One experience I will never forget. Shortly before Mount St. Helens erupted, spewing volcanic lava and ash across a hundred square miles. A climbing partner and I were gingerly making our way, crampons strapped to our boots, across the glazed ice of a forty-degree angled slope. We were roped for protection as we probed our way with ice axes across the glaciated peak, totally "whited out" by a dense cloud that enshrouded the mountain, barely able to see one another separated by no more than a few paces. Suddenly, amid rising fear and perplexity as to whether to advance or retreat, a brisk wind instantly swept away the cloud, unveiling a spectacular vista of nearly a hundred miles. Spirit Lakes, now filled with lava, glistened below where our wives picked berries.

No better picture can I convey of the dramatic effect hospitality has had in unveiling the fulness of the Christian life. It began to sweep away the cloud of selfishness and self-centeredness which enshrouded my life. Before hospitality invaded my life, becoming an essential ingredient, the Christian life was largely a creedal enterprise, secure in salvation but lacking a fulfillment that I did not even realize existed. Hospitality opened the door of my heart outward.

God's hospitality remodeling project began with a brave and persistent printer and businessman named Steve in the congregation we attended. He was determined to enter my world and reach inside to unlock the door of my isolationist heart with hospitality. He probed until he discovered a mutual interest in photography as the platform upon which to build a bridge. Steve Smith, his wife Wanda, and our families, made sure we spent time in each other's homes over the next twenty-five years. Our lives became forever intertwined, and much Kingdom ministry has been facilitated in and through each of our lives over these many years, as an outflow of simple hospitality. That spirit of hospitality was the dominant theme defining our dear friend's recent funeral.

But I was a stubborn case. So God had another weapon in His arsenal with which to break down the walls of my heart—a political campaign. Never having been previously involved in politics, I suddenly had a strong, unexplainable urge to run for the California legislature. As I walked more than one thousand miles door-to-door, introducing myself and meeting people in their homes and in every walk and circumstance, God gradually opened my eyes and heart in a new way to people made in His image. The rest is His-story. And God has a revolutionary story to write in your heart through hospitality, if you will let Him.

Heart of the Father

Hospitality expresses the heart of Father God. If a man would have the heart of God, he must have a heart of hospitality. God the Father could not have sent His only begotten Son to invite those who were estranged from Him through sin, strangers from the commonwealth of faith, into His home for eternity if He did not have an open heart of hospitality. And God expects those who are created in His image to have a similar heart.

God chose to create that "man" in His image in a split format. We are told, "So God created man in His own image, male and female created he them" (Gen. 1:27). God, in His infinite wisdom, seems to have chosen to invest aspects of His image in the male and other aspects in the female. Although each independently is created "in His image," the fulness of that image on earth is complete only when the God-like aspects of men and women are combined. While that combination does not render us "God," it does fulfill God's design for expression of Himself in humankind.

Despite the egalitarian struggle of women in our culture for equality, it is obvious, both in physical form and function as well as in general patterns of interest and emphasis across cultural boundaries, that men and women are very different, each having his and her own unique contribution to humankind. One expression of these differences is that women, by creative nature, tend as nurturers to more naturally express hospitality. So men, as with other areas of life, think, *That's women's work.*

Men somehow come to tacitly believe that to display a heart for hospitality is somehow to defile their masculinity. The biblical reality, however, is that God-like masculinity must, of necessity, display itself in a *heart* of hospitality accompanied by corresponding *acts* of hospitality to qualify as leadership material in the body of Christ (I Tim. 3:2, Tit. 1:6–8).

When was the last time you heard it expressed or saw it written in any church or parachurch context that being "given to hospitality" and being a "lover of hospitality" were an absolutely essential pre-requisite to consideration for leadership? We do not truly believe these requirements, nor do we accept them in practice, because we really do not believe they are important for men. Yet real men agree with their Creator, if they truly believe they are made in His image. Men, it's time to clean up our image to conform to the image of our Father. It is time to embrace *The POWER of Hospitality*.

Hospitality Reveals Your "Stuff"

Hospitality reflects not only God's heart but also a man's heart. Hospitality is at least one litmus test of the condition of one's heart. It is instructive that the accounts of two of Scripture's most notable men provide interesting insight on the importance of hospitality in their lives.

NOAH'S NUISANCE

But for Noah's heart of hospitality, you and I would not be here today.

"The wickedness of man was great in the earth, and every imagination of the thoughts of his heart was only evil continually" (Gen. 6:5), declared the Lord of Noah's generation. The God who created man was "grieved at his heart" (Gen. 6:6). He determined that the only hope for the man He had created was to extend an "ultimatum" of hospitality, that whoever would repent from his wicked ways and enter an ark of safety would be spared the destruction by flood necessitated by a just and holy God.

In such a time as this, Noah alone "found grace in the eyes of the Lord" (Gen. 6:8). Noah alone was capable, as "a just man, perfect in his generations," to be God's earthly agent of heavenly hospitality (Gen. 6:9). God, therefore, said to Noah, "Make thee an ark" (Gen. 6:14).

Imagine the nuisance! Noah already had plenty to do to make a living. He had a wife and family. Why should he be concerned about anyone but his family? But apparently he was, for Noah was said to be "a preacher of righteousness" (II Pet. 2:5). By preaching righteousness, it seems clear Noah urged men and women to repentance and to enter the ark, but they ignored him. Noah not only persisted in warning, but also in preparing this ark of ultimate hospitality for an entire century.

It is not difficult to understand why God tapped Noah for this incredible task. He shared God's heart of hospitality, not willing that any should perish. What for most men would have been a total nuisance became for Noah a life message. "As the days of Noah were," warned Jesus, "so also shall the coming of the Son of man be" (Matt. 24:37). Mr. Macho man, do you have a holy heart of hospitality out of which you are building an "ark" of safety for your family and others in this generation? It could be a matter of spiritual life and death. Hospitality reveals a man's vision.

ABRAHAM'S ANGELIC ANSWER TO CULTURAL CORRUPTION

Abraham was a sojourner who lived largely as a desert nomad, searching for that city with "foundations, whose builder and maker is God" (Heb. 11:10). Not only was his physical environment inhospitable; his cultural environment was so profoundly evil and corrupt that a just and holy God was required by His character to bring judgment. Sodom and Gomorrah have since been a sign of warning to any society that arrogantly refuses to repent of its wicked ways.

It was precisely in such an unwelcoming physical and moral environment that Abraham, sitting in the door of his desert tent, saw three men approach at a distance. Perhaps nothing of the account of Gen. 18 reveals more of Abraham's heart of hospitality than the words, "he ran to meet them from the tent door" (Gen. 18:2).

Abraham's hospitality was not passive but proactive. He did not wait to see if these strangers would dare to demand of him some aid or some of his time. No, he was determined there would be no strangers in his home or presence. He begged them not to pass him by. He urged them to tarry that he might display to them a holy heart of heavenly hospitality in what otherwise seemed a God-forsaken corner of earth. He saw to all of their needs.

Hospitality was foundationally important to this great father of faith. Abraham "hastened into the tent unto Sarah, and said, Make ready quickly three measures of fine meal, knead it, and make cakes upon the hearth" (Gen. 18:6). But Abraham was not willing only to delegate duties. He personally engaged in the total expression of family hospitality. Running into the herd, Abraham "fetched a calf tender and good, and gave it unto a young man; and he hasted to dress it" (Gen. 18:7). As a man of great faith, Abraham was also clearly a man of action. He put the handle of hospitality to agape love, making his life creed credible.

That was just the kind of man God was seeking to accomplish His ultimate plan of divine hospitality. He needed a man who shared His own heart of hospitality. It was precisely in this classic display of an open heart, open hand and open home that God, through these strangers, chose to secure His promise to Abraham of a son, a son through whose seed would come the Christ, who through the ark of His flesh would extend eternal hospitality to all who would enter through Him as "the door" (John 10:9).

It was not eternal hope only that God had in mind for Abraham. His divine mercy sought, through a heart of hospitality, to save the righteous from the cities of Sodom and Gomorrah, whose wickedness doomed them to destruction. When Abraham was confronted with the grievous news of God's intention, "Abraham stood yet before the Lord" (Gen. 18:22). His heart, as God's heart, yearned for the people. He pleaded, yes, even bargained, with God. When God finally brought destruction, the Scripture plainly says, "God remembered Abraham, and sent Lot out of the midst of the overthrow" (Gen. 19:29).

Abraham's faith, revealed in a godly heart displaying heavenly hospitality, gave God freedom to save Abraham's extended family from destruction. Remember, God gave man dominion in the earth (Gen. 1:28), and He is seeking a few righteous men who, on earth, will give Him access from heaven to seek and save those set for destruction. Jesus was such a man through His virgin birth. And before He ascended back to the Father He declared, "As the Father hath sent Me, even so send I you" (John 20:21).

Remarkably, Abraham "was called the Friend of God" (James 2:23). If we men would be friends of God, we cannot keep ourselves as strangers from those the Creator has made in His image.

The days in which we live are identical to the times of Noah and the Flood. The wickedness in America and throughout the earth is so profound that evangelist Billy Graham's wife, Ruth, reportedly said, "If God does not judge America, He will have to apologize to Sodom and Gomorrah." So let me ask you privately, if God is now in need of a man in your neighborhood, church, or community through whom He could extend His heart of holy hospitality to spare from temporal destruction or eternal damnation, would He choose you? If not, why? Are you willing to become that man? Why not talk to your Lord about it right now.

Hospitality Is For Patriarchs

God is not interested primarily in building a few good men who can manage to get their acts together sufficiently to escape boyhood and qualify as men. Rather, God is interested in developing patriarchs. Abraham was such a man (Heb. 7:4). I believe the only reason Noah is not specifically described as a *patriarch* is that he preceded Abraham through whom God's covenant promise of eternal redemption was to be fulfilled. In all other respects, he qualified. So profound was his righteous standard and example that the prophet Ezekiel links Noah with Daniel and Job as the Old Covenant's most righteous men, aside from Abraham (Ezek. 14:12–20).

A *man* is concerned about only himself and his family. A *patriarch*, on the other hand, has become proficient in walking righteously, applying his faith and opening his hand, heart and home in hospitality in spheres beyond his own family. He becomes that great oak of righteousness that gives shade and shelter far beyond the narrow confines of his own family. He is a man God can trust to stand in the gap for Him. In Ezekiel's day, God could not find such a man. He said, "I sought for a man among them, that should make up the hedge, and stand in the gap before Me for the land, that I should not destroy it: but I found none" (Ezek. 22:30). Has God found you in this generation? Would you like Him to find you thus? Are you willing to become a patriarch, a man God can trust to reach to others even beyond himself and his family?

Your training as a patriarch may begin with your developing a heart for hospitality. Few men, whether pastor or layman, qualify as patriarchs. Their vision is too narrow, their ways too wayward, their faith too shallow, and their hearts too self-centered. To become a patriarch, you must open your heart, open your hand, and open your home in holy hospitality.

Hospitality is Christian Living 101. Hospitality is required to follow Christ. Jesus, as our example, gave Himself to a heart of hospitality even though He had no place of His own where He could lay His head. Paul reminds us that if we would "present our bodies a living sacrifice, holy, acceptable unto God," we must be "given to hospitality" (Rom. 12:1, 13). Hospitality is a powerful and essential "weapon" for Christian warfare, and it is an essential ingredient for Christian living.

Are you a man? Will you give yourself to hospitality? The best way to start is to ask the Lord to open your heart. Then just do it. A whole new realm of life and Christian joy is around hospitality corner. Take a look. As an additional benefit, there is a great probability your wife will bless you as well, since a whole new realm of husband-and-wife relationship and mutual ministry will unfold before you. Don't miss out. Open your heart, your hand, and your home starting now.

Heart-Opening Questions
for Personal and Group Reflection

Chapter 10

1. Husband, has your wife (as mine did so many years ago) expressed a desire that your home be a haven of hospitality? Does she feel satisfied with your response, or is she frustrated, or has she just given up on her hope?

2. Men, could you relate at all to my own life story as it relates to my wife's yearning that our home be a place of hospitality? To my lack of vision? To my passive resistence? To a heart basically closed to others?

3. Can you see how hospitality expressed the heart of Father God?

4. Can you agree in principle, at this point, that if a man would have the heart of God, he must have a heart of hospitality?

5. Why do we men tend to think that hospitality is only for women?

6. Noah found grace in the eyes of the Lord for the task of spending 120 years preparing a place of hospitable safety in the midst of a violent and wicked generation. Would you find grace in the eyes of the Lord to prepare your home for end-time hospitality in our generation?

7. How did Abraham demonstrate a heart of hospitality amid the wickedness of his generation?

8. Since Paul declares being "given to" and a "lover" of hospitality as prerequisites for church leadership, do you qualify for leadership by God's standards?

9. Are you willing to become a *patriarch*, a man God can trust to reach and protect others beyond yourself and your family?

10. Are you willing to open your heart, hand and home to allow God to revolutionize your Christian walk and the life of your family through holy hospitality? Will you verbally commit to God, and your wife…today?

*H*ospitality or *E*ntertainment?

Hospitality is

first an attitude,

then an act.

A CERTAIN WOMAN NAMED MARTHA received Jesus into her house. She had a sister called Mary, who also sat at Jesus' feet, and heard His word. But Martha was cumbered about much serving, and said, "Lord, dost thou not care that my sister hath left me to serve alone? Bid her therefore that she come and help me." And Jesus answered and said unto her,

Martha, Martha, thou art careful and troubled about many things: but one thing is needful; and Mary hath chosen that good part, which shall not be taken away from her (Luke 10:38–42).

Mary or Martha?

Are you a *Mary* or a *Martha*? This is a question for men and women alike, for Jesus presented us with a classic case study of the difference between hospitality and entertainment. Martha opened her home, but her heart was not right. Many would say Martha was the hospitable one, yet Jesus said otherwise. "Mary hath chosen that good part" (Luke 10:42).

How can we clearly identify and diagnose the Mary-Martha factor? How can we develop a heart response that allows us to consistently choose "that good part?"

Many extraneous factors may bear upon my propensity to be a Mary or a Martha. One of these factors is my personality or "motivational" giftedness described in Rom. 12:6–8, that tends to establish my unique orientation toward life issues. Other factors include upbringing and the example of others.

The threshold question, however, in honestly diagnosing whether I am a Mary or a Martha is this:

> Does the focus of my time and energy reflect how I want people to think about *me*, or does it reflect how much I want people to know I am thinking about *them*?

This threshold question leads us to take a second look at the resources we discussed in an earlier chapter as the focus of our stewardship—our time, our talents, and our treasure.

THE TIME FACTOR

Time is the universal environment in which all hospitality takes place. How I view my time in connection with my desire to exercise hospitality will likely determine my life pattern on the Mary-Martha continuum. I must answer the following key questions.

1. Is the primary focus of my time and energy spent on preparation of food and environment so that I might make a good impression? Or is the primary focus of my time and energy on preparation of food and environment so that I might truly minister to the needs and comfort of my guest?

2. Do I consciously provide for energy reserve to give of myself to the purported beneficiaries of my labors? Or do I exhaust my energy reserve in preparations so I have little of myself to offer to the purported beneficiaries of my labors?

3. When friends or guests are present, am I so busy in trying to attend to such extraneous details as food and environment that I have little focused time to relax and enjoy them? Or have I consciously prepared and balanced my time so as to provide free and relaxed time to attend to friends and guests?

These are questions that are not always easy to answer, for we are prone to confuse what we *intend* to do with what we *actually* do. Patterns prevail. *Time* will always tell. As Jesus pointed out to Martha, her attitude was reflected in the way she used her time.

The Talent Factor

How I use my talents and abilities also helps reveal whether I am engaged in hospitality or entertainment. While I should always do my best (within time and financial constraints) to welcome guests and make them comfortable using my unique talents and abilities, some important questions can help measure the Mary-Martha factor.

1. Do I use my talents for talents' sake, showing off my "stuff" or abilities without regard to the needs, comfort, or sensibilities of my guests?

2. Do I use my talents for others' sake, using and channeling my talents and abilities with restraint so as not to render our time together uncomfortable or to divert attention from the guests I purport to serve?

Again, attitude is the issue. By all means, provide tasteful and beautiful decor, table settings, yard, and so forth, but not to the detriment of the relationships to be cultivated.

The Treasure Factor

Jesus made clear, "Where your treasure is, there will your heart be also" (Matt. 6:21). The concern here is not just on *what* I have, but on my *attitude* toward what I have and how I *use* what I have.

1. Is my treasure (the things I have) focused on worldly show?
2. Is my treasure (the things I have) focused on godly glow?

Attitude is as important as *action* in measuring the Mary-Martha factor. Again, the heart of the matter is my heart.

A Matter of the Heart

Southern Hospitality is a term familiar to most Americans. Perhaps because of its perceived slower pace and characteristic drawl, the American South came to be synonymous with the term *hospitality*. So when the Lord led us to relocate, after a lifetime of living in Southern California, to the former capitol of the South, Richmond, Virginia, we were ecstatic about the hospitable environment we would encounter. Our anticipation level was high, expecting to be cradled in the very womb of hospitality. We were unprepared for an unsuspecting lesson in contrasts.

Thank God for first impressions. They can be lasting. We flew into Richmond on a Wednesday evening in the summer of 1993 to speak. At 9:00 A.M. the next day, we were voicing our bid to purchase a house in foreclosure. Barely had the auctioneer's voice trailed off— "Going, going, gone"—granting a new home to our family, than a tall stranger reached his hand over my shoulder saying, "Welcome, neighbor. What just happened was a miracle!" Indeed it was, and the miracle echoes on.

John introduced himself as a neighbor "up the street." He asked where we were staying, and after some chit-chat, Kathie and I departed. That evening, we received a call from our new neighbor friend, inviting us to join him and his wife, Martha, for breakfast—at their home. After a wonderful time over cereal, fruit, conversation and coffee, we left the Gibbs home, convinced we were in hospitality heaven. Then reality set in.

Over the next year, gracious greetings by Southern gents and ladies were often followed by ungracious gaffs. The facade of geniality deteriorated often within minutes, hours, or days to mere civility. We were baffled. It was as if much of "Southern hospitality" was cultural show designed for first impressions rather than for lasting friendships. Our growing apprehension was modestly allayed when person after person, seeing our obvious heart for hospitality, warned, "Beware of Virginia hospitality. We will love you to your face and stab you in your back."

The issue is not whether genuine hospitality exists in America's South. True hospitality can be found anywhere there is a heart of true hospitality. Without the heart, that which seems to be hospitality is merely a cultural or even "Christian" show—entertainment. It is for public consumption but lacks private edification.

Praise God we did find heartfelt hospitality in both Virginia and the South. Seven years later, John and Martha Gibbs received two couples joining our family from across the nation for our daughter's wedding. For an entire week they opened their home as a haven, providing comfort, food, friendship, and lodging. New friendships developed, and the hope of holy hospitality now echoes and re-echoes from coast to coast.

The differences between true hospitality and mere entertainment are palpable. Anyone who has experienced true hospitality will clearly recognize its counterfeit. Never mistake endurance for hospitality. Never mistake entertainment for hospitality.

Following are a few additional considerations to protect our heart-set, helping us to join with Mary rather than with Martha.

1. Do I entertain? Is it entertainment for entertainment's sake, or part of a bigger and righteous purpose?
2. Do I really care for the person or people? The problem with group activities related to church, community, or club is that they often are focused on the vicarious activities of others rather than facilitating relationship and friendship among those we purport to serve. By way of illustration, consider the following contrasts:

Vicarious Activities (Pure Entertainment)	Involving Activities (Personal Interaction)
Plays	Parties
Ball games	Talent Shows
Television	Group Activities

3. Do I care about people because Jesus cares about people?

Television is a hospitality killer! Television is pure entertainment. Its active presence in a home or other setting is an almost certain reflection of a heart committed to self rather than to others. It fragments focus. It demands our attention. It reveals what I really value.

The television should <u>NEVER</u> be on in the presence of my guests. The only exception would be if their purpose in joining me is to review and/or discuss a particular program or video together. The destructive role of television in undermining our relationships is incalculable. We now have to fight their invasive influence even in restaurants. If Jesus reprimanded Martha for being overly cumbered, what would He have said to her if she insisted on keeping her TV on when He was in her home?

Group Size and Ministry Goals

Group gatherings present special problems when considering hospitality versus entertainment. The larger the group, the greater the tendency to shift to entertainment.

If the goal of the group gathering is merely to deliver information, size is relatively irrelevant because relationships are not a significant component. In reality, such group activity takes on the form of "entertainment" for all practical purposes. The smaller the group, the greater the likelihood for open-hearted interaction and relationship building. Current conviction reveals that a group of twelve is as large as one can reasonably expect to preserve relational intimacy. It should therefore come as no surprise that Jesus, the "Creator of all things," chose twelve to be with Him during His earthly ministry.

The matter of group size, as it relates to the ministry of the Church, has vast implications which we ought not to dismiss lightly. A few years ago, author William Hendricks joined me on my daily radio broadcast. In discussing his book *Exit Interviews*, Hendricks lamented that 53,000 people per week were leaving through the "back door" of America's churches. To find out why, he interviewed two dozen frustrated parishioners from coast to coast, who no longer darken church doors but remain committed to Christ. One of the three basic reasons why Christians of ten years or more are fed up includes the following:

> They do not believe the church provides true Christian
> fellowship and community, but is rather a "gospel country
> club" of Sunday back-slappers who couldn't care less about
> one another after the noon hour on Sunday.

Interestingly, these sentiments seem to echo from pulpit to pew in a variety of expressions. George Barna, in his book *Virtual America*, revealed statistics that should break your heart. While 55 percent of non-Christian Americans believe it is getting harder to make friends, 62 percent of born-again Christians believe that is true, and 73 percent of all evangelical Christians are finding it difficult to make friends. One apparent conclusion: the more RELIGION, the less RELATIONSHIP.

H.B. London, head of pastoral ministries for Focus on the Family, also joined me on *VIEWPOINT*, disclosing that at least 70 percent of pastors in America claim they have no friends.

How can we explain this disastrous trend that runs counter to the "one another" commands and expectations of biblical Christianity? We believe that one clear conclusion lies in the way we are increasingly *doing church*. From pulpit to pew, our hearts are increasingly closed to one another. Individualism reigns supreme. And our increasingly larger congregations have become theaters of entertainment.

We use deceptive slogans such as, "Small enough to care, large enough to make a difference" to justify our headlong competition with corporate America whose mantra is that "bigger is better." The Jesus model reveals quite the contrary. Yet even the most notable of America's "cell" churches pursue mega-church models, often turning cells effectively into ministry-management tools designed to usher in more and more theater-goers into larger and larger theaters for more and more entertainment.

A few observations might be appropriate for consideration by leaders at all levels. If pastors and other leaders truly had a heart of hospitality, were given to hospitality, and were lovers of hospitality, would they devise, perpetuate, and exalt a burgeoning system for doing church that is virtually calculated to undermine this fundamental operative mind and heart-set of biblical Christianity? If, indeed, such goals and practices are severely impairing, at a structural level, the ability to develop genuine loving and caring "one another" relationship, and are encouraging an entertainment mind and heart-set rather than the relational worshiping participation described and modeled by the early church (Acts 2:42–47), what spiritual force do you suppose is instigating these biblically-contrary concepts that conform to the world system?

Hospitality is neither conceived nor practiced in a vacuum. Hospitality is not just a matter of our feelings; it is a fundamental of the faith. Given the plans and patterns of America's pastors, a serious deficiency is apparent in the hospitality department. If the overseers of God's people do not share His heart for hospitality and give themselves to it, has not our spiritual leadership become fundamentally flawed? Can we expect to accomplish God's Kingdom purposes without proficiency in His Kingdom plan?

Could it be that one of the principle reasons the Spirit of God seems to be calling the Church "home" across our world is to bring us back to His design? Could it be that the Lord of the Church wants to restore the relational essence of the fellowship of believers, that genuine "one another" ministry may righteously and freely flow from a heart of hospitality? Could it be that an entertainment heart-set has gradually replaced a heart of hospitality since the days when Constantine, in the fourth century, impressed a Roman emperor's mold on the mind of the Church, leading us down the path of entertainment?

It is indeed fascinating to note that as the rhetoric of relationship pours forth from spiritual trend-setters in America, the reality of relationship is diminishing. Both George Gallup and George Barna, renowned and respected pollsters, have observed that the number of those involved in small groups have, at best, plateaued and appear to be in decline. Yet both of these spiritual and cultural observers have clearly stated that one of the most desperately needed developments for the healing of America and fulfillment of the mission of the Church is the committed involvement of our people in small groups. **Hospitality will never be fully displayed in the pews until it is portrayed from the pulpits.**

Tests for Genuine Hospitality

How can I test my heart and home, or even my group or congregation, for hospitality? How can I determine how close my intentions come to reality? Some would immediately strive to develop a quasi scientific measuring device, but that would be superficial at best, for hospitality, at root, is not a matter of the mind or measurement but is rather a matter of the spirit…of the heart. The best tests are God's tests, so for starters, we must return to Jesus' evaluation of Mary and Martha.

THE MARY-MARTHA TESTS

We began this chapter with a look at two sisters in the same home with the same Lord. Both Mary and Martha were well-intentioned.

Mary passed the test of hospitality; Martha failed. Let's see how you and I measure up.

- TEST NUMBER ONE: Am I focused on *people*—Or on *programs* and activities?
- TEST NUMBER TWO: Am I willing, in balance, to set aside the *things* I think are important to serve the *people* who are important?
- TEST NUMBER THREE: Am I excessively cumbered with *serving* to the exclusion of the people *served*?
- TEST NUMBER FOUR: Am I full of *care* and *troubled* about things?

In making your assessment, remember that a person's *perception* is his *reality*. The real issue, then, is not what I think or what you think, or what we wish others would think, but what they really *do* think. Martha thought she had it all together. She thought that because she had invited Jesus to her home, she had a handle on hospitality, but Jesus rebuked her. Would Jesus conclude, based upon your self-assessment, that you have "chosen that good part" (Luke 10:42)?

Practical Tests for Genuine Hospitality

Temporal values must always be subjugated to eternal values. Following are a few more practical ways to measure whether I have a heart of hospitality or of entertainment.

- Does the environment serve me, or do I serve the environment? This test must be applied to:

Decor	Food	Music
Cleanliness	Orderliness	Possessions

- Are material possessions a blessing or a curse on my relationship to friends and guests?
- Do I have company, visitors, guests or friends?

    Those who have *company* almost invariably think with an entertainment mind-set. Congregations that have *visitors* tend to be more close-hearted than those who welcome *guests*. Jesus said, "I call you no more servants, but friends" (John 15:15). What I *say* issues out of the way I *think*.

- Am I playing a role, performing a service, or fostering a relationship?
- Do I provide a *front-door* experience or a *back-door* experience?

    It is not the door entered that determines the perception of the guests. It is my attitude in receiving them. A *front-door* attitude almost invariably issues from an entertainment mindset; a *back-door* attitude fosters relationship.
- Do I provide a *living-room* experience or a *family-room* experience?

    Room environment sets a tone. But the tone of my heart speaks even more loudly. Ask yourself, *Why am I taking my guest into this room? Or which room would most likely make this particular guest feel comfortable for the purposes they are with me?*
- When my expectations and hopes are broken, does it ruin the experience?
    - What if someone does not show up?
    - What if someone is late?
    - What if the soufflé falls?
    - What if the candles won't light?
- Never mistake endurance for hospitality. Merely putting up with people is not the same as freely and joyfully opening your heart and home to others.

The Agony and the Ecstasy

Martha was delighted to have her Master, Jesus, in her home, but she was not delighted with His response. Nor was she pleased with the performance of her sister, Mary. Martha most likely had a very difficult time accepting and processing Jesus' appraisal of her brand of hospitality as, in effect, "entertainment." Imagine how you would feel. Yet, in a very real sense, that evaluation takes place every time a guest is purported to be welcomed into your life, whether in the home, office, club or congregation. Like it or not, our guests will evaluate the experience. And so must we if we would become like Jesus and truly have an open heart, open hand, and open home. The experience, as with Martha, may present us with both agony and ecstasy. Consider the following questions.

- What is the measure of success—or failure?
  - In response
  - In interaction
  - In feelings
  - In emotions
  - In truth
  - In relationship
- Am I measuring success or failure from
  - An entertainment mind-set?
  - A hospitality mind-set?
- Evaluate:
  - Did I accomplish the purpose, as reflected in relationship and response?
  - What did I do right?
  - What did I do wrong?
  - Was my attitude right?
  - What would Jesus say?

Questions of the Heart

In this chapter, we have explored ideas of both principle and practical application at every level of our life and ministry. Ask the Lord to reveal to you the appropriate places in your life for application. It could be revolutionary. Jesus' response to Martha was loving, yet confrontational. You may have felt like Martha as you were reading, or perhaps like Mary. Let God speak to you where you are, and then respond. Turn your agony into ecstasy the next time you have a hospitality opportunity.

Whatever you do, do not give up. Give yourself to hospitality. Become a lover of hospitality. As we close this chapter, ask yourself the following questions.

- Am I truly available to others?
- What does God want to do through me today
  – for this person,
  – for these people,
  – in this event,
  – for this season, and
  – for His Kingdom?

Let *The Power of Hospitality* change your life and those around you. Start today!

Heart-Opening Questions
for Personal and Group Reflection

Chapter 11

1. Why is true hospitality an *attitude* before it becomes an *act*?

2. Can you see yourself in the story of Mary and Martha? Where do you fit? Are you like Mary or Martha? How? How would Jesus evaluate your own life ways and attitudes when it comes to having people into your home?

3. Do you have problems with use of your time when you attempt to have people in your home?

4. Do you use your talents unselfishly to bless others, or to show off your "stuff" or abilities?

5. Does the use of your resources bring glory to God, or to yourself?

6. Why have we generally confused true hospitality with entertainment? Do you do hospitality, or do you entertain? The underlying difference between the two is attitude, isn't it?

7. How has an entertainment mindset subtly defined ministry and programs in your congregation? Changed ways will flow from changed thinking.

8. Why is it unlikely that hospitality will ever be fully *displayed* in the pews until it is *portrayed* from the pulpits?

9. Do you think the discussed "PRACTICAL TESTS FOR GENUINE HOSPITALITY" provide a good, fair, and basic gauge for testing our heart motivations? Did any areas discussed come uncomfortably close to home?

10. Have you had one or more disappointing experiences in attempts to do hospitality? Are you willing to try again to please the heart of God? Will you trust Him to give you His heart?

Chapter *12*

$\mathcal{H}$indrances to $\mathcal{H}$ospitality

*Hospitality must
happen in my heart
before it can happen
in my home.*

THE GREATEST BARRIER TO HOSPITALITY is the mistaken and unbiblical belief that to be hospitable I must be "gifted *in*" hospitality rather than "give myself *to*" hospitality. Entertainment is the greatest substitute for hospitality. But many other hindrances prevent a person from stepping into the joy of opening heart, hand and home in hospitality. Insecurity, self-centeredness, shyness, false standards, disorganization and excessive busyness are some of the controllable and changeable hindrances to becoming a blessing through hospitality. In this chapter we will review all of these issues in biblical perspective.

Attitude Barriers

For the Christian, attitudes are every bit as important as actions. Jesus' opening statement in His Sermon on the Mount zeroed in on our attitudes. That is why the first thirteen verses of Matthew 5 are called the *BEattitudes*: they are attitudes of being. Our attitudes are critical to a Christ-like life.

Actions flow from attitudes. Parents and pastors spend much of their time and energy trying to get those in their care to change their behavior, often failing to realize that the root of the behavior is the attitude out of which it issues. Jesus put it this way:

> A good man out of the good treasure of his heart
> bringeth forth good things: and an evil man out of the evil
> treasure bringeth forth evil things (Matt. 12:35).

It would seem to be a fair observation that if I have a problem or difficulty with hospitality or being hospitable, I most likely need an attitude adjustment. You and I must make the *choice;* God will help us make the *change.* Let's take a look at a few of the most common attitudinal hindrances to hospitality.

INSECURITY

You might feel insecure about hospitality for a number of reasons. You may just feel generally insecure about your place in life and with others. On the other hand, you may have little or no hospitality experience, or may even have had an unpleasant experience. These issues may be inhibiting factors, but they ought not and need not be barriers.

If you are generally insecure, this feeling is often the result of wrong thinking about yourself. Excessive SELF-focus will frustrate your ability to be concerned about others. God warns us not to think of ourselves "more highly" than we ought to think (Rom. 12:3), but before you can know whether you might be in danger of thinking *more* highly than you should, you must first know how highly you *ought* to think. You might even paralyze yourself with *false humility*, pretending to think less highly of yourself on the outside than you really think on the inside.

You can do it! God would not require you to give yourself to hospitality if you were incapable. If you are made in the image of God, you are capable of opening your heart, hand and home in hospitality. You make the choice, and God will help you change. That is true for pastor and people alike.

You may feel inexperienced or have had a bad experience. Perhaps your heart has been responding as you have been reading, and you are saying, *Yes, I want to do this, but I don't know how to get started.* Find someone to guide and mentor you. Perhaps you already know of someone who seems to demonstrate hospitality easily. Go to the person. Explain your desire. Ask if you can tag along, if you can just be present, or if you can help with preparations. Ask questions.

Kathie has informally mentored in hospitality many women with differing educational, ethnic, and socio-economic backgrounds. Those times invested together have built and expanded precious relationships, even including the wives of pastors and politicians. I will never forget sharing a meal time in our home with a group of Christians who wanted to make a difference in our state and nation. After we had concluded our afternoon together, our local state representative and his wife lingered after others left. Kathie discovered the wife in our kitchen with tears streaming down her face, confessing her profound feelings of inadequacy to do hospitality and begging for assistance. It was sheer delight for Kathie to let a little of her experience rub off on a new friend. They shared time together, and hope for hospitality was born. That dear lady has periodically prodded us to get a book written to multiply the blessing and joy of hospitality for others. Kathie has had similar experiences with pastors' wives who yearn for someone to come alongside and open the door to and for them in hospitality.

Remember, You can do all things through Christ who strengthens you (Phil. 4:13). You make the choice; God will help you make the change, even through the helping hand of one of His hospitable servants.

Too Shy

For many years we struggled with this problem in a variety of settings. Shyness is one expression of insecurity that usually finds its root in excessive self focus. An inferiority complex and a superiority complex have the same root; they reflect a wrong view of self and others.

While not wanting to be overly simplistic, here are two ideas that will help if you perceive shyness as an inhibiting factor to hospitality. First, you must recognize and admit that you are made in the image of God and that God would not require something of you that you were incapable of doing. Second, you must ask the Lord to reveal to you the root of wrong thinking, be willing to admit it, and turn from it. This we had to do many years ago, and it was as if we were being released from prison. Finally, you must choose to act on what you know you ought to do. Take the first step of hospitality by faith. Open your heart first. Extend a caring hand. As a world-famous psychiatrist once said, "Happiness is a door opening outwards."

I Can't

The "I can't" excuse is a *feeling* rather than a *fact*. It is often a camouflage for feelings of insecurity or shyness. But it may also be rooted in false standards and expectations of what is required to be hospitable. It should be sufficient to respond to you, if you feel you can't give yourself to hospitality, by asking, *Are you a Christian*? If your answer is, "Yes," hospitality is an essential ingredient of what it means to be a Christian and exercise agape love. You *can* do all things through Christ who strengthens you (Phil 4:13). Begin by faith. Feelings will follow.

It's Not My Responsibility

This is undoubtedly the most serious hindrance to hospitality issuing from attitude. It reflects a composite of serious spiritual heart conditions that tend to reinforce one another. This particular problem is more than a mere hindrance; it is a virtually impenetrable barrier that requires nothing short of spiritual heart surgery. It is also a mind- and heart-set that is rapidly becoming dominant not only in the American nation but also in the American church. Of even greater concern should be the unholy synergy that begins to interplay in the heart, creating a spiritual problem with consequences greater than the sum of its parts that echoes throughout the society until it becomes the dominant message.

Following are just a few of the spiritually-rooted heart issues and attitudes tangled in the *I'm not responsible* excuse.

Pride	Possessiveness
Selfishness	Independence
Self-centeredness	Compassionlessness
Isolationism	Callousness
Individualism	Bitterness
Greed	Hatred

Note that each of these characteristics is antagonistic to the very heart and soul of the Christian faith as reflected in the entire Bible. But perhaps the most fundamental flaw in this excuse is that it is, in effect, an outright denial that anyone other than myself is made in the image of God. In practical reality, to deny that I am responsible to others because *they* are not made in the image of God is to deny that *I* am made in God's image as well and, therefore, to deny that I am even accountable to God as anything but a mere animal.

Particular and pointed attention is being given to this specific excuse because, as a nation, America is being consumed by a spirit of individualism that has seriously invaded the Church House. As early as the 1830s French observer, Alexis de Tocqueville, noted a different strain of freedom and liberty gaining sway in American society from the mutuality of covenant community so beautifully expressed by the Pilgrims and Puritans. He coined the word *individualism* to describe this new idea permeating the culture.

"Individualism," said de Tocqueville, " is a calm and considered feeling which disposes each citizen to isolate himself from the mass of his fellows and withdraw into the circle of family and friends; with this little society to look after itself."

In his book *Habits of the Heart* (1985), sociologist Robert Bellah notes, "Tocqueville saw the isolation to which Americans are prone as ominous for the future of our freedom." And so it has become. As a secular prophet, de Tocqueville described one hundred and seventy years ago our present dilemma and the nature of the consequences.

Bellah, reflecting on de Tocqueville's observations, observed in *Habits of the Heart,*

> Such folks [individualists] owe no man anything and hardly expect anything from anybody. They form the habit of thinking of themselves in isolation and imagine that their whole destiny is in their hands. Finally, such people come to forget their ancestors, but also their descendants, as well as isolating themselves from their contemporaries. Each man is forever thrown back on himself alone, and there is danger that he be shut up in the solitude of his own heart.

Fellow Christians and Americans, our worship at the altar of libertarian individualism has not saved us but enslaved us. We have forsaken God's liberty in favor of man's license. Our greatest blessing has become a curse. "Liberty and justice for all" has become liberty and justice for *me*. The chains of our slavery are being forged on the anvil of our selfish hearts. Like Pontius Pilate of old, we ceremonially wash our hands within the isolation of our minds and say to our neighbor and society, "It's not my responsibility." Entire congregations now collectivize this myopic, self-focused outlook, paralyzing the true love of God from meaningful expression through our hands, homes and congregations.

This message urging you to exercise hospitality from the heart comes at a crisis moment for our country as we sit poised not only on the cusp of a new millennium but also on the near edge of Christ's Second Coming. This is not a self-help book, but a prophetic-hope message to a people in deep distress. Consider these words prayerfully in your own heart. (For more extensive discussion of this issue with specific application to American Christians, see my book *Renewing the Soul of America* (© 2002, Elijah Books), specifically the chapters entitled "My Brother's Keeper," "Compassion that Counts," and "A Civil Body Politic."

False Standards

One of the most common hindrances to hospitality is **false standards**. These false standards are constructed in the mind and become the attitudinal filter through which I view the entire subject of hospitality. They become the "dictionary" by which the word *hospitality* is defined and interpreted in my mind.

False standards for hospitality are framed around false expectations about hospitality and what it takes to be hospitable. These false expectations reveal misunderstandings about hospitality and usually become apparent in excuses why I cannot do hospitality. Following are a few of the most common such excuses:

My house is too small.
But I live in an apartment.
I'm not a talented decorator like Mrs. _____.
I'm just not a good organizer.
I'm living on Social Security.
I'm single.
But they wouldn't want to come to my house.
Yes, but I'm too old.
I'm just too young.

Can you relate to any of these excuses? Perhaps you could add another one to the list. At root, hospitality is not about the state of your *home* but about the condition of your *heart*. Hospitality depends not on your *capability* but on your *availability*.

Be encouraged! Jesus was hospitality incarnate, yet the Scriptures tell us "the Son of man hath not where to lay His head" (Matt. 8:20). Now that could present a problem for most of us, but Jesus' heart was so open in hospitality that He found ways to "receive" people wherever He went, even helping them to open their homes. Take heart! Open your hand. Open your home, whatever and wherever it may be. It is not your *home* but your *heart* that is being tried, tested and proved.

Ann, a dear single lady, came with concern to Kathie after we had been teaching these principles of hospitality. She said that her heart had been convicted and challenged, that she wanted to do hospitality, but she said, "I only live in a small rented room." Kathie wisely responded, "Well fix it up as warmly as you can and ask the Lord who you should invite." After a few more helpful hints about how to create a welcoming environment inexpensively, Kathie sent her on her way with hope rooted in faith and love. It was a breakthrough experience for Ann. She later reported excitedly how God had used her to reach to someone else—stretching beyond her fears by faith.

This could be a breakthrough day or week for you as well, regardless of your circumstances. Just open your heart, open your hand, and open your home. Don't let false standards and wrong expectations rob you of the joy of hospitality. Men, join your wives in this exciting expression of God's heart.

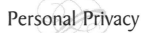

Personal Privacy

Many people lose out on the joy of hospitality by withdrawing from people into their private cocoons. This practice is becoming increasingly common and may well have become the norm in America. Withdrawal for personal privacy is driven by a composite of forces and attitudes such as individualism, isolationism and independence that have come to define American life, even among Christians.

The demands of our fast-paced existence and the clamor of so many voices in our culture for attention cause us to retreat into our private world, far "from the madding crowd." Yet a counterphenomena is also revealing our desire to be with people, as huge numbers throng to ever-multiplying malls, not only to shop but also to meet their God-given need for human society. We would rather meet people generically at the mall than specifically in our homes. Why is that? The answer, we believe, is spelled C-O-M-M-I-T-M-E-N-T.

All of us need to retreat from the noise and pressure of life. Even Jesus found it necessary to withdraw from the crowds and demands of people to be restored in quietude with His Father. Yet, He withdrew not to avoid people or commitment to them, but to be more effective in giving more of Himself to those whom God placed in His daily path. The issue is attitude. Am I reluctant to have people in my home because I really don't want to be bothered? Is it because I just want to protect my personal privacy? Jesus would never wall Himself off from others for such carnal purposes. An open home reflects an open heart. A closed home to preserve personal privacy reveals a closed heart. This is of particular concern for those involved in public ministry. There is a time for privacy, but we must be known for an open heart, open hand and open home.

If you have developed a life pattern of withdrawing from others to protect your personal privacy, an attitude assessment is in order. Selfishness by any other name still smells the same. If you are unwilling to love and open yourself and your home to those you *can* see, how can you say you love God, whom you *can't* see (I John 4:20)? If my home is not open to others, it is not open to Jesus. And if my home is not open to Jesus, there is cause for serious question as to whether He has my heart.

Behavioral Barriers

Attitudes always drive behaviors. You and I tend to act in certain ways and patterns because we tend to think that way. A behavioral change, therefore, usually requires an attitudinal change.

A number of hindrances to hospitality, although connected to our attitude and thoughts, are of such a nature as to truly be *controllable* barriers. These might include such excuses as "I'm too busy," "I'm too disorganized," or "My house is too dirty."

Let's look briefly at these excuses.

Too Busy

Busyness is the hallmark of western, and particularly American, society. Pastor and people alike are busy. Both homemakers and home-breakers wear busyness as a badge of honor. But busyness can be both a boon and a bane. Excessive busyness is a barrier to holy hospitality. A life schedule that hinders hospitality loudly declares, *I do not have time for you.*

Thankfully, busyness need not be a terminal disease. The remedy for a hyperventilated schedule is to remove some things from my schedule. That requires a reassessment of my priorities. Since the Scriptures require those who call themselves *Christian* to give themselves to hospitality as a basic ingredient and expression of life in Christ, hospitality must become a priority in my schedule. Often, this barrier can be bulldozed away by merely *choosing* to be a *doer* of hospitality and letting the growing joy of reaching to others replace the adrenaline addiction of treadmill existence.

I must make the choice; God will help me make the change. But one thing is certain: if I am too busy for hospitality, I am indeed *too busy*. To be too busy to open my heart and hand to welcome people into my home is to be too busy for Jesus.

Too Disorderly

Some folk just seem to have a knack for getting everything in just the right place. Others of us seem to be devoid of the ability to get anything into what would appear to be a right place. Some of us are neatnicks, and others couldn't seem to care less. Yet, if my household is too disorderly or downright dirty, I am most likely going to be hindered in the practice of hospitality.

Who wants to invite someone into their home when the sink and counters are continually strewn with dirty dishes, beds are unmade, the air reeks from mounds of unwashed clothes, and strata of dust could measure decades of homemaking dereliction? And even if an invited one came, would he or she want to return? Your time together should not be remembered by foul smells but by sweet fellowship.

Does the way you live reveal something of God's cleansing, restoring work in your life? Would your guests know it? Does your family know it by the way you faithfully follow through with your household responsibilities? For good reason it has been said, "Cleanliness is next to godliness." Internal cleansing by God's grace gradually reveals itself externally by our cleaning up our disorderly ways and practices. This principle has proven to be true in almost every culture.

If you struggle in this area, ask someone you know who has a better handle on their household to help you learn to turn your disorder into godly order. Your family, friends, and guests will be blessed, and a new world of unhindered hospitality will open before you.

Too Disorganized

A common complaint of many, especially women, is that they feel they lack sufficient organizational skills to fulfill even the simplest acts of hospitality in their homes. Often, these feelings are not based in fact but are borne out of comparison with someone who is renowned for having a super-organized home. Insecurity sets in and hinders hospitality.

Disorganization can lead to disorderly conditions in the home and life that severely impair freedom in reaching respectfully to others. More often, however, disorganization leads to frustration and a generalized feeling of inadequacy to display hospitality genuinely in the home. Many women allow themselves to become paralyzed by this sense of disorganizational incapacity. Do you relate to this intimidating frustration? If so, there is hope.

First, step out by faith. You can practice hospitality by faith. Leap over the wall of fear and frustration by faith. Determine to do hospitality. Then do it. You will grow more confident with each opportunity you embrace by faith. Remember, *practice makes perfect*.

Second, seek out someone you deem to be more organized, experienced, or talented in true hospitality (not entertainment). Ask if he or she can assist you or give you some pointers. Don't be ashamed.

Kathie has been plied by wives of pastors and politicians seeking help with the hindrance of disorganization. Whole new relationships have been born out of these times of discipling in hospitality.

A Final Word of Encouragement

God has ordained hospitality as a foundational life practice for His people. Hospitality is a universal calling. You can do all things through Christ who strengthens you (Phil. 4:13).

Hospitality is holy. Don't let unholy hindrances prevent you from the joy of blessing others through *The POWER of Hospitality*.

Heart-Opening Questions
for Personal and Group Reflection

Chapter 12

1. Why is the greatest *barrier* to hospitality the belief that I must be "gifted *IN*" hospitality rather than "give myself *TO*" hospitality?

2. Why is entertainment the greatest *substitute* for true hospitality?

3. Why are attitudes the greatest *hindrances* to hospitality?

4. What attitudinal barriers come between you and the true, effective, and fulfilling practice of hospitality?

5. Does anyone in your life truly practice hospitality from the heart (rather than entertainment) who could mentor you?

6. Do you battle with "false standards" that hinder your practice of hospitality? What are they?

7. Do you think your home is to be used solely as your private retreat from the world? Is this attitude consistent with God's ownership of your home or time?

8. Do you have behavioral patterns that hinder you in practicing hospitality? What are they? Are you willing to place them before God and allow Him to work with you in changing these patterns that prevent you from experiencing the fulfillment and joy that comes from giving yourself to hospitality?

9. Do you believe you can do *all things* through Christ who strengthens you (Phil. 4:13)?

10. Practice makes perfect! Are you willing to begin practicing holy hospitality? Your heart and home will never again be the same!

The Hope of Hospitality

The world brings us
therapy; God brings
us hospitality.

WHEN HOPE IS LOST, all seems lost. Many lose faith for loss of hope. And hope is intimately connected to hospitality.

It has often been said, "People don't care how much you know until they know how much you care." But many wonder, *Does anyone care at all?* Hospitality provides a hope-filled link between our faith in God and our required love of those created in His image. In this chapter we will explore how hospitality opens people everywhere. You will read stories of men and women whose lives have been opened through hospitality to provide hope, in turn, to others.

Hospitality Opens People Everywhere

TED AND LINDA

Ted was tough. He was a businessman, rising in the ranks of the business world. He was a big man with big plans and big problems. Those problems seemed to defy solution, presenting barriers in his relationship to God, family, and others, including his wife. Ted and his wife, Linda came to my office somewhat reluctantly for counsel on a variety of troubling issues. We talked, but instead of preaching at him, I hugged him—right there in my law office. It was a hug of holy hospitality. It revealed that my heart was open to Ted beyond the transfer of mere information. And that hug of hospitality broke barriers. For Ted, it opened a channel of relationship both to the Lord and others. We became friends. Ted and Linda traveled with our family and several others to Israel, where my daughters began to refer to them as "Uncle Ted" and "Aunt Linda." Our lives will forever be connected, and eternal destiny was shaped through a simple hug displaying hospitality. Yet, that hug of hope most likely never would have taken place had it not been for Steve and Wanda.

STEVE AND WANDA

We first met Steve and Wanda at a large church in Pasadena, California. Steve was a successful entrepreneur in his own business. I was just two years into law practice and both Kathie and I had college or advanced degrees. At that time, I was definitely not known as a "people person," but the Smiths invited us to their home as an extension of their heart for hospitality—a largely foreign concept to me.

Steve had no idea how tough reaching me would be. He tried everything he knew. He was baffled until he discovered that he and I shared an interest in photography. Photography became a connecting link by which a businessman without advanced formal education could reach the heart of a fledgling lawyer for what would prove to be a dramatically unfolding holy purpose. Our lives became intertwined for kingdom purposes for more than twenty-five years.

Hospitality became a dominant theme of our hearts and homes revealed in what we set our hands to do. Thousands of hearts have been opened to Christ's love through Steve and Wanda's hospitality. Steve has since passed from this life, but his hospitable influence continues. Thousands now will read the results of Steve and Wanda's holy hospitality, and that hospitality will echo throughout eternity as you now pick up the mantle. Truly, hospitality opens people everywhere.

The Hope of a Hug

Hugs are regular happenings in many cultures, but in America and much of the rest of Western culture, touch is often taboo. The absence of touch has revealed itself in unnecessary touchiness and is partly an expression of the progressive disease of individualism that eats like a cancer into our relationships. A hug, as an expression of an open heart, will accomplish what no handshake will ever do. Because our greatest need is to be loved, we all yearn for a holy hug. The shell of the hardest man can be broken with a hug from an open heart of hospitality.

There are many other ways to give hospitable hugs than an actual physical hug of the arms. One such way is a "hug on paper." Cindy and Shean are famous for hugs on paper, yet they are a continent apart.

Cindy is a secretary and office manager par excellent. But she also acts as God's heavenly secretary, sending little notes of love to those in her ever-expanding spheres of influence. Kathie and I have been the recipient of many such notes, as have hundreds of others. They always seem to come at critical moments when we need a hug from God. Have you ever needed such a hug? Why not consider delivering one today? It might even become a habit, expressing the hope of hospitality to someone on God's heart at the moment. Has someone come across your mind lately? Maybe God put him or her there. Give a hug on paper.

It has been said that poetry, like music, is the language of God. Shean is gifted in poetry. Not only does she give hugs on paper, but they are also often expressed in poetic meter and rhyme. If you are thus gifted, give your gift. Hospitality opens the heart to provide hope—yes even through hugs on paper and in poetry.

The Hope of a Haven

"Home is where the heart is," we say, and where the heart is there is a haven of hospitality. Christ offers the home of the Father as a haven of rest, and we, as His sons and daughters, must model the Father's hospitality.

Everyone of every race and every culture needs a haven. A haven provides hope for restoration, recoupment, reconciliation, revival, a night's rest, and eternal rest. Your cabin in the mountains, at the beach, in the desert, or on the lake can provide a hospitable haven of hope for a weary minister, a worn missionary, or a washed-up marriage.

When Kathie and I were more flush financially when I was practicing law, we purchased property in Lake Arrowhead, California, with the vision of using our resources to offer a place of retreat to others. We began implementing the vision by inviting others even while things were in a state of relative disarray and development. Our home was an open haven even with the ceilings being re-plastered and plastic draping the walls. The desperate need for a haven cannot await perfect circumstances.

The evening before I wrote this chapter, Chris called from Northern Virginia to ask if we knew of a hotel he might possibly stay the evening for a conference which was beginning that evening in Richmond. All hotels and motels with which he was familiar were booked. The Holy Spirit whispered in my ear, "You have two unoccupied bedrooms upstairs that will provide wonderful and private accommodations." Kathie agreed, and Chris and I enjoyed wonderful fellowship that evening that provided a haven of hope to discuss difficult circumstances, answering a need which might otherwise have gone unmet.

Four months earlier, Chris had invited me to join him and minister to and with a small group of men at Wintergreen in the Blue Ridge Mountains. It was a needed time for men to open their hearts to one another for hard-core discipleship. During an afternoon break, Tony, a retired marine geologist and geophysicist, and I took a lengthy walk amid icy wind and light snow, but our hearts were strangely warmed.

We shared together much of our vastly different spiritual sojourns, and I related to Tony how God had touched my hardened heart in the area of hospitality. He acknowledged that God had been moving in his own heart for a number of years, and that he and his wife, Pat, had dedicated their home to a ministry of hospitality. Tony's own words reflect how hospitality has become an obedient response to God's heart in providing a needed haven for His servants.

Tony's Story

OBEDIENCE WINS

My wife and I built our dream house for our retirement years in the Shenandoah Mountains of Virginia. The home is everything we ever wanted and more. It is truly a gift from God. Knowing that it is only by His grace that our dream could be realized, we dedicated our new home to the Lord. After we moved in, we went through each room and dedicated it to the Lord and His purposes.

We have used the home for Christian hospitality ever since, but our obedience was really tried once. In the fall of 2000, our church held its annual missionary conference. As with all such conferences, the guest missionaries needed homes to stay in. We signed up to house a couple with one child that would stay here two nights. Before we signed up to house this family, we were approached by a member of the housing committee to see if we would be interested in housing a young missionary couple with three small children who would stay here for five nights. I told the committee member that we had been through our child rearing years and were not interested in having young children, other than our own grandchildren, in our home for that many days.

Well, it seems that everyone in the church had either signed up for another family or just did not have the room for such a large family because as the conference approached, a home for this family had still not been found. My wife and I really did not want the noise and confusion of several very young children for so many days, but our house was certainly large enough to house this family. We discussed the situation and decided that since we had dedicated our home to the Lord, we needed to be obedient to His call for hospitality. We agreed to take in this larger family for the five-night stay rather than the couple and one child for two nights.

Again, the Lord demonstrated His blessing on those who obey. The family was great! We had a wonderful time with them and their three children. We became the best of friends and really hated to see them leave after the five-day visit. They became as close as another son and daughter and we gained three great "foster" grandchildren. We hope to visit this couple in a year or so on their mission field of Thailand.

Again, we learned the old and very true story; the Lord blesses those who obey His commands. I believe this is especially true with hospitality. All of our guests have brought a blessing, but this young couple and their three children were a very special blessing that we will never forget. Our lives have been so enriched through knowing and loving them!

How would God use your home as an earthly haven of hope for others on their journey to His heavenly haven? This path becomes more and more exciting the more our hearts are opened. Give it a try! The Scriptures declare that when we cry, He "maketh the storm a calm" and "bringeth them into their desired havens" (Ps. 107:28–30). Why not make your hand God's hand extended?

The Hope of Healing

Healing is rooted in hope. And our Creator, in His infinite wisdom, has designed those made in His image to hope. But hope, in a very real sense, is rooted in a heart of hospitality.

If, as we protest, America was destined to disciple the nations to proclaim the hope of the gospel of Christ to an estranged world, we should reasonably expect that Pilgrims and Puritans would have infused the land with God's heart of hospitality. Indeed they did. So pervasive was this theme that America herself became known as a haven of hope through a heart of hospitality despite the insidious growth of individualism that threatened to suffocate it. This great hope for America as a haven for healing was perhaps best expressed secularly in the words of Emma Lazarus, daughter of Jewish immigrants, who, in words that have become a classic of our commonwealth, passionately declared in 1883:

> Give me your tired, your poor,
> Your huddled masses yearning to breathe free,
> The wretched refuse of your teeming shore.
> Send these, the homeless, tempest-tossed to me.
> I lift my lamp beside the golden door!

John Winthrop, godly attorney and first governor of the Massachusetts Bay Colony, set forth the spiritual vision of a covenantal community displaying holy hospitality as an expression of the true love of God revealed in the love of the brethren. In his ***Model of Christian Charity,*** penned June 12, 1630, Winthrop set forth what is perhaps the best expression of the Puritan ideal of what America was to become—a vision for a covenant community revealing holy hospitality. Listen with your heart to his words:

> That which most people in churches only profess as a
> truth, we bring into familiar and constant practice; we must
> love one another with a pure heart and fervently; we must
> bear one another's burdens; we must not look on our own
> things but also on the things of our brethren. Nor must we
> think that the Lord will bear with our failings...
> But if we neglect to observe these articles...and—dissembling with our God—shall embrace this present world and

prosecute our carnal intentions, seeking great things for ourselves and our posterity, the Lord will surely break out in
wrath against us and be revenged of such a perjured people,
and will make us to know the price of the breach of such a
covenant.

To this end we must delight in each other, make others'
conditions our own and rejoice together, mourn together,
labor and suffer together, always having before our eyes our
commission and common work, our community as members of the same body.

For almost four hundred years, we as a people have gradually
and collectively drifted far from the words of Winthrop, embracing
individualism rather than the heart of Christian charity and hospitality envisioned and enacted by our Christian forebearers. The consequences have echoed through the collective membranes of the
American mind and have wreaked havoc in our hearts and homes.
Hope has become a casualty. As Pearl S. Buck wrote in the *New York
Times* in 1941, "When hope is taken away from a people, moral
degeneration follows swiftly after."

The searing influence of unrestrained individualism on our heart
of hospitality has cauterized our moral imagination and sealed over
the flow of moral truth. Our collective pain is palpable. We need God's
truth so bad it hurts, but we hurt so bad we can't hear the truth. What
prescription of hope will speak to this growing horror? **The world
brings us therapy; God brings us hospitality**. We crave credible relationships to translate truth that will provide hope. That is what Jesus
did, and as our Lord said just before He ascended back to the Father,
"As the Father hath sent me, even so send I you" (John 20:21).

Joe and Liz were renowned throughout the city for their professional status. But the high and the mighty are not exactly a haven of
hope in the midst of the storm. When painful marital problems
developed, they had no place to turn for hope and healing, and they
were not participants in a covenantal community of true Christians.
They had, however, been welcomed a number of times into the home

of Christian neighbors, also professionals, just to develop relation-ship. Joe and Liz independently and without the knowledge of the other, let their hearts be led by the warm remembrance of earlier hospitality. They each returned to their Christian neighbors' home for help. Hope was restored, and healing brought reconciliation. Hospitality truly opens hearts everywhere. It even provides hope and healing for hurting marriages.

The Hope of Happiness

It has been said that "Happiness is a door opening outward." If that be true, it should not be surprising that true and lasting happiness escapes most Americans, even Christians, in this generation. As we plunge headlong into our "rights" of "life, liberty, and the pursuit of happiness," individualism welcomes us with open yet unfulfilling arms that leave us empty. Hospitality is God's divine prescription of hope for happiness on earth as we, on earth, reveal His heart for hospitality in heaven.

There is peace in the practice of hospitality. As Kathie and I have given ourselves to hospitality these many years, we have discovered a joy and fulfillment that translates into inner peace. As we share with others the hope of hospitality, many report a transformation in their own hearts and homes much like opening a hidden door to an entirely new realm of happiness that had been shrouded by a dense fog of preoccupation with self. Perhaps that is why Sir Thomas Browne in *Christian Morals* observes,

> To enjoy true happiness we must travel into a very far country, even out of ourselves.

As the writing of this chapter approached conclusion, we were invited to share some of these thoughts with a congregation in Northern Virginia in preparation for our annual National Day of Prayer. Kathie and I were privileged to experience firsthand the warmth of hospitality by Tony and Pat, who earlier in this chapter revealed their open heart and open hand, opening their home as a haven of hospitality to a missionary family. Perched high in the Blue Ridge Mountains overlooking the Shenandoah Valley, their home provided a breathtaking view that alone stirred the heart. There, on their couch, was a small pillow with a message that also gripped our hearts as it will yours: "The heart is happiest when it beats for others."

Hope of a Home

Home is the ultimate place of hope this side of heaven. In the home resides the hope of the family, the church, and the nation. "No genuine observer can decide otherwise than that the homes of a nation are the bulwarks of personal and national safety." Perhaps this is why Thomas Jefferson wrote, "The happiness of the domestic fireside is the first boon of Heaven."

"Just a lookin' for a home" is the cry of most people, regardless of their pedigree or position. But as Edgar A. Guest has so aptly stated in his classic poem, "It takes a heap o' livin' to make a house a home." One of the essential elements of that "livin'" is hospitality. Without a heart of hospitality, no house will be a home, and hope will not be found there. "Happy is the house that shelters a friend," wrote Ralph Waldo Emerson. And those who open their homes in hospitality secure not only happiness in their home but hope in the heart of the strangers welcomed there. Hope for the traveler, hope for the homeless, hope for the hungry and hope for the heartbroken can all be found in a home happy with hospitality. Is hope being provided from your home?

"Home, in one form or another, is the great object of life." Heaven as our home is the ultimate and final hope. Hospitality provides the hope of Heaven. **Hospitality allows your home to serve as a half-way house for God to welcome into His home strangers to the "commonwealth of faith."** Jesus said, "In my father's house are many rooms...." "I go to prepare a place for you, that where I am, there you may be also." Therefore, "Let not your heart be troubled." Now that is the final hope of home! Will others find the hope of an eternal home because hospitality graces your home? Let *The POWER of Hospitality* in your home guide the way to Christ's home.

HOSPITALITY

OPENS

PEOPLE

EVERYWHERE

"And now abideth FAITH, HOPE, and LOVE" (I Cor. 13:13).

Hospitality spells H-O-P-E. Hospitality is God's divinely ordained glue, linking FAITH and LOVE. Hospitality is hope in action. Hospitality provides

> HOPE for reconciliation to God;
> HOPE for racial reconciliation;
> HOPE for reconciling marriages;
> HOPE for rebuilding community;
> HOPE for realizing a discipled nation; and
> HOPE for revival.
> - Restoration of TRUTH will be the MIND of revival but
> - Restoration of HOSPITALITY, as a tangible expression of agape love, will be the HEART of revival.

Revive us, O Lord, with your heart of hospitality that hope may abound on earth, preparing the way to your home in heaven.

Let's close this chapter with a fireplace motto that you may want to make a part of your home:

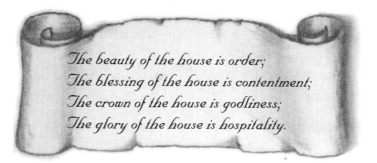

The beauty of the house is order;
The blessing of the house is contentment;
The crown of the house is godliness;
The glory of the house is hospitality.

Heart-Opening Questions
for Personal and Group Reflection
Chapter 13

1. In what ways is *hope* intimately connected to hospitality?

2. Why does hospitality open people everywhere? Can you think of examples in your own life or that of someone else?

3. Do you agree that a hug can be a genuine expression of hospitality? Why can a hug do what no handshake could ever do?

4. Have you ever received a note that was a true expression of someone's open, hospitable heart toward you? How did that make you feel?

5. Do you know of someone whose home is a haven for others in the time of storm? Is your home such a haven? Why not? Would you like it to be? What steps are you willing to take to make that a reality?

6. America became a haven of hope because of a holy vision of her early founders for God-breathed hospitality. As you read the words of attorney John Winthrop from his "Model of Christian Charity," what thoughts went through your mind? Where is our nation, your church, your home today in comparison to those visionary words penned in 1630? Will you commit to read Winthrop's entire *Model of Christian Charity* included in the Appendix of this book?

7. Why is "Happiness a door opening outward?"

8. It has been said that "Home, in one form or another, is the great object of life." Can you see how hospitality can provide the hope of Heaven by allowing your home to be a half-way house to welcome strangers into the "commonwealth of faith?"

9. Have others found hope of an eternal home because hospitality graces your home?

Chapter *14*

End-Time Hospitality

Can we be raptured

to Christ's home if we

refuse to open our home?

GOD'S HEART IS BROKEN over the broken hearts of His sons and daughters. From the Church house to the White House, America's heart is broken. Few subjects are of a more pressing, practical, or potent nature for the Church or the healing of America than that of hospitality. Yet, hospitality is also an essential for end-time preparation.

The Hope of Hospitality

Hospitality means to reach to strangers. A stranger is anyone who is unknown, unfamiliar, unacquainted, or not admitted to fellowship.

Our world and our churches are packed with strangers. At least 70 percent of our pastors admit to being strangers in the midst of the crowd. A holy disillusionment is brewing from pulpit to pew. Jesus is coming back. He is ironing out the wrinkles in the Bride's gown. He expects us to be fully reconciled—ONE!

The hope of our healing is rooted deeply in the Father's heart of hospitality. The very gospel is good news precisely because it tangibly translates God's heart of hospitality. We are all estranged—sinners, strangers from God. The Father's open heart of hospitality opened His divine hand, sending His only Son "across the tracks"of time into a sinfully unpleasant place called Earth, to extend an invitation to join Him for an eternal marriage supper in His home. Christ declared, "In my Father's house are many mansions: I go to prepare a place for you…that where I am, there ye may be also" (John 14:2–3).

Reconciliation began in Egypt. God called Moses and then Israel to flee Egypt as strangers so that He could welcome them to His Promised Land.

End-Time Hospitality

God loves strangers! "Cursed be he that perverteth the judgment of the stranger," warned Moses (Deut. 27:19). God's heart never changed. Malachi closed the Old Covenant, declaring,

> I will come near to you to judgment; and I will be a **swift witness against those that…turn aside the stranger**, and fear not Me, saith the Lord of Hosts. For I am the Lord, I change not" (Mal. 3:5–6a).

Jesus was hospitality incarnate. Watch Him reach to the outcast, to the poor, to the tax collector, to the sinner. Peter, apostle to the Jews, warned, **"The end of all things is at hand"** (I Pet. 4:7). In that end-time plea, he commanded, **"Use hospitality one to another without grudging"** (I Pet 4:9). The great apostle to the gentiles, Paul, drove home the same message:

> **Let love be without dissimulation:** Be kindly affectioned one to another with brotherly love,...**given to hospitality** (Rom. 12:9-10, 13b).

Notice! Paul did not say "gifted in" hospitality. We are told to give ourselves *TO* hospitality. So elementary and foundational is this principle in the Kingdom that Paul required each person in leadership to be "a lover of hospitality" (Titus 1:8).

Hospitality is the tangible translation of agape love we talk so much about. It is the key that unlocks the door to genuine Body life. It is the single most powerful evangelistic tool, since statistics clearly reveal that more than 70 percent of all persons come to Christ, not through crusades or programs but through relationships.

Hospitality is the "grease" that lubricates and activates all legitimate ministry. There is no true ministry without hospitality. Hospitality is the nondelegable, unavoidable essence and manifestation of true Christian love. Purported ministry without it, regardless of appearances, is a cheap organizational counterfeit.

Truth without relationship born of hospitality is void of reality. God could have sent a flying scroll, but instead He sent a suffering servant to "flesh out" the truth. Jesus declared Himself to be "the Truth" (John 14:6). "The Word was made flesh, and dwelt among us" in divine hospitality, so that "we beheld His glory...full of grace and truth" (John 1:14). That is what will bring integrity to our message. Preachment without hospitable relationship is a perversion of God's plan and purpose.

Preaching, teaching and living biblical hospitality will revolutionize the Church as we know it. It gives the necessary "handle" to effectuate and activate the love of God we profess to offer. It is the window through which we can reach an alienated world of strangers from the "commonwealth of faith." Jesus will not return until we give ourselves to hospitality. Therefore, hospitality must become a priority for those awaiting Messiah's return on the near edge of the Second Coming. This will require reassessing our individual and collective viewpoints, bringing them in line with God's historic viewpoint on strangerhood. Our thinking will then change as well as many of our personal and corporate plans and practices.

Institutionalized Strangerhood

A STERN REPRIMAND FOR ISRAEL

God loves strangers! Israel suffered strangerhood in Egypt for four hundred years. God heard their cry and their groaning. And He sent Moses to deliver them. But they were a tough bunch. They were perpetually tempted to enforce strangerhood on those journeying with them.

After a generation of wilderness wandering—out of Egypt in the flesh but groveling there in the spirit—Israel received a stiff rebuke from Moses.

> Circumcise therefore the foreskin of your heart, and be
> no more stiff-necked (Deut. 10:16).

Now what attitudes and behaviors does this language conjure in your mind as meriting such a stern reprimand? Adultery? Thievery? Idolatry? These would certainly have earned God's wrath. Yet those were not God's concerns here. Prayerfully listen to Moses' pronouncement. Read it aloud.

> For the Lord your God is God of gods, and Lord of
> lords...He doth execute the judgment of the fatherless and
> widow, and **loveth the stranger,** in giving him food and rai-
> ment. **Love ye therefore the stranger: for ye were strangers
> in the land of Egypt.** Thou shalt fear the Lord thy God; Him
> thou shalt serve (Deut. 10:17–20).

A FINAL CALL TO THE CHURCH

Our God is unchanging. He still loves the stranger. His message to His children has never changed; neither have His children. We are still stiffnecked, aren't we? For at least seventeen centuries we have developed traditions and practices to institutionalize strangerhood in the Church, even in the name of Christ.

The very way we "do church" has, in effect, become institution-alized strangerhood. We have developed it into an art form. And Yahweh, Jehovah—the Lord of lords and God of gods—addresses His children, wooing and warning before the Second Coming of Christ, "LOVE THE STRANGER!" "Grieve Me no longer!" "Come out of Egypt." Could this be His final call?

A Clever Sleight of Hand

Satan is very clever. By the third century, he found a way, in religious disguise, to build a box that would paralyze the effectiveness of the Church for seventeen centuries. The Roman emperor Constantine converted an empire to Christianity by imperial fiat. With the apparent blessing that eliminated rampant persecution came a curse.

Politically decreed faith replaced personally conveyed faith. Cathedrals relegated the Church to boxes with four walls. An open heart's door was replaced by a massive "church" door. The haven of the home took a backseat to the haven of the "sanctuary."

Stained glass replaced clear windows. The Church could not see the world, nor the world the Church. Beautiful buildings stole the beauty of the Body of Christ. "Come see our building" became the Kingdom cry, casting a deep shadow over the natural haven of the heart in homes where body life had once thrived. Men bowed in shrines of wood and stone while the life of "living stones" that make up the Church was smothered in ecclesiasticism and all but snuffed out.

Men and women who had worshiped in synagogues and from house to house in the first century were now relegated to "God's house." Once accountability thrived as they looked each other in the eye, breaking bread from home to home. Now the cold pallor of strangerhood hovered over the spirit of hospitality. Worshipers gathered in rows rather than in relationship. The collective effect was devastating.

Hierarchies heralded the demise of elders and servant pastors, who had made tents by day and loved the brethren, not by trade but by a living truth that constrained them. Instead of the Lord "adding to the Church such as should be saved," the Church added such as should become members of glorified country clubs. Back-slapping churchgoers replaced warm-hearted, hugging families.

"Come to my church" obscured "Go into all the world." The building obscured the Body. Programs of the Church obscured the people of God. The corporeal body became a corporation. Big became better. Love was largely lost in the lurch. Institutionalization paralyzed the people. The heart was left at home. Men became strangers to their brothers in Christ and were isolated even from their own flesh, as families became divided by age and sex for the "efficient propagation of the gospel." It was a clever sleight of hand—all so religious. Deception is still deception.

FEELING STRANGE, ACTING STRANGELY

The sense of the covenantal community disintegrated. The back of men's heads in pews structured out the glory of God to be seen on faces. Strangerhood was now structured in the Church. And the Spirit of God was grieved.

Home remains where the heart is. And God still calls us to leave Egypt. When we "leave Egypt," we must again open our hearts to the "strangers" among us. But in many respects, the entire Body of Christ has become a "stranger." We feel strange with one another and treat each other strangely. From congregation to congregation and even within our own congregations, we do not know one another. Many neither care nor know how to care for one another.

Love has become "organizational" rather than organismal. Our programmed style of caring often renders faceless the objects of our care. The Master still yearns for us to bring the poor to our own house and to feed the hungry with our own food (Is. 58:7). He wants to eradicate strangerhood at the table of His truth. He yearns for us in the final moments of history to truly come out of Egypt.

Where is Your Heart?

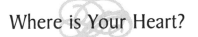

The "I AM" is stirring by His Spirit to create a holy disillusionment with institutionalized "churchianity." He is calling His church home, for "Home is where the heart is." Through house-churches, small-group and cell ministry, touching one another's lives "from house to house," He is breaking us out of the "house of bondage" of institutionalized worship. His purpose is to restore the relational gospel of a Savior who was the "Word made flesh"—the very incarnation of the divine heart of hospitality that "dwelt among us"—that we might again "behold His glory, full of grace and truth." The Father's heart will not allow His Son's prayer to go unanswered: "Father, that they all may be one; that the world may believe that thou has sent me" (John 17:21).

It is time to come out of Egypt. It is time to restore a spirit of holy hospitality. Integrate your faith, your hope, your love. Let there be no more strangers among the true "household of faith." Open your heart; then open your hand; and open your home. It will change the way you think and live! It will revolutionize the way we "do" church. It will profoundly influence our nation and the world. And it will prepare our hearts to conform to the welcoming hospitality in Christ's eternal home. We must prepare for our Lord's soon return. "The end of all things is at hand," warned the Apostle Peter. Therefore, "Use hospitality to one another without grudging" (I Pet. 4:7,9).

Mary and Joseph found no room in the inn. Will your brother and sister find room in the inn of your heart and home? Remember! Home is where the heart is. Where is your heart? Have a heart. Open your hand and home!

Can we be raptured to Christ's home in the heavens if we refuse to open our homes on earth? Do not answer too quickly. For if we do not love those we *can* see, how can we say we love God whom we *cannot* see? (See I John 4:20–21). The Father asks you today, "Do you love Me?" His response echoes through the centuries: "Then love the stranger."

My Prayer for a Heart of Hospitality

Lord,

I love you! I am so blessed to be your child. Truly you have caused the lines to fall unto me in pleasant places. You have brought and continue to bring rest to my soul.

I am most grateful for a spouse and family that love you and seek to serve you. Help us all to walk in love toward each other and those you have placed in the spheres of our influence. We want to be ambassadors of your love and grace. We want our home to be an embassy for Christ. Help us to walk out this calling faithfully.

Continue to reveal your divine heart of hospitality to and through me and my family. Help me, help us, to make your love tangible to all whose lives we touch. Open my eyes to see people the way you see them. Open my heart that it becomes your heart, open my hand that it becomes your hand extended, and open my home that it becomes a vestibule of your Kingdom, welcoming others into your eternal home. Help me to be an effective steward of the resources you entrust to me so that I might better fulfill your call to holy hospitality.

By faith, I give myself to hospitality. And by your love, I will be a lover of hospitality. Keep this vision for holy hospitality always before my eyes. Work it deep within my heart. Thank you for opening your heart, hand, and home of hospitality to me. Help me now to open my heart, my hand, and my home as an end-time expression of your love in partnership with your end-time purposes. I know I am called for such a time as this, and by your grace, my home will become an embassy welcoming many into your eternal kingdom, preparing the way of the Lord.

In Jesus' name I pray,

Amen

Heart-Opening Questions
for Personal and Group Reflection

Chapter 14

1. Are you convinced, at this point, that there are few subjects of a more pressing, practical, or potent nature for the Church or the healing of America than that of hospitality?

2. Do you believe that we are either in or close to the end times?

3. Why is hospitality essential for end-time preparation?

4. How is the Gospel itself rooted in and defined by hospitality?

5. Why has God continuously expressed a heart for the stranger?

6. Why is truth, without relationship born of hospitality, void of reality?

7. Why is preaching, without hospitable relationship, a perversion of God's plan and purpose?

8. How has the Church institutionalized strangerhood?

9. How does the practice of hospitality reflect, at least in part, our coming out of Egypt?

10. Peter said, "The end of all things is at hand." Therefore, "Use hospitality to one another without grudging (I Pet. 4:7, 9). Are you prepared to get on board with this mandated end-time practice? When will you start?

11. Mary and Joseph found no room in the inn. Will those God brings across your path find room in the inn of your heart and home?

12. Can we be raptured to Christ's home in the heavens if we refuse to open our homes on earth? Don't answer too quickly! It may just reveal if our hearts are truly converted, if we are truly saved. Salvation is not revealed in an idle creed but in a new breed whose converted hearts compel them to do the will of the Father (Matt. 7:21–23). Blessings to you as you become a doer of the Word and not only a hearer (James 1:22).

Chapter *15*

$\mathcal{R}$eceiving $\mathcal{H}$ospitality

Every occasion

offering hospitality

provides occasion

for receiving it.

IT IS MORE BLESSED to give than to receive," declared Jesus (Acts 20:35), yet where there is giving, there must be gracious receiving. Godly giving without godly receiving is grotesque. Such a thing could only be rooted in ungratefulness.

What Would Jesus Do?

Open hearts will open doors. When those doors of hospitality begin to swing open, many of us who have never crossed the threshold of another's home will be blessed with that opportunity. But for many, that opportunity may be pregnant with not only anticipation but also apprehension.

Questions begin to bombard the mind. How should we dress? How will we be able to have meaningful conversation? Why are they inviting us? What do we do with the kids? What will be expected of me? What if they have animals I fear or to which I am allergic? What if the place is filthy? Or what if those inviting me are completely outside my life experience or economic position?

Since every occasion offering hospitality provides an occasion for receiving it, these questions are to be expected as normal and part of our human experience. Many of the questions provide us with a test of our love of God and our love of those created in His image. Our answer will determine our testimony. Without a test, there is no testimony.

God's purpose for His sons and daughters is that you and I be increasingly conformed to the image of Jesus, His only begotten Son (Rom. 8:29). God must place us in situations that mold us and provide opportunity for us to respond as Jesus would in the same or similar circumstances. Never have the words made classic by Charles Sheldon been more appropriate: "What Would Jesus Do?"

Hospitality Without Partiality

What did Jesus do? What did Jesus teach by precept and practice concerning our relationships with others? How did Jesus receive open acts of hospitality? Scripture provides us with memorable insights.

SIMON THE LEPER

The day before Jesus' crucifixion, while the chief priests were conspiring against Him, Jesus was the recipient of hospitality from a most unusual source. Matthew records, "Jesus was in Bethany, in the house of Simon the leper" (Matt. 26:6). In Middle Eastern society, lepers were outcasts. They were feared and despised. Their disease was loathsome and even viewed as a "type" of sin. Yet Jesus was in a leper's house. Had Simon been healed? We are not told. But Jesus received his hospitality.

There is yet another reason why Jesus might have been "turned off" by Simon. It appears that Simon was the father of Judas Iscariot, who was to betray Jesus that very day (John 12:4; Matt. 26:6-15). Jesus knew who would betray Him (Matt. 26:23–25). Yet He did not allow that association to deter Him from receiving Simon's hospitality. This is astounding! What a challenge to pastor and people! The love of God constrained Him.

WOMAN OF ILL REPUTE

Reputation can rub off in the estimation of many, yet Jesus refused to allow the undesirable reputation of one who would bestow hospitality to prevent receiving the expression of her heart. Luke reports that "a woman in the city, which was a sinner" came to another's home where Jesus had come to eat and began weeping and washing His feet with her tears (Luke 7:37–38). Now washing the feet was truly a servant act of hospitality in dry and dusty Israel.

Luke notes, "when the Pharisee which had bidden [invited] him saw it, he spoke within himself, "This man, if he were a prophet, would have known who and what manner of woman this is…for she is a sinner" (Luke 7:39). Jesus, knowing his thoughts, responded with a parable resulting in the classic conclusion, *He who is forgiven much loves much.* Jesus drove the message of hospitality home to this pharisee who prided himself on the openness of his home, saying,

> Simon, seest thou this woman? I entered into thine house, thou gavest me no water for my feet: but she hath washed my feet with tears…. Thou gavest me no kiss [common hospitable practice for men in the Middle East]: but this woman, since the time I came in, hath not ceased to kiss my feet. My head with oil, thou didst not anoint: but this woman hath anointed my feet with ointment (Luke 7:44–46).

A woman of ill repute among the religious establishment received salvation that day for her heart of hospitality reflecting the openness of her heart to Jesus. Hers was not a faith of creed but of deed and truth. And Jesus, to the astonishment of this craftsman of religious creed, declared to the woman, "Thy faith hath saved thee; go in peace" (Luke 7:50).

True hospitality can reveal repentance and open the door to the Father's house through salvation. We dare not elevate ourselves and our reputation over that of the only begotten Son of God. Jesus did not go to the prostitute's home. She would not have expected that. But He gladly received her hospitality. What would you do?

Zacchaeus the Tax Collector

Politics separates many a man from the Master. Politics also separates many of the Master's men and women from those whose hearts might otherwise willingly receive the hospitable gift of salvation. Such was potentially the case for Zacchaeus, a Jew who had become rich by collecting taxes from his own people on behalf of the Roman Empire. Here was a man despised for his politics and power, "chief among the publicans" (Luke 19:2). But "he sought to see Jesus" (Luke 19:3).

People pressed Jesus everywhere because of His miracles and because He taught "as one who had authority" and not as the institutional religious establishment. Zacchaeus, because he was of short stature, put pride aside and climbed a tree to see Jesus. This act revealed the openness of a seeking heart, which fact did not escape the Lord. When Jesus saw him, He said loudly and publicly, "Zacchaeus, make haste, and come down; for today I must abide at thy house" (Luke 19:5).

Sometimes circumstances require you to invite yourself into another's home or life experience, not for your own purposes but for the need which God reveals in the person's life. Jesus had measured the man well, because Zacchaeus "made haste, and came down, and received Him joyfully" (Luke 19:6). Zaccheaus received Jesus. Jesus, knowing the potential political cost to His reputation among the power brokers of the day, was willing to sacrifice temporal values for an eternal victory.

The backlash was immediate, "And when they saw it, they all murmured, saying that He was gone to be a guest with a man that is a sinner" (Luke 19:7). But Jesus looked beyond the outward appearance to the heart. Do you? This kind of applied truth is rugged for our business-as-usual churchianity. It may "tax" our belief in the Truth. Zacchaeus was so deeply moved by Jesus' willingness to be in relationship that He repented on the spot. Jesus' willingness to be received by a despicable tax collector resulted in that tax collector being received into the Father's house. "Today," declared Jesus, "is salvation come to this house" (Luke 19:9).

As the culture wars rage in the American political realm, and as party politics seems to define the temporal order, might a little of *The POWER of Hospitality* be more powerful than much of our posturing and power politics? Breaking bread might be more effective than banging heads. While we must stand for truth, being willing to sit in relationship without regard to reputation might just allow the one who declared himself to be "The Truth" to bring salvation to the scene. Jesus did not rebuke Zacchaeus for his politics and practices. He was merely received into his home and heart by extending a hand of hospitality.

Partiality perverts hospitality, both on the giving and the receiving ends. Hospitality given or received with partiality reveals a heart self-focused rather than servant-focused. If there come into your assembly a man in goodly apparel and also a poor man with unpleasant raiment, and you provide a good and honorable place for the one who wears the latest style but ignore or treat the poor man with dishonor, "Are ye not then partial?" asks James, the brother of Jesus (James 2:2–4). If we have "respect to persons," James warns, we "commit sin" (James 2:9). Aren't you glad God is no respecter of persons? His hospitality is genuine.

Guidelines for Receiving Graciously

Do's

- Do express enthusiasm for an invitation. Work out your own fleshly reservations privately.
- Do recognize and express gratefulness for another's expression of hospitality, however small it may seem.

- Do make every effort to find areas of interest and need in those who would open their home to you.
- Do show interest in your hosts' family and children.
- Do give of yourself, opening your own heart to meaningful relationship.
- Do contribute what you can.
- Do promptly write a note of thanks and appreciation.

Don'ts

- Do not let pride get in the way of accepting or receiving hospitality. You may just be in the presence of "angels" unawares.
- Do not show open displeasure over things that fail to meet your standard in choice of food, food preparation, order, cleanliness, manners, etc.
- Do not be critical.
- Do not extend hospitality only to those who can reciprocate.
- Do not expect your own hospitality to be reciprocated.

The key is to receive hospitality as "Jesus with skin on." As Christ's body, we are to be the incarnation or fleshing-out of Christ even as Christ was the "Word made flesh" (John 1:14). "As the Father hath sent Me," said Jesus, "even so send I you" (John 20:21).

Responding to Hospitality

Receiving hospitality includes responding to hospitality. What should I do after someone has reached to me with open heart and hand? Must I reciprocate in kind?

Network marketers and salesmen talk often of the "Law of Reciprocity." If you do something for someone, that person will feel a natural obligation to reciprocate in some way or "return the favor." This can serve as needed provocation for some of us to do that which we know we ought to do. But checking the true motive of the heart is important. Am I responding out of a mere sense of obligation; or am

I grateful for this extra incentive to do that which, in my heart, I know I both ought to do and want to do? Never mistake endurance for hospitality.

Receiving hospitality does not require that I reciprocate in every instance to those who have opened their heart and home. But the best honor I can give to one who has shown me hospitality is to show myself hospitable, to extend hospitality to someone else. Consider writing to someone who has opened heart and home to you, thanking them for the inspiration given to enable you to do the same for someone else. Can you imagine the multiplied blessing that will begin to echo among the brethren?

Jesus graciously gave and received hospitality. If we are truly His disciples, we can do no less. In fact, **our first act of hospitality is to receive Christ and His Holy Spirit into our lives.**

Rejecting Hospitality

Hospitality is God's divine design for exchange of relationship. It is the *modus operandi* —M.O., or mode of operation—of His eternal home and heart. God, therefore, expects hospitality to be the "M.O." of both our hearts and homes as His children. When that "M.O." is violated, the Father is not pleased, to put it mildly.

Because extension of hospitality is so intimately connected with the will and ways of our Father, to fail to give or receive hospitality by His sons and daughters created in His image is tantamount to desecrating His image and is a direct affront to God himself. In fact, rejecting hospitality can be downright dangerous. Scripture actually records that it makes God furious.

To offer hospitality to someone requires that I open my heart in love, open my hand in generosity, and open my home in acceptance and fellowship. It requires great transparency and holy risk with the reward of relationship. Rejection of offered hospitality is, in effect, an open rejection of one made in God's image. For this reason, we must be extremely cautious about rejecting proferred hospitality, probing carefully the motivation of our own hearts. Rejecting hospitality is not to be done casually and is not without potential consequence, both temporal and eternal.

The gravity of rejecting hospitality is driven home by Jesus in His "Parable of the Great Supper" (Lk. 14:12–24). "A certain man made a great supper," said Jesus, "and bade many." He sent his servant to bid all who were invited to come when everything was ready. But one after another, those who had been invited made excuses why they couldn't come. When the report of rejected hospitality got back, "the master of the house, being angry, said to his servant, Go out into the highways and hedges, and compel them to come in that my house may be filled."

It is well understood that the "master of the house" in the parable referred to the Father, the servant being Christ, the servant son. And by extension, as Christ's brethren, you and I are bidden to extend the Father's hand of hospitality to join Him, through repentance, at the final Wedding Supper of the Lamb. As it is written, "Blessed are they which are called unto the marriage supper of the Lamb (Rev. 19:9).

But note carefully! It is not actually those that are invited who are blessed but those who accept the invitation. The master (God the Father) was furious with those who rejected His hospitality, declaring, "That none of those men which were bidden shall taste of my supper" (Lk. 14:24).

The quickest way to incur God's wrath is to reject His gracious offer of hospitality. For this reason, rejection of the Father's invitation of hospitality to His home is an "unpardonable sin." It is a sin that cannot be forgiven, because the only way to repent is to accept the invitation. Rejection of the invitation is rejection of the Holy Spirit, whom the Father has sent into the earth to extend His invitation.

For this reason, Jesus warned, "All manner of sin and blasphemy shall be forgiven unto men, but whosoever speaketh against the Holy Spirit, it shall not be forgiven him, neither in this world, neither in the world to come" (Matt. 12:31–32). For this reason also God's wrath was upon the religious leaders of God's chosen people who, throughout history, rejected God's messengers, the prophets, and Christ Himself. Stephen, the first martyr of the Church, infuriated them by accurately calling them "stiff necked" and "uncircumcised in heart," declaring, "ye do always resist [the invitation of] the Holy Spirit: as your fathers did, so do ye" (Acts 7:51–52).

If God is infuriated by those who reject His invitation because they don't like the nature of the invitation, don't like the messenger, don't like his clothing, or don't think his status or education measure up, what should we expect His response to be to His own children who claim His name but reject honorable offers of hospitality by those made in God's image, using the same or similar excuses?

To give may be more blessed than to receive, but if there is to be a giver, there must be a receiver with an open heart. Who knows but what God is bringing answers to prayer, new vistas for ministry, a new Kingdom connection, needed conviction, or any of a host of other blessing possibilities your way through an unsuspected, unusual, or even seemingly less-than-desirable invitation. It could be an appointment with destiny for you or the other person or family. Seize the moment. God will smile and say, "That's my son." "That's my daughter."

Heart-Opening Questions
for Personal and Group Reflection

Chapter 15

1. How is it that open hearts open doors?

2. With every giving there must be a receiving. When was the last time you received hospitality? Was it a good, unpleasant, or awkward experience? Why? Were you an active participant or a passive receptor?

3. The words "What would Jesus do?" have been popularized based upon Charles Sheldon's classic book *In His Steps*. So, how did Jesus receive hospitality? Give some examples.

4. Aren't you glad Jesus is no respecter of persons? But are you? What would keep you from receiving hospitality from another? Political alliances? Social status? Neighborhood? Racial difference? Reputation? What would Jesus do in your shoes? Can we be *pure* without being *partial*?

5. Which of the "Guidelines for Receiving Graciously" cause you the most difficulty? Why?

6. Are you willing to extend hospitality without it being reciprocated? Would you be willing to extend hospitality repeatedly to various persons or families without any reciprocation?

7. Why are you willing to do hospitality? Is it for what you can *get*, or for what you can *give*?

8. Are you willing to express heart-felt gratefulness for another's efforts at hospitality even if it falls far short of your desires or expectations? What do you think Jesus would do?

9. Why is endurance of others not the same as hospitality?

10. What is the best way you can honor another person who has shown you hospitality?

Chapter  16

The Key
of Hospitality

Hospitality is a
divinely designed
key to the door of
the heart.

THE HEART IS LIKE A PRISON. Those inside prison walls cannot get out for lack of a key. Those outside the prison who desire access to those inside cannot gain access for lack of a key. Whoever holds the key controls access both in and out.

Similarly, the doors to our hearts are often, if not usually, locked shut. Just as sin and selfishness lock men and women away from the rest of society in prison, so sin and *SELF*-ish-ness lock off our hearts from one another and from God. Whoever holds the key has freedom of access, whether in or out.

207

Keys of the Kingdom

The word *key* appears just eight times in all of Scripture. The Hebrew word for *key* literally means "an opener." Jesus, in speaking to Peter together with the other disciples, said, "I will give unto thee the keys of the Kingdom of Heaven" (Matt. 16:19). Completing this handing over of spiritual keys, Jesus told His followers that whatever they would "bind" or lock up on earth would be done, just as it was in Heaven. He completed the picture by saying that whatever they would "loose" or unlock on earth would be done, having already been done according to their authority in Heaven.

Interestingly, these "keys of the kingdom" are never specifically delineated or defined anywhere in Scripture. That means you and I must discern accurately and spiritually what these keys are and use them appropriately, binding or locking up where necessary and loosing or unlocking where needed. It would seem, then, that whatever tools God has expressly given us to accomplish this locking and loosing on earth are the "keys of the Kingdom." These obviously include, among other things, the "Word of God," the "Name of the Lord," and the "Prayer of Faith." We are convinced that these keys also include *The POWER of Hospitality*, for we are expressly commanded to give ourselves to hospitality (Rom. 12:13; I Tim. 3:2). Why is it that hospitality seems so little used and is little more than a vague concept to many Christians?

Keys Seem Insignificant

Virtually all keys are comparatively insignificant. You undoubtedly possess many keys. Take a look at a few of them. Most keys are relatively nondescript. One would not normally go out of his or her way merely to buy a key so as to possess the key. The true value of the key lies not in itself but in where it will allow you to go or in what it will allow you to use or accomplish.

The "Word of God" is a key that gives access to the mind and heart of God. A Bible never used is a key owned for its own sake. It does absolutely no good. According to George Gallup, well over 90 percent of Americans own Bibles, and the average American owns at least four, yet Gallup says we are a nation of "biblical illiterates." We pride ourselves in owning "keys" but seldom use them appropriately. A Bible seems so insignificant in the face of personal, national, or international problems.

The "Name of the Lord" is claimed by 86 percent of Americans who claim to be "Christian," at least in moral precept. More than 40 percent of us claim to be "born-again," wearing the name of Jesus as a badge of identity, yet many are utterly ignorant of how to use the name of Jesus as the Scriptures portray, a key unlocking the power of God in the earth. While we revere the name of Jesus, it just seems so relatively insignificant when we have political and technological power at our disposal. Prayer also, while acknowledged as an essential "key," is given relatively short shrift by many Christians and even pastors. Why? In reality, it just doesn't seem to us to be operationally significant in the face of the onslaught of problems that bombard modern man, especially when we have a plethora of purportedly "spiritual" seminars that really dispense self-help in the name of Christ.

The same is true of hospitality. It seems so insignificant, doesn't it? The truth is that hospitality has appeared so insignificant to our spiritual leaders that it is seldom, if ever, taught by precept from the pulpit, and it is demonstrated even less by example. Hospitality just does not seem to register on the spiritual "Richter Scale," even though our lives, ministries, families, and nation are being shaken for lack of it.

The Kingdom of God is driven by and becomes operational through "keys" that seem of little relative value—a name, a word, a prayer, faith as little as a grain of mustard seed, and, yes, hospitality. Perhaps this is what the Apostle Paul had in mind when he said, "God hath chosen the foolish things of the world to confound the wise" (I Cor. 1:27).

A Key Gives Us Access

A key may seem small and insignificant, but it gives access to power, places, and people. When a man or woman is symbolically given the "keys to the city" by the mayor, that person is given open access to power, places, privilege and people. The keys to your car give you access to power for transportation in style and speed not otherwise available. The keys to your home give you access into your home and keep others out. The password on your computer is a "key" that grants access to a world of information that would otherwise be closed to you. It allows you entrance, but keeps others out.

Similarly, the "keys of the kingdom" give us access to realms not otherwise available. Power, places, and people are accessed by these "kingdom keys." Salvation itself functions as a key, allowing access to God Himself as well as to His home (Rev. 3:20; John 14:1–3). Remember, Jesus said, "I am the door; by Me if any man enter in, he shall be saved" (John 10:9). Salvation through faith in Christ and personal repentance is the only key that unlocks the door. Only a thief tries to get in some other way (John 10:1).

To what otherwise inaccessible realms, then, does hospitality open the door? The heart! God is seeking access to the hearts of men and women in your neighborhood, city, place of work—even in your own home and family.

Because the heart of man is "desperately wicked" (Jer. 17:9), it is also locked up in pride and evil ways (Mark 7:21–23) and is paralyzed by fear and bondage (Heb. 2:14–15). Because God created man in His own image, He knows precisely the divinely created and ordained "key" to unlock the door of men's hearts that otherwise remain inaccessible to both God and man. One key is *The POWER of Hospitality*. It may well be the most potent key we have in this "post-modern" age, where Truth is deemed unknowable or non-existent.

Hospitality—Key to the Heart

When man, through sin and broken relationship, was estranged from God, the doors to men's hearts were slammed shut and locked tight. We became "lost" to God's household and locked off from those created in His image. Because all of us have sinned and become estranged from God (Rom. 3:23), that makes for a lot of locked doors. A spiritual locksmith was required to gain access to so many hearts. Imagine the challenge!

But God, in the fulness of time, opened His great heart of hospitality, extended His hand and sent forth the very essence of Himself made flesh, Jesus, to express in both word and deed an open invitation from His Father's heart to join Him in His home forever (John 14:1–3). Jesus was the "key" made flesh. Jesus incarnated or "fleshed out" God's heart of hospitality. You could call it "down-to-earth hospitality."

The key of hospitality entered and began turning the locks of hearts. It was a universal key. Men and women began to allow their Creator back into their hearts and homes. As they did so, their own lives became duplications of the Father's heavenly-manifested key. The doors to the hearts of husbands and wives, fathers and mothers began to open. Whole families received the warmth of heavenly hospitality. Neighborhoods and entire cities followed.

The joy of restored relationships with God and man was beyond anything before experienced. Those that gladly received the liberating life of restoration by holy hospitality threw open the doors of their own hearts and homes to others. The numbers grew rapidly, made "believers" by this amazing good news of God's hospitality displayed tangibly through the hospitable warmth and genuine love of neighbors and even former enemies. They began to break bread together from house to house (Acts 2:46). They did not get together weekly to fulfill organizational demand but gathered daily to revel in a gospel revealed in relational reality.

The key had unlocked the door. The love of Christ constrained them. They were able, even glad, to endure persecution for the truth, when they were wrapped in the holy hospitality of the Messiah who had been sent as the Father's living expression to "tabernacle" or live among men (John 1:14). God was not doing a religious thing *for* them, like the priests. Now God was demonstrating His desire to be *with* them (Matt. 1:23).

They were no longer to be strangers in religious robes but friends in relational righteousness (John 15:13–15). Organizational trappings and stifling religious formality began to give way to heart-felt relational expression. The home became an epicenter of ministry. The heart was there. They began to freely share what they had with others. No longer owners but trustees, they saw themselves as having things in common. After all, the key had unlocked the door to their hearts and homes, and those who believed came together as often as they could. No one lacked what they needed (Acts 2:41–51).

To as many as received this incredible offer of divine hospitality and turned from their own pride and sinful ways that kept them separated from God and one another, God gave the privilege to become as His own sons and daughters, welcoming them into His household (John 1:12). No wonder we are told to "do good to all men, but especially unto them who are of the household of faith" (Gal. 6:10). God's hospitality was the key to men's hearts, but the story does not end there.

The Story Never Ends

Warmed by *The POWER of Hospitality* of the One they called "Emmanuel" (Matt. 1:23) and His open-hearted, truth-bearing friends, those who joined with them followed their pattern. Opening heart and home in hospitality, they extended their hand in fellowship to all who would allow the key to open their hearts, while continuing through open heart, hand and home to use the key of holy hospitality to gain entrance into the hearts of others, the locks of whose hearts seemed frozen. Truth and mercy kissed each other, turning sterile religion into heart-warming relationship.

Behold how they loved one another! Openness of heart, hand and home brought a palpable oneness and accord, the envy of those outside. With gladness and singleness of heart they dined together daily, praising God and having favor with all the people (Acts 1:46–47).

Yet the story continues. Emmanuel, having revealed the meaning of "God with us" (Matt. 1:23), declared to His disciples after His crucifixion and resurrection, "As the Father hath sent Me, even so send I you" (John 20:21). The key has been put in our hands. Holy hospitality is the divine key maximizing access from the portals of heaven to the portals of men on earth to communicate the greatest news of all time—God's hospitable invitation to join Him in His home for eternity. "Loving God, loving each other; and the story never ends!"

From Your House to God's House

You and I hold the amazing key of the Kingdom in our hearts and hands. Multitudes are in the valley of decision (Joel 3:14). They are deciding daily whether to accept or reject God's salvation invitation to His eternal home. One day, God Himself will finally close the door, just as He did when the door of invitation to Noah's ark slammed shut. Many are waiting to see our earthly demonstration of the heavenly *POWER of Hospitality*. But they will never experience it unless you unlock the door of your own heart, hand and home in a display of down-to-earth hospitality. Hospitality is a divinely designed key to the door of the heart.

The story is told of a certain Levite from the tribe of Ephraim who journeyed to Bethlehem-Judah. As dusk fell, his servant begged him to stop for the night in the city of the Jebusites who were not of Israel but of the ungodly Canaanites. The Levite insisted they should not lodge there but pass on to Gibeah which belonged to the tribe of Benjamin. But as they turned in to lodge at Gibeah, like Mary and

Joseph did centuries later, "there was no man that took them into his house to lodge." Finally, an old man passed by, inquiring why they sat in the street, to which the Levite responded, "I am now going to the house of the Lord; and there is no man that receiveth me to his house" (Judges 19:1–18).

Untold millions on the near edge of Christ's Second Coming who, like the Levite, are in the valley of decision trying to "go to the house of the Lord," but "there is no man [or woman] that receiveth them to his house." The key to your heart and home may be the key to God's eternal home for a sojourner in your sphere of influence. But you must open the door with that little, seemingly insignificant, key of hospitality.

The story of the Levite and his traveling companions becomes one of the most horrific accounts of the entire Scripture. The entire city composed of covenant sons of Abraham was so outrageously inhospitable and dishonorable that the other tribes of Israel nearly destroyed the entire tribe of Benjamin from inheritance among the twelve tribes. It was a near duplication of the inhospitable heart revealed in the grossly evil conduct of Sodom, which God Himself destroyed.

In this dangerous and sinful world, how will people who want to get to God's house get there safely? Could it be that God's plan is for them to go by way of your house? What will be our excuse on that certain and soon-coming day of judgment when men and women destined for the gross inhospitality of hell and eternal fire say, "I tried to get to the house of the Lord, but there was no one to take me into his or her house?"

You and I hold the key to welcome wayfaring strangers into the commonwealth of faith. Your heart, hand and home are God's ordained access points for His Holy Spirit to reach locked hearts. "Where there is room in the heart, there is always room in the house." Is there room in your heart and home for down-to-earth hospitality?

Heart-Opening Questions
for Personal and Group Reflection

Chapter 16

1. In what ways is the heart like a prison?

2. What are some of the things a key allows you to do?

3. Since keys are so small and seemingly insignificant, why are they so powerful?

4. Do you think that hospitality could well be one of the "keys of the kingdom?" Why, or why not?

5. Why do you think the "key" of hospitality is so seldom used by both pastor and people?

6. How did God the Father use hospitality as a "key" to gain access to men's hearts on earth?

7. How did Jesus use hospitality to open the hearts of men?

8. Have you ever considered that an open door to your house may provide the key to someone's destiny?

9. How would your congregation change if everyone, beginning with the pastor, purposely began to insert the key of divine hospitality into the doors of people's hearts and lives?

10. Has this chapter inspired you to activate hospitality in your life? How? What ideas has the Holy Spirit birthed in your mind and heart?

If I would preach

hospitality, I must

practice hospitality.

HOSPITALITY IS GLORIOUS, but not glamorous. According to *Christianity Today*, "Hospitality is an unglamourous subject that doesn't get much attention from the pulpit." Yet, as we have seen, hospitality is at the very heart of the gospel.

How could Christian leadership for centuries have missed such a simple, yet profound, fundamental for our living out the life of Christ, particularly in Western culture? How might the message of hospitality affect my ministry, my congregation, my city, or even my own family? How might hospitality bridge the laity-clergy gap that has, for seventeen centuries, frustrated the fulfillment of the biblical

217

vision of the priesthood of all believers? These and many other questions will be explored in this chapter, providing pastoral perspective for all believers who must become "Priests of the Lord: Ministers of our God" (Isaiah 61:6), to fulfill God's plan and purpose for His church.

Hospitality can revolutionize the way we "do church." Simple, old-fashioned hospitality is more effective for church planting, is more transforming than social service programs, and has untapped potential for discipleship, not to mention hope for a host of other issues that have baffled the best of men.

Restoring Hebraic Roots

How could Christian leadership, since the early Church of the first and second centuries, have largely lost the profound simplicity of hospitality at the heart of the gospel? The simple answer is that the viewpoint of the Church and its leaders changed dramatically. And viewpoint determines destiny.

The Church was born in Jerusalem on the Day of Pentecost. Pentecost was a Jewish feast celebrated fifty days after the Feast of Passover and the Feast of Unleavened Bread, and the Feast of First Fruits. Pentecost was followed by the Feast of Trumpets and the Feast of Tabernacles, both of which were celebrated by Jesus, His apostles, and the celebrated Apostle Paul, all of which were Jewish. The Jews were the descendants of the Hebrew people, who, because they were the seed of Abraham, had been delivered from the bondage of Egypt to display God's eternal plan and purpose as a covenantal community before the nations of the earth in a place called the Promised Land.

Strangers (gentiles) were to be "grafted in" to this holy relational community whose hearts were rooted in the home and whose religion was rooted in relationship (Rom. 11:17). The "Feasts of the Lord" were open to all who embraced the "God of Abraham, Isaac, and Israel," whether Jew or Gentile, and the more important was the feast to the faith, the greater was the reveling in relationship, culminating with the most joyous of all, the Feast of Tabernacles.

It was into such a spiritual environment that Yeshua (Christ) was presented as the "Word made flesh," "tabernacled among us," who welcomed all who would receive Him to His Father's eternal home. It was in this same Hebraic environment that the Church was born, Yeshua having promised to all who come into relationship with the Father through Christ participation in the granddaddy of all feasts, the "Wedding Supper of the Lamb" in the New Jerusalem.

As the Church began to spread through preaching and persecution, invading Gentile realms in other lands, Gentile thinking and ways invaded the Church. Predominant among the influences were Greek thinking and Roman organization. For the revered Greek, the mind mattered most, and relationship was of remote relevancy. Hellenistic or Greek influence rapidly replaced the Hebraic heart. God's Truth became not so much faith to be *practiced* but facts to be *pondered* and *protected*.

For gentile Christians, it became more "kosher" to think like a Greek than like a Jew. The same process eroded Hebraic practice. As Christianity spread throughout the Roman Empire, so did the Roman Empire spread its ways and practices among Christians. Roman structures and organizational ways replaced Hebraic synagogues and relational patterns of worship. Even the Hebraic "Feasts of the Lord," which God called "MY feasts" (Lev. 23:2), were replaced by pagan feasts reframed and reformatted to encompass Christian purpose.

With radical changes of thought and practice among followers of Christ came radical rejection of the Hebraic practices and ultimately radical persecution of the Jews, severing the Hebraic roots of the Church while laying the foundation for seventeen centuries of abandonment of the very heart and soul of first-century Christianity. The Spirit of God has been grieved. It is indeed difficult to make our Jewish friends "jealous" if Gentiles totally abandon the very Hebraic undergirdings of the Church (Rom. 10:19; 11:1).

We must remember that the early followers of Christ were not called "Christians," but were considered a Jewish sect. They were merely Jews who embraced Yeshua as the promised Messiah. God is bringing a correction in our viewpoints that will bring course correction. It is part of the Holy Spirit's "preparing the way" for our Lord's return. Much is at stake. Changed attitudes will be reflected in changed actions, which will help us accomplish many of our much-sought-after hopes and dreams for our families, our congregations, our cities, and our nations.

Virtually all of the sub-topics that are discussed in this chapter have a direct or at least indirect link to the adoption of a Greek mind-set or Roman operational set coupled with rejection of a Hebraic heart-set. Our future success will depend significantly on the degree to which we restore the Hebraic roots that open our hearts hospitably to others.

Equipping the Saints

Nowhere is the substitution of the Greek mind for the Hebraic heart more prevalent in practice than among pastors. In fact, those of us who pastor have become perhaps the primary perpetrators and propagators of a purely cognitive approach to the practice of Christian faith. While what we believe is truly important, how we live is of equal or greater importance. The great gap between what we say we believe and how we really live opens us and our flocks to self-deception (James 1:22).

In few places is this gap more apparent than in the practice (or lack thereof) of hospitality. If my *home* is not open to the people, it is indeed a stretch to convince others that my *heart* is truly open to them. Is what I *say* reflected in what I *do*? While statistics do not always tell the whole truth, the fact that at least 70 percent of pastors admit they have no friends reveals a significant disconnect between our sincere desire to practice agape love and our failure to practice hospitality. If the head believes in agape love, the heart must open our hands and homes in acts of hospitality.

What we do as pastors becomes critically important in considering what the people in our care will both believe and do. The apostle

Paul states that apostles, prophets, evangelists, pastors, and teachers are given to the Church to "perfect" or "equip" the saints for the work of ministry and for the edifying of the Body of Christ (Eph. 4:11–12). Paul also advised Timothy and Titus that overseers in the Body should be "given to" and "lovers of" hospitality (I Tim. 3:2; Tit. 1:5–8), as living examples so that the entire church would be "given to" hospitality (Rom. 12:13).

When hospitality begins to invade and issue from a pastor's heart, new hope and healing flows from his ministry, and his home becomes a revitalized haven for his family, the faithful, and those who would enter the family of God.

Discipling Sons and Daughters

To *preach* hospitality, I must *practice* hospitality. And if I would practice hospitality, I will soon preach hospitality. As has been so frequently said, "Preach, and if necessary, use words."

Hospitality must become one of the essentials of Christian discipleship because it is essential to the heart of God. One reason hospitality has been so easily overlooked in all of our best efforts at teaching and transmitting the faith to our spiritual sons and daughters is that hospitality is not something you *believe* but something you *do*. Our Greek thinking has so enshrouded our minds that we have convinced not only ourselves but also others that God is concerned solely with our *believing* rather than with our *behaving*. Such thinking has fostered moral relativity while frustrating ministry relationships.

If we would be *touched* with hospitality, we must *teach* hospitality. This book is an effort to transmit both the principle and the practice of hospitality to pastor and people alike. Hopefully, it has spoken to your heart and opened new vision. Undoubtedly, many thoughts have crossed your mind with fresh illustrations of how the actual display of someone's open heart, open hand, and open home have deeply affected your life or that of someone around you. Such illustrations, fleshing out the faith, are powerful in reaching the heart of your congregation. But nothing is more powerful in teaching hospitality than your example of hospitality. Like so many other things, hospitality is better caught than taught, but it still needs to be taught as a fundamental expression of our faith in Christ.

No discipleship is complete without meaningful focus on the practice of hospitality. Hospitality gives us a "handle" on agape love. It requires not only *teaching* but also *training*. It envelopes every aspect of our Christian walk. Once one gains a vision for *The POWER of Hospitality*, many other aspects of our walk with Christ begin to take new and clearer focus. Forgiveness, reconciliation of every type, fellowship, reaching the lost, and virtually every other aspect of ministry and relationship take on new significance and meaning.

Hospitality is not only a powerful tool to place in the hands of our spiritual sons and daughters but is also an essential part of the training of our own children. It has been an incredible blessing to see our daughters, each in her own way, initiating various expressions of hospitality as young adults. They participated in many practical ways since early childhood as Mom and Dad grew in the practice of opening our hands, hearts, and home to others. We did; they watched. Then we did it together. We watched while they did. And now they are reaping the rewards of an open heart and open home as they live out hospitality, each in her own unique way.

The heart of our faith is revealed in a heart of hospitality. Let's get serious about training our children and discipling the saints in this essential expression of God's grace to us. May no Christian magazine ever again need to ask, "Whatever Happened to Hospitality?"

Reaching the Lost

Contrary to popular expression or belief, the heart of the "Great Commission" is not *evangelism* but *discipleship*. Our Lord, before His ascension, declared that because "All power is given unto me in heaven and in earth," we must

Go therefore, and teach [make disciples of] all nations, baptizing them…and teaching them to observe [obey] all things whatsoever I have commanded you" (Matt. 28:18–20).

As Jim Russell so aptly states in *Awakening the Giant*, we have been astoundingly successful at evangelizing America (at least to appearances), but we have profoundly failed at discipleship. We have introduced America to the God of our fathers, but we have failed to teach Americans to obey the God of our fathers. This has resulted in a massive disconnect between our *profession* of the faith and our *practice* of the faith.

Is evangelistic preaching in our congregations or crusades the key to winning the world for Christ? Researcher George Barna says an emphatic "No." "The most common means to salvation," writes Barna, "is through the personal ministry of a Christian friend." In fact, evangelism through personal relationship produces almost twice as many converts as do sermons, church services and evangelistic events combined. Barna therefore exhorts, "Equip the saints to do the work of evangelism. Even without a public platform, they may be the most effective preachers of all."

Herein lies a huge problem. If at least 70 percent of all pastors admit they have no friends, and the pastoral heart is not "given to" and a "lover of" hospitality, how does such a pastor equip saints for relational reaching to the unsaved? Perhaps we need to reassess our priorities in preparing ourselves to prepare the people.

Congregational Growth and Retention

According to William Hendricks in *Exit Interviews*, confirmed in lengthy discussion on *VIEWPOINT*, the author's daily radio broadcast, 53,000 people per week are leaving the back door of America's churches. That is an astounding 2,756,000 per year. No wonder the church in America has not grown more than a net 1 percent in the last generation. This figure has been recited in so many seminars and books as to be virtually indisputable.

This is indeed a devastating commentary for a nation whose spiritual leaders like to see themselves as setting the pace for world evangelism and discipleship. One pastor unabashedly declared privately, "I don't care how many go out the back door as long as I keep more coming in the front door."

Why are so many leaving disgusted or disillusioned? Aside from the fact many increasingly feel they are not receiving a full dose of the "full counsel of God," most of them are frustrated by the lack of meaningful, heart-felt fellowship and by a sense that they have no meaningful place in the Body but for dropping a gift in the plate and filling a pew. Absent is the heart of hospitality that creates a womb of acceptance for those who cannot or will not crash their way through the barriers of lifeless institutionalism to carve out a niche in a cavern of crowded loneliness.

Hospitality is God's special heaven-like glue to bind the Body of Christ together in agape love. Individual Christians are described as being "lively stones" comprising a temple for Christ's indwelling (I Pet. 2:5). Collectively, we are seen as a wall of stones making up a "spiritual house." But what causes those stones to firmly hang together? Is it a mere creed or confession of faith? Or is there a catalyst that causes the creedal and confessional mortar to bind those individual "stones" to one another?

Open hearts, open hands, and open homes displaying holy hospitality are the catalytic agents that will assist and help to effectuate the agape love we know and preach should be the bond of the brethren. Shouldn't it be displayed among those who profess to model the methods and message of the Master? Was that an "Amen" I heard? Pastoral hospitality breeds congregational hospitality. Congregational relationship binds hearts for congregational retention.

Does your congregation welcome people with *greeters*? Greeters are good, but they are only gatekeepers. If people are welcomed through the gates but are not welcomed into the homes of the people, the facade of hospitality is betrayed by the lack of hospitable fellowship. Organizational welcome will never suffice for the yearning for relational warmth.

Ministry Relationships

The majority of true biblical ministry follows the Master's methods of relationship, which were intensely personal. Relationships, American style, are *pragmatic* rather than *personal*. They are most often *organizational* rather than *organismal*. That leads pastors and parachurch leaders to develop purported relationships in large groups rather than in intimate face-to-face fellowship. The people in our congregations tend to follow our pattern. The result is often frustration and failure at virtually every level of attempted relationship over time. This dramatically affects our ability to shoulder the mantle of ministry together, for we are not truly *together*. Consider the impact of this illusory form of relationship and what might happen if we truly developed an open heart of hospitality with one another revealed first through our homes.

CONGREGATIONAL UNITY

A true heart of hospitality revealed in open homes will not only facilitate relationships that foster retention but will also, perhaps more importantly, build a strong bond of unity within the congregation.

Nothing is more beautiful to behold than the affectionate love of the brethren. Yet, that love is often more of pretense by public or organizational show than issuing out of a personal and private relational glow. Programs are often the organizational shortcut to the longer-term building of enduring relationship. When members of a congregation and their pastor make a practice of regularly opening their homes to one another—not just to their favorite few but to strangers—God's heart of hospitality intertwines with ours, and "a threefold cord is not quickly broken" (Eccl. 4:12).

CITY–CHURCH UNITY

Across America and around the world there is a clear move of God to see the city-wide church reborn. There is a growing call and increasing desire for unity among pastors and people across racial, denominational, and congregational lines. This movement in the twenty-first century is essentially a revival of the practice of the early church in the first century A.D. It is another clear manifestation of the soon-return of Christ, for He will not return for a Church with spot, wrinkle, or any such thing (Eph. 5:27).

The Church of the first century was identified not primarily by congregation but by city. Elders were to be appointed in every city, not necessarily in every congregation (Titus 1:5). Church governance and ministry was on a city-wide basis, enabling church discipline, ministry, and relationships to be fully operational. Only in such a context can Jesus' plan for resolving differences among professing Christians described in Matt. 18:15–17 be fully implemented and effective.

Only when pastors and people throughout a city are at one with God in Christ revealed in their oneness both in faith and fellowship with one another can Jesus' *High Priestly Prayer* of John 17 that "they be one" become a reality. Since it is not likely that our Lord's prayer of John 17 will go unanswered by the Father before Christ's return, we should well anticipate that pastor and people alike must find themselves leaping over and demolishing walls of individualism, congregationalism, racism and denominationalism. Each of these walls are "isms" that frustrate or replace, in whole or in part, our oneness in Christ. Our various cultures must decrease, and Christ must increase.

There is no more important or prophetic application of our call to holy hospitality than in the cooperative fulfillment of Christ's Bride to, in fact and fellowship, truly become His Body. That will require relationships at a level not yet practiced or experienced among individualistic Americans and American congregations and their pastors. It will require nothing less than an outpouring of heavenly hospitality on earth, opening our hearts, hands and homes to one another across congregational, racial and denominational lines.

Pastors, given to and loving hospitality, must take the lead. The "Pastor-to-Pastor" plan for building relationships outlined in Appendix 1 is a proven method that my wife and I used to help pastors and their wives begin to develop these Kingdom relationships.

Building relationships requires that we *value* relationships. We must learn to value the *person* rather than *position* and power.

Organizational substitutes give the illusion of progress because of the more public display of activity. Pastors' gatherings, city-wide congregational gatherings or celebrations, and even pulpit exchanges are good but are no substitute for time spent as couples in one another's homes. Pastor Wayne Mancari in Richmond, Virginia, became convinced that organizational time was no substitute for relational time. He dedicated himself to meet and fellowship individually with one new pastor every week. After several years of faithful dedication, he has built relational bridges across every conceivable barrier to at least 250 pastors in the metro area.

Relationship is an investment. We must pursue the Truth together in building relationships. If we give ourselves to hospitality, opening our hearts and homes to one another, eternity will pay dividends in proportion to the time invested. Are you beginning to catch the vision?

Bridging the Clergy-Laity Divide

The Roman emperor, Constantine, gave the Church a kind of spiritual constipation by injecting the pagan priesthood into early-church practice to solidify the political power of the empire. While changing times and seasons of the Church to conform to pagan practice, he also dealt a death-blow to the priesthood of all believers that has paralyzed the mission of the Church for seventeen centuries. Interestingly, church leaders in this last generation are increasingly acknowledging this point to be true, but centuries of unbiblical tradition continue to dictate practice.

The POWER of Hospitality can play a significant part in restoring the priesthood of all believers, breaking down the artificial clergy-laity divide. Pastors who have been told by professors or other colleagues, by either direct instruction or example, that to maintain position and power you must maintain separation from the flock can now freely build true relationship among the people. The pastor and his wife can invite a couple or family each week or month into their home, or be invited into the homes of others.

Public teaching on hospitality paves the way for private practice of hospitality. Relationship will free us from organizational bondage that frustrates the free flow of ministry. Try it!

Restoring Our Inner Cities

The cities of the world are drawing the peoples of the world like a giant magnet. America is no exception. The teeming masses of "faceless" people are exploding, creating relational time bombs of multitudes in a sea of crowded loneliness. Into the vortex of this human maelstrom, Christ calls His Church for such a time as this, the final harvest.

Would Jesus deal differently today than He did at His first coming amidst the seething hatred of Roman occupation? Or would He again minister relationally among the people, one on one. Would He tender the bulk of His time to twelve, walking with them and breaking bread together, or would He form a multitiered organization to fire a spiritual shotgun in a bulk-mail or computer campaign, never looking into the face of those whom He wanted to see the face of God?

Since the very heart of the Gospel is the expression of God's heart of hospitality to those who are strangers to the commonwealth of Christian faith, it would seem that Christ would not replace the *relational* connection of the first century with an *organizational* connection in the twenty-first century. Since Christ did not call us to make converts but to make disciples, what would happen if we invested our time and resources directly into people, empowering them with *The POWER of Hospitality* to reach relationally into their own spheres of life with the Good News. The priesthood of all believers would become a reality, and people rather than programs might pierce even to the boiling inner cities of our land.

Since our inner cities have baffled church growth and evangelistic experts, perhaps God would honor our simple following of Jesus' and the apostles' simple example. It may not be grandiose, it may not report well to nonprofit or denominational constituencies for America's organizational fund-raising, but the relational connection may be just the heart condition of holy hospitality that would bring hope and healing to our inner cities. And what works in the inner cities will also affect suburbia, for *hospitality reaches people everywhere.*

License to Lead

The Church around the world seemingly adores the Apostle Paul. From his epistles we glean much of the doctrine to which we cling. We have parsed his words nearly to the subatomic level. How, then, did we miss his explicit words concerning hospitality?

To Christians generally, Paul writes that we should be "given to" hospitality (Rom. 12:13). To leaders or overseers Paul makes abundantly clear that we must be "given to" and be "lovers of" hospitality (I Tim. 3:2; Titus 1:6-8). Those who satisfy the requirements concerning hospitality and meet the other criteria that Paul lists in these passages are granted a "license to lead." But if we fail to have and exercise *The Power of Hospitality,* we are unqualified to lead or oversee the work of God. The obvious question then is, "Are you qualified?"

When hospitality becomes an active and essential part of your ministry life, your ministry enjoyment and fulfillment will dramatically increase, as will your effectiveness. Your spouse will even feel the difference, as will your children. A whole new realm of opportunity may just be waiting for you to open the door of your heart. Blessings to you as you begin.

The Power to Change Your Community

ONE PASTOR'S TESTIMONY

Hospitality is one of the most substantive aspects of the practice of our faith. Clearly, in these end times, the Father is restoring what it really means to be a follower of Christ. Chuck and Kathie Crismier are being used by God to awaken the Church to the practical reality of a living faith through the simple, yet powerful practice of hospitality.

Several years ago, my wife and I met the Crismiers, and our lives have never been the same. We gathered in one another's homes regularly for over a year, centered around a meal that facilitated intimate sharing that was almost always revealing, healing and restoring. As a young couple who lived in the inner-city one block from public housing, we didn't fit the typical mode for "hospitality" as often misdefined as only for the "have a cup of tea" class of people. Refreshingly enough, the Crismiers helped us discover that true hospitality is more in what is in the heart than what type of china you can set out on the table. Yet they were also able to challenge us to be intentional in treating all guests as royalty even at our economic level.

We believe the heart of the Lord is excited that through the saints being freshly encouraged in the grace of hospitality, the fields that have been ready for harvest will have a fresh supply of laborers who will open their hearts and homes to those in need of the living Saviour; Jesus the Christ.

It is essential that hospitality be fully restored to its rightful place in the lives of believers in modeling the love of Christ in a tangible way, in the church and to the world. Both the declaration of Christ to love one another and the requirement in scripture for leadership to be hospitable lead to an outworking of our faith for the world to know the Father sent the Son. Hospitality: open heart + open hand + open home = changed lives for Christ, which equals a changed community!

Thanks, Chuck and Kathie, for living out HOSPITALITY AS A MODEL to the church for those who will receive this challenge to see "covenant community" restored to our world through believers living out hospitality as a lifestyle.

Don Coleman
Inner-city pastor, Richmond, Virginia

Heart-Opening Questions
for Personal and Group Reflection

Chapter 17

1. Why do you think hospitality has received such little attention from pastors in our pulpits?

2. How could Christian leadership for centuries have missed the simple, yet fundamental significance of hospitality in our living out the life of Christ? Why has hospitality been most notably absent in Western culture?

3. In what significant way did the viewpoint of the Church change from the first century to the twenty-first century?

4. Why is the Holy Spirit stirring up interest in and remembrance of the Hebraic roots of the Christian faith some twenty centuries after the birth century of the Church?

5. What are some basic differences between the Greco-Roman mindset and the Hebraic heart-set? Can you see how recovering a Hebraic heart-set could have significant ramifications for how we look at and do ministry?

6. Why is it that pastors, perhaps more than any other group, have been the propagators of a Greco-Roman mindset? How has that affected the flock and the Church's expression of the faith? Might this have anything to do with why 70 percent of pastors admit to having no friends and why the majority of pastor's wives feel the ministry is a threat to their marriage and family?

7. Do you agree that, "If I would PREACH hospitality, I must PRACTICE hospitality"? Why, or why not?

8. How can pastors best disciple the flock in hospitality?

9. How would genuine hospitality increase congregational growth and retention?

10. In what ways might hospitality assist in achieving Christian unity in your city?

11. Why might hospitality be appropriately called, "A license to lead?"

Can God Be Serious?

*Hospitality is a
quintessential
expression of God's
heart and character.*

A CLOSED HEART CAN BE DEADLY! Just ask Nabal. Unfortunately, though, you won't be able to connect with him for he is dead. He died suddenly, judged for a closed and hardened heart. Here is his shocking story, which you will also find in I Samuel 23.

Running for His Life

Nabal was the head of his home. He was a very prosperous man, a hard-driving businessman. He also had a caring and good-looking wife, Abigail. The Bible says she was "a woman of good understanding and of a beautiful countenance." In fact, the Scriptures describe Nabal as "very great." He lived in Maon, but his possessions were in Carmel. Nabal was a rancher with three thousand sheep and a thousand goats, a prominent man indeed. Our story catches him shearing his sheep, and he had many shearers in the vast fields to help him. But someone else needed his help. It would require an open heart and an open hand, and God was watching.

David was running for his life. Samuel had anointed him king, but Saul sought his life. David, together with his men, were hiding in the wilderness. Saul, because of his rebellion, had lost favor with God, but David had favor both with God and the people. Yet he would not find favor with Nabal.

In need of supplies, David sent ten of his young men to solicit Nabal's help. David knew Nabal's shearers were out in the fields. He advised his young men to assure Nabal of David's good will and intentions, showing how the shearers had been protected, surrounded as they were by David's men in the wilderness. How would Nabal respond? His heart would be revealed in his hand.

A Hand Without A Heart

With respect and courtesy, David's men sought Nabal's assistance. Both David's plight and Nabal's prosperity and prominence were well known. What was not known was the condition of Nabal's heart. Listen to Nabal's response to David's request.

> Who is David? And who is the son of Jesse? There be
> many servants now a days that break away every man from
> his master.
> Shall I then take *my* bread, and *my* water, and *my* flesh
> that I have killed for *my* shearers, and give it unto men,
> whom I know not whence they be?

So the young men returned to David in the wilderness to report the failure of their mission. David was furious and ordered his men to gird on their swords, intent on destroying Nabal for his gross inhospitality. But God intervened, prompting Abigail, Nabal's wife, to intercede with David not to take matters into his own hands to effect judgment on Nabal's unrighteousness.

The Scripture says Abigail was a woman "of good understanding." She implored David not to sully his anointing by returning vengeance for Nabal's evil. She described her husband's heart and attitude in making her plea to David with words that should cause pause for every professing Christian man or woman. Hopefully these words find no affinity with you or anyone in your home.

> Let not my lord, I pray thee, regard this man of Belial,
> even Nabal: for as his name is, so is he, Nabal is his name,
> and folly is with him.

Abigail, having heard the request of David's men and the despicable response of her husband reflecting the ongoing state of his hardened heart and revealing his affinity with Satan's household, then extended her hand with all that was needed by David's wilderness company, revealing her own heart of hospitality. David blessed Abigail for her wisdom and godly appeal, which prevented him from taking God's work of vengeance upon himself. And "David received of her hand that which she had brought him."

Struck Dead

Nabal may have been a prominent head of his home, but he had no heart. It was his life pattern. He claimed that all with which God had blessed him was his own. Four times he repeats, "my bread," "my water," "my flesh," and "my shearers." His own wife knew his ways well. What does your wife think of your ways? How about your God?

Abigail returned to Nabal and found him squandering the resources God had given him that could well have been shared without any significant impact to his own needs. The Bible says, "…and behold, he held a feast in his house, like the feast of a king." Nabal's heart was merry within him" in his drunken state, so Abigail delayed in reporting to him how she had saved him from certain death at the hands of David's men.

"But it came to pass in the morning, when the wine was gone out of Nabal, and his wife had told him these things, that his heart died within him, and he became as a stone." Spiritually, his heart was already stone. He was a walking dead man, despite his vast wealth and prominence. His heart was not open to God or man. He was a self-made man who hoarded everything for himself.

This is one of the least taught passages of Scripture, undoubtedly because its profound significance has not been understood. But why has it not been understood? The passage seems plain on its face. Most likely it is because we, as Christ's church, have not truly valued hospitality. We have not grasped our Creator's viewpoint. We have neither appreciated nor practiced hospitality as foundational to the Christian life. Neither have we considered the seriousness with which God views its absence in our lives.

Now we get a shocking glimpse of the solemnity with which God viewed the hardness of Nabal's heart and his refusal to extend hospitality. Let these words sink into your soul:

> And it came to pass about ten days after, that *the Lord smote Nabal that he died.*

God killed Nabal for refusing to extend hospitality. This is one of just a handful of incidents throughout the entire Bible that God himself is said to have struck a man that he died. From our point of view, it seems extreme, because we place so little comparative value on hospitality. But from God's viewpoint, hospitality is a quintessential expression of His heart and character. To refuse to freely open one's heart, hand and home to man made in His image is an open affront to the character of God and is a head-on assault against the two great commandments…thou shalt love the Lord thy God with all thine heart, and love thy neighbor as thyself.

Grace Was Extended

Let there be no more Nabals among pastor or people. If your life remains in you, grace is extended to be and become a man or woman of hospitality. But do not delay! God granted Nabal only ten days to change his ways. The unrepentant stubbornness and hardness of his heart brought down the heavy hand of a holy God as a living parable for every generation. He was struck dead as an eternal demonstration linking God's demand that we display love with His holiness and justice.

Hospitality is a nondelegable and nonavoidable duty for every true disciple of Christ. Neither is it a matter of mere pedigree. The record reflects that Nabal was "of the house of Caleb." Do you remember Joshua and Caleb? They were the only two adults out of 600,000 men that God delivered from the bondage of Egypt who were allowed into the Promised Land. God said that Caleb was allowed into the Promised Land "because he had another spirit" and "hath followed me fully" (Num. 14:24). Do you have that "other spirit"? Positions and pedigrees do not count. The only thing that counts is "following God fully."

Excluded From the Congregation

Can God really take hospitality this seriously? Given the relatively minimal attention given to hospitality by the Church since the first century, and even less by the Church in America in the past several generations referred to as the "American Century," it would come as no surprise that you may be surprised. But that does not alter the obvious reality of God's mind on the matter.

Again, your opening of heart, hand and home to others, especially to strangers, is of such magnitude in God's mind because it is a practical or functional reflection of His very essence. God is love (I John 4:8). And we are to be "followers (or imitators) of God, as dear children; and walk in love..." (Ephesians 5:1–2). "He that loveth not, knoweth not God; for God is love" (I John 4:8). Hospitality gives real-life definition to agape love. Without the reality of hospitality, agape love remains, in large measure, an abstraction. Therefore, for reality in your spirituality, practice hospitality in your locality.

We close this chapter with another brief account revealing the inescapable seriousness of God's mind and heart on this matter. This historical record may well challenge your sensibilities and understanding of the God we claim to love and serve. But He has not changed His essence or character. He loves and gives Himself to hospitality but rejects those created in His image who refuse to follow His example.

We return now to Israel's epic journey out of Egypt, out of the "house of bondage." Their trek to the Promised Land led through the territory of the Amorites and Moabites. The account can be found in Numbers 21–24.

As Israel approached the land of the Amorites, Moses sent messengers to Sihon, their king, saying, "Let me pass through thy land: we will not drink of the waters of the well: but we will go along the king's highway, until we be past thy borders" (Num. 21:21–22). Sihon had opportunity to extend elementary hospitality to Israel, but he refused. Even though Moses graciously asked only for the simple right to pass through, Sihon could have said, "Yes, you may pass through, and feel free to water your flocks and followers." Instead, he rejected Israel's polite request out of hand. Therefore, "Israel smote him with the point of the sword" (Numb. 21:24). But the story does not end there.

Israel then headed toward Moab. When the king of Moab saw what Israel had done to the Amorites when they refused hospitable passage, Balak hired a prophet, Balaam, to curse Israel and bless Moab. Balaam tried to pray out from under the known will of God five times so as to reap the promised rewards from Balak to curse Israel. But God would not let him get by with it, speaking to Balaam even through the mouth of a donkey. Balaam thus became a curse and a byword to Israel to this day. But God perceived Moab's actions to hire Balaam and curse Israel as a fundamental act of gross inhospitality.

When Moses was preparing to pass the baton of leadership to Joshua to lead Israel into the Promised Land, God gave Moses instructions for the people upon their entry into that land "flowing with milk and honey." You can find those instructions in the book of Deuteronomy.

Consider these astoundingly forceful and seemingly harsh words from the heart of God:

> An Amorite or Moabite shall...not enter into the congregation of the Lord for ever (Deut. 23:3).

Why would God prohibit the children of Amon and Moab from entering the congregation? And forever? God must have considered the attitudes and actions of these peoples particularly heinous, especially offensive. Indeed He did! Here are our God's precise words delivered by Moses. This is our loving and just Creator's specific reason for refusing entrance into the worshiping congregation:

> Because they met you not with bread and with water in the way, when ye came forth out of Egypt (Deut. 23:4).

What If I Disregard God's View?

It was almost exactly one thousand years after Moses instructed Israel before entering the Promised Land that Nehemiah's heart was gripped with urgency to rebuild the walls of Jerusalem. Judah had been captive under Persian domination. Artexerxes reigned in Shushan, and Nehemiah found favor in his eyes, receiving permission to journey to Jerusalem to rebuild because "Jerusalem lieth waste."

After rebuilding the walls "because the people have a mind to work," Israel assembled with prayer and fasting, separating themselves from the strangers and confessing their sins. They stood, read in the book of the law, and worshiped. They read in the book of Moses in the audience of the people; and therein was found written, that the Amonite and the Moabite should not come into the congregation of God forever; because they met not the children of Israel with bread and with water" (Neh. 13:1–2).

Israel and Judah had long since forgotten the words of the Lord through Moses. Now they were seeking God's blessing to be restored to His people. And they were confronted with reality from God's viewpoint. They had, for hundreds of years, gradually mixed with the Amonites and Moabites, even in marriage, all of which God had strictly prohibited. Now what should they do?

Should they respond as American Christians, saying, "Oh well. God is loving. He will overlook this. Besides, it's really not all that bad, is it? I mean, God couldn't possibly expect us to correct such a mess, could He? To separate wouldn't be very loving, would it? A loving and gracious God would never expect that, would he? Someone's feelings might be hurt."

Fortunately, Nehemiah and Ezra were not Americans and did not think as modern American Christians. They feared God. They knew that Israel had exchanged their own will for God's will and were willing to admit it. They also set about to sever the Amonites and Moabites from the congregation. "They separated from Israel all the mixed multitude" when they heard the law [instructions] (Neh. 13:3). They even had to sever marriages with the Moabites and Amonites. Ezra records that "all the people sat in the street of the house of God trembling because of this matter." And they responded to Ezra and Nehemiah, saying, "As thou has said, so must we do" (Ezra 10:12).

This is the only place in the entire Bible where God apparently approved as His "mandatory" will "putting away" of a spouse. This was true, as noted by Ezra, even though "some of them had wives by whom they had children" (Ezra 10:44). The blatant refusal of the Amonites and Moabites to extend basic hospitality to Israel on the

way to the Promised Land was to have severe and continuing consequences forever, notwithstanding Israel's drifting viewpoint away
from the "God of our Fathers."

You may say, "Well, that doesn't leave me with very good feelings. I just don't understand why God would require that of people."
Ultimately, we must let faith override feelings, shouldn't we? Some of
us may just have to begin our new journey of hospitality by faith,
trusting that when God, our Creator, declares and demonstrates it to
be of such fundamental importance, it must be extremely important
regardless of whether I currently understand it.

The Challenge

When all is said and done, God's desire is that we freely and
rejoicingly offer *The POWER of Hospitality*, not primarily out of fear
of divine judgment or correction. But when we do not fully understand or agree with God's viewpoint on this or any other matter, it is
time, as the Apostle Paul stated, to cast down our own reasonings and
thoughts which exalt themselves against what God has said, "bringing into captivity every thought to the obedience of Christ" (II Cor.
10:3–5).

Will you, by faith, embrace and begin to empower others with
The POWER of Hospitality? Destiny, both temporal and eternal, lies in
the balance. Let us grasp with renewed vision and purpose this amazing heavenly key of hospitality that God has entrusted to us, using
our hearts, hands and homes to open the door to His eternal home
on the near edge of the Second Coming.

Time is passing quickly! Let *The POWER of Hospitality* revolutionize your life, family, congregation and city to prepare the way of
the Lord for history's final hour.

Heart-Opening Questions
for Personal and Group Reflection

Chapter 18

1. How did the story of Nabal, Abigail and David affect you?

2. Have you found yourself thinking like Nabal, "That's *my* food, *my* house, *my* money, *my* time" to justify closing yourself to others in your mind?

3. If David had come to your house with a similar request that he brought to Nabal, how would you have responded?

4. Why did God strike Nabal dead? Do you think God was unjust? Does this reveal the seriousness with which God views the matter of hospitality?

5. Why is hospitality a nondelegable, nonavoidable duty to every disciple of Christ?

6. Why did God exclude the Amorites and Moabites from the congregation?

7. What consequences could occur in your life if you refuse to open your heart, hand and home in hospitality?

8. In what ways has this chapter or this book changed your thinking?

9. Do you now believe *The POWER of Hospitality* could well revolutionize your life, family, congregation and city?

10. Are you willing to begin and commit to a new journey of hospitality by faith? Remember, a journey begins with the first step.

Chapter *19*

The Power of Hospitality

Hospitality is the relational conduit through which mercy and truth can meet and kiss each other.

THE POWER OF HOSPITALITY is not only supported and exhorted by biblical principle, but it is brought to life by believing practice. In this chapter, your heart will be stirred by the lives of others who chose, sometimes against considerable odds, to reach out with an open heart, open hand and open home to touch the lives of others. We believe your life will also be empowered as you experience *The POWER of Hospitality* through their lives and example.

Hospitality Changed My Life!

The story of the prodigal is my story. "He was lost, and is found." That's my life.

Growing up I had few friends. From the age of ten, I carried adult responsibilities which were often overwhelming. I cleaned two houses for $5 each. At home, I cleaned the entire house. By age twelve, I also did all the laundry and cooked all dinners. During the summers, I was the one who cared for my two brothers and baby sister. I knew no other life.

In 1980, my husband and I accepted Christ as our Savior. Soon we were folded into the "Faith Builders" class at the rapidly growing Faith Community Church in Covina, California. As an adult, I had only one friend, but my life was about to change.

The servant leaders of the Faith Builder's class made me feel so welcomed and comfortable. Chuck and Kathie Crismier were wonderful leaders by their example. To talk the talk is easy, but to walk the walk is a commitment.

Chuck was then an attorney who served as one of the several volunteer pastors. Chuck and Kathie's message and teaching were both inspiring and challenging. But for me, the most life-changing teaching was on hospitality.

Hospitality changed my life! I began opening my home to individuals, couples and families. The rewards definitely outweighed the work. My husband, Rick, joined in.

As we began to open our home to others, invitations to others' homes began coming to us. This was a whole new experience. Through hospitality, I began to develop new friends and experienced a new level of intimacy with others who were virtual strangers. I had not only friends, but also prayer warriors at my side. People cared about me and my family, all because of a simple dinner invitation.

So many people seem to want others to care about them, but they won't take the first step. I learned how to take the first step, and my whole life and attitude changed. My home and family have been blessed emotionally, financially and spiritually because of our reaching to others in hospitality. And, in turn, we have been blessed because of other's hospitality. I am confident their lives have been blessed as well.

Hospitality is a whole new way of living. You cannot get to know someone intimately by seeing them at church. A glib, "Hi, how are you?" just doesn't cut it. Opening your home and heart is the only way! So when you see those familiar—or even unfamiliar—faces, take a risk to have your own spirit lifted. Invite someone to your home so God's blessing can fill both of your lives. It will change your life just as it has mine.

Dee Ann Larsen

Busy mother and wife of a paving contractor

Hospitality: A "Doing" Ministry

Hospitality, I believe, is a very practical tool that God desires to use to bless people, love, soften and even heal people. I believe that God can work through hospitality in ways that preaching cannot. Hospitality is a "doing" ministry, not a "hearing" or a "saying" ministry. I have been fortunate enough to have examples in my life of people—real people—who have practiced hospitality. These people have shown me that it does not take a lot of money, great skills, fantastic houses, or anything too great. Hospitality takes a willing (and humble) heart, a decided mind, hands that are willing to work and serve, and an open home. No place is too small: even Jesus practiced hospitality at others homes or in an upper room!

Years ago, in the mid-1980s, when I was a new believer, the Lord showed me a scripture that was soon to become a blessing: "Let the love of the brethren continue. Do not neglect to show hospitality to strangers, for by this some have entertained angels without knowing it" (Heb. 13:1–2). The occasion was a weekend trip to a "sister church" in Northern Virginia that I attended to hear some of the Church leaders speak. Different families opened their homes to house members from the "sister church" in Richmond, Virginia, overnight. Another single guy and I stayed with a family that put us up for the night and fed us while we were there. I remember lying down for the night and reading Hebrews 13:1–2, knowing that I was to share that scripture with my host and hostess. As I did, the tears began to fall from their eyes and I knew that the Lord had touched them in some way.

Hospitality has changed my life and has helped me to know others better. We have people into our home regularly. And you never know—maybe by practicing hospitality I have entertained some angels!

Bill Landrum
Heating and Air Conditioning Technician

Jump-Starting Hospitality

Hospitality brings fear and cold chills to most of us. It certainly did to me until my husband jump-started our own brand of hospitality. Let me start at the beginning. My mother was one to invite anyone over who didn't have a place to go. It could be a holiday or just a Sunday afternoon bowl of popcorn. It didn't matter. If you didn't have a place to go, you could go to Mom's. After Todd and I got married, we had couples over to our home and had a "no utensils spaghetti dinner." The utensils were plastic gloves. What fun!

We would have sports parties when the major tournaments were on. We enjoyed having people over.

About eighteen years ago, we left our home state of South Dakota and moved to Florida, and then on to Virginia, where we joined a large church in Richmond. A lot of the people there were very successful, up-and-coming business people who had nice, big houses. We, on the other hand, were living in a very small rental house out in the country. We loved the country part, but the very small house did not fit my idea of hospitality. My idea was that as soon as God gave me a nicer home, I then could have people over properly.

Then came the jump-start. One day in Sunday School, I heard my dear husband say that we would be having a volleyball party at our house in a couple of weeks. My mouth dropped, but I kept my composure and thought, "*Oh, this is not good!*" But on the way home from church that day, I thought, *How will God know that I will invite people over if He gives me a big house when I won't have people over in a small house.* Right then, my heart changed as did my attitude, and we planned the best volleyball party we could pull together. Well, about one hundred people were at our little rancher house with one bathroom, and we had the best time. We had volleyball for all ages. We had sack races, three-legged races and other games for the children. The adults played with the children, and all went home tired and saying they wanted to come back for more.

God did a huge work in my heart that day, and we went on to sponsor more events at that house for another year or so. And guess what? God blessed us with a bigger house and a bigger yard. But my heart had already changed. It didn't matter what house we were in.

Opening our home became a way of life. We started to keep track and decided it was just too much work. We have people over as often as we can. We host an annual Thanksgiving dinner that our children think is the best holiday of the year. Last year, on the way to our house, one of the couples that has come since we started called to see if they could bring along a friend of the family. We shuffled some chairs, got out another plate and said, "Yeah, come on." We now have people who look vaguely familiar come up to us as we are shopping in a store and say, "I've been at your house," or "I rode your zip-line the last time I was there."

So, the question is, how do you do hospitality? You start. That's all it takes, a start. As you can see, it doesn't need to be perfect in your mind. It certainly wasn't perfect in my mind when we started. But people need to get together just to talk and relax and get to know one another in homes away from a church setting. I now see all kinds of people whom I would love to invite over. When we do invite them over, *we* are the ones who are blessed.

Todd and Jill VanderPol
Small Business Owners

The Power of a Note

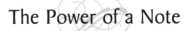

I was new to the church and was looking for a way to "get my feet wet" by helping in the women's ministry. One activity for which I volunteered was sending notes to express sympathy, support or thank you's. I soon had occasion to send a thank you to "Eddie," who does all the custodial work for the church as an act of giving to the Lord's work. I did not yet know him but had seen his dedication and acknowledged this fact in my note. The next time I went to church, several people told me that "Eddie" wanted to know who the lady was who sent this note. He said that it made all his work worthwhile. I met him and heard the same message from him. I found out that he was a recent widower, and serving the church was both helping him to fill an empty place and was providing a way of serving his Lord.

I felt very humbled that a small act that I did as an "assignment" could have such a profound affect on that dear man. I learned a lesson about the importance of small things, whether it be a note, a word of kindness, or other ways of acknowledging a person's relevance to others. We all need recognition. I've sent "Eddie" many thank you's since that time, and I am often reminded to send notes to others as the Lord brings them to mind. "Eddie" recently brought in an album displaying all the cards I and others have sent. What a humbling yet joyous experience!

Connie Markva
Homemaker

A Single Man Sold on Hospitality

I am a single man...never married. I have become convinced that being "given" to hospitality includes singles. By this I mean that singles can participate by having people in their homes, not just waiting to be invited. There seems to be no expectation for singles to be given to hospitality. As a single man, though, I have been challenged to think differently, thanks to the godly example of my pastor and his wife.

I suppose it is particularly unusual for a single man to practice hospitality. Yet, there is great blessing in doing so. Yes, it does involve work, like preparing meals, ensuring that the home is comfortable and inviting, and cleaning the house before and after guests leave. That is probably the biggest reason single guys are not known for their hospitality—usually their dwelling places are a mess! Plus, we think more about social activities and going out and having fun. There is nothing wrong with that, but a lot of these activities can distract from one of the main objectives of hospitality—building relationships.

It is easy to get caught up in the **doing** of socializing and never connect with people on a deeper level or with non singles. Even though there is some merit to separating groups based on sex, interests and needs, much is lost by not encouraging groups to interact through hospitality. One of the greatest blessings that I have experienced in practicing hospitality is the opportunity to build meaningful relationships with families, older couples, teenagers, children and people of a different race. It truly fosters community and strengthens the spiritual family when these groups interact. Through hospitality, I see where God uses me to influence the children and teenagers of the families in my fellowship. I actually feel as if I play a small role in rearing them, as if I were a big brother. Of course, I am greatly encouraged by watching godly examples of parenting and grandparenting by fellowshipping with those who are my age and older.

Another aspect of hospitality that has influenced my life is how I view my home. It is not a castle for me to hide myself from the world, but rather an embassy to be used to bring people to Christ. We all know that the residence of an ambassador is called an embassy. How much more are the homes of ambassadors for Christ to be embassies of His Kingdom and Government.

When I started looking for a house, I wanted to find a place that would be conducive to hospitality. The den of my house is what sold it. I could see it as a wonderful room to fill with people, and it has been used on many occasions for just that. I want my house and yard to look nice and comfortable, not to show off but to create an environment of blessing. Every aspect of decorating is centered on hospitality—how the furniture is arranged, and the kind of furniture that is purchased. Is it comfortable? Is the lighting sufficient? Is the home comfortable and inviting? Is it a place that people would feel welcome? Obviously, our attitudes and the opening of our hearts are the most important factors in creating that environment, but who wants to sit on something that is uncomfortable or causes hygiene concerns? Who wants to walk up to a house where the yard looks like a tornado hit?

Another factor in my looking for a house was ministry potential. Where could I live to impact the neighbors most? My mission field is my neighborhood. I have enjoyed getting to know my neighbors by having cookouts, open houses at Christmas time and inviting them over for dinner. Introducing them to my Christian friends and family has also influenced them for the Kingdom. What a great way for my unsaved neighbors to meet other believers. I believe that the continued practice of hospitality and prayer for my neighbors will yield a harvest.

William Hendricks
Mortgage Broker

Heart-Changing Transformation

It has been my joy to work in a missions-minded suburban church as a secretary for many years. I had the pleasure of seeing hundreds of people come and go on missions trips during those years, and then one day, for the first time, the Lord prompted me to go on my first mission trip and my first trip to New York City. It was like the "country come to town." To say it was a life-changing experience does not do justice to the heart-changing transformation that happened to me.

In New York City, we had the opportunity to serve the homeless right where they live—in cardboard boxes on the streets of the city. Homeless? The boxes were their home. It was my first experience in receiving hospitality from homeless individuals who were gracious and welcoming in receiving our presence and our food and drink.

I returned home with a heart that was changed in many ways, including my concern for the homeless population and a new and deep love for my own city and the diversity of culture and race. For the first time in her life, this white, suburban church secretary was experiencing the heart of God for the lost and the needy. I felt the Lord reminding me of something I had learned from *Experiencing God* by Henry Blackaby: "Find out what I am doing and join me in it." The Lord gently reminded me, "You don't have to take Me to the city; I am already there." That was a relief, because I knew He wanted me to become involved in what He was doing in Richmond, but I didn't know anyone or where to begin.

I began with what I had in my hands. My husband, Charlie, had been involved in Promise Keepers and had developed some friendships with a few black pastors in our inner city. The Lord prompted me to invite one of those pastors and his wife to dinner at our home. We had never had a black couple over for dinner simply because I did not know any black couples. It was a very enjoyable evening, and from that night, we were "friends," and the Lord opened the door for us to trust one another enough to do ministry together. That would not have happened without the time spent sharing each other's lives and breaking down dividing walls.

God now has opened doors for me to extend ministry city wide and to help others open their hearts, hands and homes across racial and denominational lines to those in need.

Gwen Mansini
Director Urban and Home Missions
Mechanicsville Christian Center

The "Prophet's Chamber"

One of the greatest pleasures for me is to entertain members of the Body of Christ who are visiting the area in which I live. So often, missionaries, ministers, pastors and their wives or evangelists and friends from out of town need a place to call "home" for a few days. They need a place of peace and a quiet place of restoration for their souls. Hospitality in these cases is a special delight, as I know I am serving those who serve the

Lord in full-time ministry. This is the very heart of God—to provide food, shelter and rest for those who serve Him.

When I invite people to my home, I am inviting them to receive a blessing that is a bit of the character of our Lord. My parents taught me to receive guests and honor them as such. That instruction has been deepened throughout the years as I grew in the understanding of the nature of God. It gives me great delight to entertain new friends. As I prepare my home for their arrival, I pray over the atmosphere, that it might be a place of safety and refuge, if needed, as well as a place of joy and love. I pray that they will feel welcome and know they are free to be themselves, just as if they were in their own home. This is the very essence of hospitality—to be made welcome and comfortable enough to "kick off their shoes."

As I prepare the food, I try to take into account the likes and dislikes of those who will be eating with me. I prepare the meals with the thought of pleasing them and that they will enjoy the flavors of each item. It delights my heart to see my guests enjoying what is before them. Everyone likes to know they are remembered and that their special likes and dislikes are taken into account. Hospitality embodies this remembering of the individual. They are made to feel "special" and important, which they are.

Nothing knits hearts together in deep friendship more quickly than the opportunity to share deepest needs and prayer requests around the "table of hospitality." People feel safe and sheltered, which is what our Heavenly Father wants us to feel when we are in His presence, sharing His table. Secrets are confided, tears of healing flow and hurts are wiped away with love and gentleness when hospitality is present. Hospitality makes welcome those who are strangers to my family. Once they have been in my home, they are no longer strangers and are welcome to return again and again.

Gerie Martin
Loaves and Fishes Ministry

Stretching Beyond the Home

Having been reared in a home where hospitality was practiced as an integral part of our lives, it was natural that in my home as a married woman, my husband and I would continue the practice of hospitality. Over the thirteen years of our marriage, we have opened our home to both friends and family who needed places to live for a time. We have had many out-of-state and foreign visitors, and even strangers stay with us for differing lengths of time. We have also had many individuals, families, and groups in our home for meals and fellowship. In fact, several years ago we sold our home and moved to a home which boasted an open floor plan more geared to having others in our home. We have made many choices in our home based on our mission and purpose to having others in our home. These things we have enjoyed and continue to enjoy greatly, and we are always on the lookout for new people we can invite into our home to get to know better.

In the past few years, as my husband has read the Proverbs 31 passage regarding a virtuous woman over me each week, I have been very challenged by the words, "She stretcheth out her hand to the poor; yea, she reacheth forth her hands to the needy" (Prov. 31:20). Over these years, I have come to see that hospitality is much more than just opening your home to people. Hospitality also encompasses opening your heart and your hand. This is definitely part of opening your home effectively, but it can also mean stretching beyond your home into someone else's home or need. I have felt God call me to help supply some of the physical needs of widows, children who at the time were feeling like orphans, and others in need. I recently felt extremely blessed to help pack the belongings of a newlywed couple who were moving from their apartment because the wife was pregnant and on total bed rest. She obviously could not pack to move, and the husband was working as hard as he could to provide for her. As I packed their things into boxes, I found myself thinking, *This is hospitality! I am opening my heart and my hand toward these people!*

I now have a much broader vision for hospitality. I am no longer just looking for people to invite home. I am also looking for people to whom I can offer hospitality in their territory rather than mine. Reaching forth your hand outside of your home will never take the place of bringing people into your home. However, I am beginning to feel that just bringing people into my home is not all that God requires of me to fulfill His admonition to "Use hospitality one to another without grudging" (I Peter 4:9).

As I look back, I can see clearly the example my parents set for me in all areas of hospitality. I hope my children will follow this legacy of hospitality which my parents set and which my husband and I continue—opening our hearts, hands and home.

Nicole Akyeampong, homemaker
Administrative Assistant, Save America Ministries

The Hospitality of Adoption

AN AMAZING THIRTY-YEAR FAMILY ADVENTURE

Hospitality seems to define much of our lives. Neither Neil nor I grew up in homes that entertained much, but he is very gregarious and loves people, drawing us into a pattern of an open home. Even though my cooking skills were not well developed, we started bringing people home after church regularly. Our Sundays did not seem complete if we were not sharing time and food with others.

Perhaps this helped prepare me for a thought planted in my heart that I would someday like to adopt a child after we had some the usual way. I don't recall when I first shared this dream with Neil, but he was receptive. We had our two boys, Craig and Kurt, and had lost a baby girl between them. The doctor said that for me to carry another child to term would be unlikely, so my deep desire for a little girl led us to adoption. We encountered obstacles trying to adopt within the United States, so we sought out an agency that placed children from Korea. The Lord's hand was obviously at work leading us to this agency.

This began a challenging but oh-so-rewarding adventure for us. Mundane would never describe the years that followed. I was a bit scared too, concerned that I might not be up to the test of total commitment to this child. Neil was stalwart, always confident and reassuring that we were fulfilling God's will for our lives. Much prayer had preceded even our initial foray into adoption, and God gave us confidence to proceed.

Craig was nearly eleven and Kurt seven-and-a-half years old when Sarah arrived. They were thrilled with this little sister and set about to make her smile and be happy. We observed the potential for a spoiled little girl who might live up to her name Sarah, meaning "princess." So we decided we needed another child, preferably a girl. Fourteen months later, two siblings—Susan, age four, and Christy, fourteen months—arrived and added to the joy of the family. While I was still struggling to adjust to the added time demands (absolutely positive that I was living proof of the "Peter Principle," having bitten off more than I could chew), I overheard Kurt telling his dad that it wasn't fair to adopt only girls. Couldn't we get a boy? Then we'd have three of each. Neil responded by saying that now was not the time to talk to Mom about that, maybe later.

I never cease to be amazed at how God works. The idea of a boy germinated, and our hearts were prepared. We decided that a boy between the ages of Kurt and Sarah would be ideal, so we contacted the adoption agency. They later informed us that all the waiting boys that age had at least one older male sibling, except one who had a younger sister. Our instinct was to say yes to the brother and sister immediately, but we knew we needed to pray about it. That night, the Lord gave Neil Psalms 127 and 128. The Lord says children are a heritage from the Lord and that happy is the man who has a quiver full of them. His children are like olive plants.

Thankfully, we had this confirmation from the Lord because we had challenging times ahead. The immigration regulations at the time restricted the number of children who could be brought over for adoption to two (we already had three because of siblings). Through the arduous efforts of Neil and a congressional staffer, however, we managed to get a private bill passed by Congress to allow the children to be ours.

When we discovered the ordeal ahead to get these children to the United States, it would have been easy to give up and say we don't need this grief. However, as was the case in each adoption, once we saw the pictures of these children living in an orphanage in Korea, we took each one into our hearts and wove him or her into the fabric of our everyday living. God's love is a special love and enables us to do and be more than we can achieve in our own strength.

In November 1976, after nineteen months of waiting, David, age nine, and Julie, five-and-a-half, joined us. To prepare for them, we had added a two-story addition to our home. The next year, we heard of a ten-year-old boy who was already processed to come to the United States, but the applying family had decided he was too old. The agency was able to bring him over and place him with us. So Keith became a part of our family, finally balancing out four boys and four girls. We found the dynamics of absorbing older children into the family structure to be far more demanding, but everyone adjusted. That same year, the TV show *Eight is Enough*, came out. We decided maybe that was a sign!

In 1974, we had become part of a house-church, meeting mostly in homes, including ours. The brethren were very supportive in every way during our times of preparation and adjustment. The children were used to having a lot of people in our home and seemed to thrive on the fellowship as we did. Even the children would invite people home after church, sometimes without asking permission. We had to set guidelines fast, but their budding hospitality blessed our hearts.

Our oldest son, Craig, was a people person from toddler age. Our next door neighbor called him her little "Yenta." He kept her informed of everything he heard and observed in the apartment building. As he grew older, he exhibited great hospitality and generosity which have continued into adult-hood. When he left for college, the floodgates seemed to open to young people coming to live with us for varying lengths of time. At first, they were students whom Craig knew coming to the Washington D.C. area to do internships on Capitol Hill, student teaching, or starting a job and just needing a jumpstart to get their feet on the ground. Friends of some of our other children followed suit. The word seemed to spread that we had an open-door policy to Christian young people. Twenty-four years later, this practice continues.

We have been rewarded greatly and have learned a lot. Having people here constantly, with the physical and emo-tional demands entailed, has been a growing experience for me especially. I have learned a lot about my weaknesses— not a pleasant thing. God has used certain people to spur my growth. On one occasion, a young man came to live with us, wormed his way into my heart, and later married one of our daughters. When he joined our revolving house-hold, there was a young woman here whom he, along with everyone else, found irritating. One evening he asked me if I knew how long she was staying and if there was a way to expedite her departure. My response was that I didn't think she'd leave until I could get my own attitude and reactions readjusted.

We have had a number of uncomfortable situations, sometimes outright rebellious attitudes and ungodly behavior, that have required intervention and correction. If I get discouraged and start thinking, *I don't need this in my life,* God seems to send along a jewel who truly loves the Lord, and we miss greatly when he or she moves on.

Some of our greatest enjoyment has come from fellowship around the dinner table. So much laughter and also opportunities for learning from one another. Sharing the Word (my husband is always a teacher) and discussing public policy are the norm around here. When our youngest daughters, then in high school, went to Colorado for a two-week session about the Christian world-view, they "complained" that the teaching sessions were just like the discussions around our dinner table. Another call, this time with excitement, informed us that one of the guest speakers was a man from South Africa who had spoken at a meeting in our home.

We have many enduring relationships with some of the people who have lived with us. There is an extended-family feeling. Some of them we'd love to "adopt."

A few years ago, we joined a Bed and Breakfast Club which brings people our age whom we've never met to stay with us for from one to three nights. We never know what God will do or whom He will use. I try to keep in mind Hebrews 13:2: "Do not forget to entertain strangers, for by so doing some have unwittingly entertained angels."

Neil and Connie Markva
Patent Attorney and Homemaker

Receiving Can Be Humbling

Our wedding was set. Since my husband travels a bit with work and had to go to Orlando anyway, we decided to make Florida our honeymoon destination. We would be there for him to do his job, and we'd be able to take advantage of the fact that his airline ticket and our hotel accommodations for three nights were covered. We are on a very tight budget, so it seemed like a great plan!

When we arrived at the Orlando airport and met the van that was to take us to the hotel, out jumped some familiar co-workers with these words to greet us: "The job is canceled. The hurricane that's coming is a category-four. You should try to catch the next flight out of here."

We were stunned. Catch the next flight to where? This was our honeymoon. We were planning to stay at the hotel the next three nights (for free), and then to spend the four days and three nights that followed at one of those resorts where you agree to listen to a ninety-minute sales presentation in exchange for romantic hotel accommodations and tickets to Universal Studios. What we didn't fully comprehend was that, rather than running our own agenda, we were about to run into Hurricane Charley. And Charley didn't care one iota about our agenda.

Since the job got canceled and the employees were told to leave Orlando and go home, the company no longer needed to pay for hotel accommodations for its' employees. We quickly recalled an R.S.V.P. we'd received from an old college buddy and his wife which had a note scribbled on it, inviting us to their home, should we ever find ourselves in Orlando. I called our friends, whose immediate response to the sound of my voice was, "When do you want to come over? Our guesthouse is open." Our gracious friends drove to our hotel, picked us up, and brought us to their home.

Before any of this, Chuck Crismier had invited us to contribute our thoughts on hospitality. It was something we figured we'd discuss and write during our honeymoon week in Florida sunshine. But God must've thought it a clever opportunity for us to receive a five-and-a-half day object lesson to teach us how little we really knew about the subject.

Charley hit that night, Friday the thirteenth, and took out a lot of tree limbs, along with all the electricity: lights, air conditioning (did we mention that this was August in Florida?), refrigerator, and stove. He closed down the resort where we were planning to stay at the end of the week. So, there we were, literally at the mercy of our friends, like it or not, receiving their generous hospitality. We felt extremely grateful. We felt humbled. As each day followed the next, we wondered if we were (or at what point we would certainly become) a burden. We began to feel guilty. We felt helpless to change the situation and so jumped at every opportunity to pay them back. We took them out to restaurants for meals that were not in our budget to buy. We babysat one evening so they could go on a date. It was an unusual honeymoon activity, but we were desperately trying to express our gratitude and relieve our guilt.

Our friends were wonderful. They balanced paying attention to us with casually living their own daily lives (as much as possible in a disaster area). They made their home and car accessible to us and enveloped us with loving warmth and openness. They never gave us the impression that they expected us to reimburse them somehow. At the same time, they were gracious enough to take us up on many of our offers to reciprocate and serve them.

They had needs, too. After all, it was their refrigerator and stove that were dead. Sometimes they disappeared when mealtime would approach, probably to relieve the pressure they may have perceived we felt to purchase all the meals for all of us. Or maybe we were driving them a little bit crazy, and they actually escaped for a respite. Who knows? What became clear to us, however, is that we were fighting an inner battle to distinguish our own genuine expressions of gratitude from those nasty feelings of obligation to "pay back."

We've recognized from this experience that receiving hospitality can be a very humbling experience. It takes some skill and sensitivity (like our friends demonstrated) for that humbling not to turn into humiliation. Knowing what it feels like to be in a position of need, where receiving someone's hospitality is a necessity, we have become more empathetic to our future guests. "Freely you have received; freely give." Evidently, Jesus knew those feelings, too.

Dave and Holly Eaton
Graphic Designer & Author

Holy Spirit-Empowered Hospitality

When I meet someone for the first time, my first instinct is to see when we can have them over to the house to get to know them better. My husband went home to be with the Lord recently, and after practicing hospitality with him more than thirty years, I now feel strongly that every "single" believer must work on the skills of becoming excellent at sharing his or her home in this great privilege that the Lord of hospitality has given us.

I believe it is part of our job as believers who are employed by God to be His hand extended to a hurting world. It is best done in a warm and loving home than anywhere else. People are more relaxed in a home setting. After going through necessary grieving following Steve's passing, I am constantly reaching to others in Jesus' name, bringing neighbors and new strangers I meet into my home, just as we always did. If our homes are built on the right stuff, we then will have precious and pleasant homes in which to have people and give the gift of hospitality to them.

The man of the home is the one who establishes the good foundation in his home with his family. Our children ministered to our guests right along with us when we had them in our home, because my husband taught and trained them in the Word of God and His example of loving people. Most of the times we would partake of the Lord's Supper. During that time our daughters often had a chance to pray with us. Sometimes Steve had them actually pray over the person who was our guest, because they could pray as well as their father. This practice ministered much more than another adult praying over their needs, and those prayers would be answered, too! Hospitality trained our daughters in ministry, which is part of our job as Christian parents (Prov. 22:6).

After we received empowerment by the Holy Spirit in 1979, our lives changed dramatically as we had a heightened awareness of our new unseen guest (the Holy Spirit) in our lives and our home. Steve led us as we prayed. We anointed the four corners of our home with oil and sanctified every room for His service. So the Holy Spirit did come, externally into the very rooms of our home and internally in the rooms of our hearts.

One summer we had a pastor and his wife and two children from Africa stay with us for a month and a half. The day they left we were all crying. Then the very next day we had a wedding for a good friend in our backyard! No problem, the Holy Spirit was in charge and helped us orchestrate the whole thing without missing a beat. If I hadn't used the "Helper" all of my life, I don't know what I would have done.

Rahab was given protection because of her hospitality to the spies from Israel (Josh. 6:17). If you want your home to be protected from the enemy, use it in hospitality, and I believe it will be protected in a special way by Jehovah-Nissi.

Are we willing, on the spur of the moment, to put someone up for the night in our guest rooms? I find that many people have lovely homes built with guest rooms in them and yet they rarely use them for strangers. Lydia did in Acts 16:13–15. She constrained them to stay in her home overnight. I am sure she made them a delicious breakfast in the morning before they left too. It was such a blessing to have people stay in our home. Most times when they left we felt an emptiness inside as they drove away, because our hearts had connected with theirs in a very special way during their stay.

Matthew 25:35 says, "For I was hungry and you gave me something to eat, I was thirsty and you gave me something to drink, I was a stranger and you invited me in." We must let the Holy Spirit break our "Practice of the Presence of Self." He does this by forging Himself into our inner beings and giving us a servant's heart.

As I look back over our years as a family together in our wonderful Cape Cod home in California, some of the most precious memories are when we practiced the sweet gift of hospitality together in our home. Glory be to the Lord!

Wanda Smith
Mother, Grandmother, Homemaker

What a God Strategy!

As a pastoring couple, my wife, Carla, and I have majored in hospitality for many years. When we sensed a call to encourage and help develop the city-wide church here in Richmond—for there is really only one Church in Richmond—our dining room table became the location for many miracles of the heart. We have found that when one Christian truly touches the heart of another Christian under the power of the Holy Spirit, miracles happen. These are quiet miracles of love that produce much freshness in God's Kingdom.

Because we value hospitality so much, when I received an inheritance from my parents, we were able to add a section to our house that increased the size of our dining room and living room. We also purchased a large table for the dining room and then sought the Lord for whom we would invite to it.

The first dinner we scheduled for this larger table was a meeting of Christian leaders from all parts of the city. No one was asking me to do this; I just felt a sense of urgency from the Lord about it. It was as though the Body of Christ needed ligaments if it was to be anything more than dry bones, and my job was to allow ligaments to form on the Body of Christ around our big table.

By and large, the people we first invited around that table were only distantly aware of each other, and they came from very diverse backgrounds. About half were people who cared for the poor; the other half were business leaders.

Five months later, I received an email that described the miracle of the heart that occurred around the expanded table. The letter was from Gwen Mansini, who helps coordinate ministries to the poor in our community.

I don't know if you know this, but I want to thank you again for the gift of hospitality that you and Carla extended to a group of leaders to have dinner around your table this past year. The evening that Charlie and I were there, along with others from…other churches, including Buddy Childress and Geronimo Aguilar, was a landmark event. At the moment, none of us could have ever known what God was doing.

At that dinner Buddy got to know Geronimo and asked him to speak at an evangelistic outreach of Needles Eye Ministries. Buddy heard Geronimo speak, share his testimony, and heard Geronimo's heart for the poor…. Buddy then asked Geronimo to speak at four Needle's Eye luncheons. With each luncheon, the numbers increased. The last luncheon was the largest crowd ever, more than 150. These were powerful meetings. I believe seventeen people responded to receive Christ.

...This happened because you and Carla were humbly obedient to the Lord to open your hearts and homes to a few leaders so that they might get to know one another. What a simple strategy. What a God strategy!

Doug and Carla McMurray
Presbyterian Pastor

PART II

The *Art* and *Practice* of *Hospitality*

by Kathie Crismier

Practical ideas, tools, pointers and encouragement, enabling you to practice hospitality with confidence as never before.

Chapter *20*

Getting Started

For reality in

your spirituality,

practice hospitality

in your locality.

YOU HAVE BEEN CULTIVATING a *heart* of hospitality; you recognize the power of hospitality; and you have decided to **do** hospitality. Now what? It's time for the *art* of hospitality.

Each of us has special abilities and talents. What are yours? Identify your attributes and strengths as an individual or as a couple. Discuss with your spouse how together you can begin to serve others through hospitality. It can be enlightening when we talk to our mates about this area of ministry. Ideas begin to springboard into reality! Let your hearts be united to begin expressing together this divinely designed plan to reach to others.

Start where you both feel comfortable. Decide what each person will do—what your goals are—who you will invite. Then do it! Believe me, hospitality can evolve into some really exciting relationships. Be open to the Lord's leading.

You may begin by having one or two people over, or you may feel more comfortable with four to six guests. I never imagined I could enjoy serving one hundred guests in our home, but we have done it often and enjoyed it immensely. But large groups are not for everyone, so relax. Most expressions of hospitality are one-on-one or in small, intimate gatherings. Remember your goals. They often change with the size of a group.

Your goals might be one or more of the following:

- Welcoming new neighbors
- Reaching to an unbelieving neighbor
- Ministering to a hurting marriage
- Loving a newly married couple
- Helping new people meet "the gang"
- Encouraging others to reach out and show God's love
- Getting people together just for a good time of fun
- Reaching to a homeless or needy person
- Getting to know a visitor or new member in your congregation
- Providing a haven for a visiting speaker

Whatever your goals may be, evaluate after your gathering to see if you met them and how you can come closer next time. Remember to give each guest an opportunity to share. It can be a thoroughly enjoyable experience getting to know new people.

Some gatherings may not seem superspiritual, and perhaps they are not. Nevertheless, we all need to learn to have fun and laugh in these serious days in which we live. I heard a man say at one of our gatherings that he had no idea Christians had so much fun! That is ministry! How does the world see you? He dedicated his life to Christ and, three years later, took over major ministry responsibilities after growing through dedicated discipleship. It all began over an informal meal.

I personally enjoy making our parties or get-togethers very festive. I go all out to create an atmosphere. People feel special and enjoy the added effort. I enjoy creating a theme, but if that is not your thing, enjoy doing it your own way. If you enjoy the gathering, it is likely others will too. If you feel pressured and harried, your guests will pick up on it. So, do what makes **you** comfortable and your guests will feel comfortable.

Remember, hospitality is reaching to others, giving of yourself to make others feel welcome, happy, comfortable and special. Ministry takes place when others are confident that you have their best interests at heart. Let's get started!

Focus on Others

I love the word *hospitality*. It refreshes with feelings and memories of warmth, love, acceptance and belonging. Hospitality is serving others, meeting their needs, reaching to strangers. The term *entertaining* often sends messages of fear: "I won't measure up," "putting on the dog," or "too much work."

Scripture tells us to "love thy neighbor as thy self" (Mark 12:31; Lev. 19:18). To do this, we must ask God to give us a love for others and a desire to reach out beyond ourselves, even to strangers. Making ourselves available to others means having an awareness of their needs. For most of us, this means spending time alone with God, asking for a new sensitivity to those around us.

So much of our lives is spent meeting our own needs and desires. Focus on ourselves seems to be a progressive disease that smothers the love of God in our lives. We need to ask God to show us how to reach out and love others as He would have us do. We need new eyes and the key to unlock our heart.

Being Genuine

True hospitality requires being *genuine* with others. It calls us to opening our hearts as well as our homes to bring a sense of caring and acceptance to others. I discovered that what really matters is not what I serve my guests but my acceptance of them and my willingness to risk sharing my thoughts, feelings and surroundings. I must become vulnerable.

My husband, Chuck, and I learned a secret. We did not know how to really love others enough. So we asked God to give us a supernatural love for others. I was amazed! God did exactly that. I no longer saw people as "unlovely" or "not as good as" or "better than." God began to give us His kind of love for all people.

We lose out when we judge others by educational, cultural, financial, or social differences. The people who have meant the most to us in the last twenty-five years have been, for the most part, different from us in these areas. Man looks on the outer appearance, but God looks on the heart (I Sam. 16:7). God has been revealing to us His secret. We now choose to look on the heart. It is amazing what happens. It is almost like being released from a self-imposed prison. It is hard to imagine greater joy and fulfillment.

We so often put the focus on our performance. God wants us to reach out and love others into His presence. That is what hospitality is—reaching out with an open heart, open hand and open home.

Stretching Heart and Home

God answers prayers, but not always the way we expect. Soon after we asked for this supernatural love, God gave us a big test. One Sunday morning, a man off the street came into the group where we were ministering. He was looking for food, not for a handout. His dignity was at issue. Both Chuck and I felt that we needed to respond. So we took him home. He had obviously not bathed and we had to breathe through our mouths all eighteen miles of our ride home. Our girls treated him like everyone else. They talked with him in the car. We ate lunch together out on the patio and encouraged him to share his story. What an experience we all had! We were learning to love as Christ asked us to. After lunch, he stacked wood, and we all returned to church that evening. I do not know what happened to that man, but I do know what happened to our family. That began a new journey of love for us, a challenge to our comfort zone.

At the opposite end of the spectrum, a few years ago we received a phone call asking if we would host a dinner for a presidential candidate. By this time, I was ready for anything. We made plans on just a few days' notice. But the next day we got word that the candidate had dropped out of the race. What I realized was that we can do anything God asks of us if we are "willing" to be obedient. He wants our obedience above all else. God is not looking for *ability*, but for *availability*.

God may never ask you to feed a man off the street or a presidential candidate, but the question is, would you be willing? Begin today and see where God leads you in the ministry of hospitality. Be willing to be stretched.

For the Christian, hospitality is not really a choice. It is a command...a choice to obey. In I Peter 4:9, we are called to "Use hospitality one to another without grudging." God knew we would come up with a long list of excuses, so He tells us to just do it. Be obedient. Hebrews 13:1–2 kindly counsels, "let brotherly love continue."

Heart for the Stranger

Do not forget to entertain strangers, for by doing so some have unwittingly entertained angels (Heb. 13:2). We are prone to be hospitable to those we know. God exhorts us to reach beyond ourselves and our circle of friends, first to others who share in faith, and then to strangers from the faith. It will bring unexpected blessings. "Love the stranger, for you were strangers in the land of Egypt," exhorted Moses. Many are strangers from the Commonwealth of Faith, and many within the Body of Christ often feel like strangers.

Throughout Scripture, we see evidence of the importance of hospitality and how they entertained the stranger. Jesus was welcomed into the homes of many.

We have evidence that early in our nation's history hospitality was highly esteemed. Some of our forefathers, such as George Washington, nearly went bankrupt from doing so much hospitality. People were welcomed into the family life for a meal or for several-day stays as they traveled through. In many instances, this was how news was spread, and guests were a welcome and interesting addition to their lives. Today, we stay in high-rise hotels, dine alone, and rarely interact with those in the city we visit. We stay to ourselves.

Life and values have changed, and, along with the change, we have lost the value of relationships. In many of our cities today, we can go about our lives and rarely speak to those with whom we have contact, other than to ask for directions. We can go to the bank, market, gas station, dry cleaners, etc., and speak very few words to conduct our business, never having really touched a life or been light and salt to a lost and dying world.

Touching Lives

There is a great reward in helping others feel welcome on the planet through a smile or kind word of encouragement, even in passing.

Our culture today has become so caught up in materialism that we have lost the art of communicating with those around us. We feel important and valuable only if our schedule is full. But are we touching lives? Are we making a difference by our actions with others? Many of us are lonely little islands, getting up, going to work, doing our job, going home, watching television, going to bed, and most often not relating to others, even in our own family. Then we wonder why we feel lonely in a crowd. Our communities are filled with lonely individuals living in bubbles, bumping up against each other but not knowing how to relate and interact with one another. Reaching out and touching people brings fulfillment into our lives that has kingdom value.

Now that we have established that hospitality is a mandate from God, how do we joyfully begin this act of obedience? Begin by asking God to give you the desire to be obedient and to do hospitality. Ask Him for a heart of hospitality. Begin to think hospitality. Ask Him how He wants you to begin. Then begin. Begin developing the *art* of hospitality. The art of hospitality flows from a *heart* of hospitality. The art must reflect the heart.

Encourage Your Children to Do Hospitality

As I spoke to a women's group on hospitality, one mother said that she was going to help her seven year old to have a tea party for her friends. This is a wonderful way to train your children in hospitality and manners. It means more when they welcome their friends, and it is amazing how much they observe and imitate.

My husband and I have enjoyed greeting our guests in theme costumes for larger parties from time to time. Now our children are asking when we can do another costume party. It adds to the atmosphere and excitement, and your guests feel special. Whether it is a show, or a flow of love, is a matter of my attitude.

Our teenage daughters wanted to do a formal sit-down dinner for their new friends during our first Christmas season in Richmond, Virginia. So we sent our invitations and planned our menu. I had to be creative quickly because our living room furniture and lamps had not yet arrived. We set up portable tables in the living room with a lot of candles for light. My husband, married daughter and I served the food, and our two high school daughters and their friends were really ministered to by the fact that the whole family participated in the evening. The next Christmas season, many of those kids asked if we were going to do it again. That's success! They experienced a womb of love and acceptance.

The purpose of the particular party was to invite those kids into a Christian home to experience the love and support of a Christian family. We gathered them together around the fireplace in the gathering room after dinner and asked each to share what Christmas meant to them. It gave our girls an opportunity to share their hearts on the meaning of Christ's birth.

Parties can be a great seed-planting opportunity around the Holy Holidays or Feast Days. Don't miss the opportunity. The world is more receptive at Thanksgiving, Christmas, Passover and even the Fourth of July. Take every opportunity. There is no lack of opportunity—only lack of courage. So take courage, take heart, and start.

Get Started

Here are just a few ideas to prime the pump of your thinking. One idea may just lead to another.

- Tea on the terrace, deck or patio
- A harvest party
- An ice cream social—everyone brings toppings
- Small group theme dinners are fun and help break down barriers. Focus on a particular country.
- A cook-out on the deck or patio
- Fourth of July neighborhood parade
- Easter sunrise breakfast. Plant a cross in the yard, and after breakfast share the Resurrection story. Have neighborhood children put on a Resurrection play for their parents after breakfast. We did this one year, and every neighbor showed up with their delicious breakfast contribution, which I had coordinated. I served the main dish and decorated. Chuck coordinated activities for the children and families focused on the Resurrection. Everyone was moved by the early-morning worshipful adventure and enjoyed their kids in the play.

Don't forget to be creative in reaching out to business colleagues and work associates.

Be Creative—Don't Compare

Be obedient in all you do, responding to the leading of the Lord. All creativity comes from Him. Go for it!

Avoid comparing what you do with what others do. God calls each of us differently. Early in our marriage, Steve and Wanda Smith, close friends, were very influential in teaching Chuck and me about hospitality. They did it not so much by words as by example. We felt loved and cared for and enjoyed their hospitality. When we made a decision to "do" hospitality, we did it using our gifts and talents and listening to God's creativity. We didn't try to do what they did.

After buying our second home, we "subpoenaed" neighbors for a Christmas open-house. We discovered two neighbors who had lived across from each other for seventeen years. They met each other for the first time as they walk to our open house. We all had a wonderful time, and we planned another event—a Fourth of July parade. All of the children decorated their bikes, trikes, wagons, skates, etc., and off we went with music on tape. Adults garbed in red, white, and blue joined the parade, one couple pushing a wheel barrow with a Bible, flags, and Declaration of Independence. We marched several blocks back to a house with a pool where we swam and ate and built relationships.

We fostered other gatherings during our eleven years in that neighborhood. These built relationships which gave later opportunities to share in more private settings why we had victory over circumstances. When others shared similar situations, we were then part of their lives to share God's heart and hope.

Years later, we were reviewing several of these events with friends who had earlier modeled hospitality for us. They lamented that they hadn't done such things and felt they had failed. But God showed them how He uses us each differently. We don't all do all the same things all the time. That was one season of our lives. We need to listen to the Lord and do what He places in our hearts to do. Our means and focus may change over time and with circumstances. Our goal is to reach out and love in the name of the Lord.

Shifting Seasons of Service

Expressions of hospitality change with needs and the seasons of our lives, but the heart for hospitality seeks every opportunity. Chuck and I did not grow up in homes where hospitality was a way of life. We had to learn to practice hospitality, because God showed us it was important.

When we moved into our first home, I began a women's Bible study for neighbors in a heavily racially mixed neighborhood. It was a precious experience. We later gathered a group of twelve people once a month for a potluck supper and Bible Study on Sunday evenings in place of evening services.

When we bought our second home, Chuck was chairman of the Pasadena Christian Business Men's Chapter. I was shocked when he announced that he felt we should have a summer outreach dinner for the CBMC men and their spouses at our home. But, being an obedient Christian wife, I set about to plan that outdoor event for one hundred guests. Our state senator, a Christian, was to speak. I had my favorite restaurant make a lasagna. I made the green salad in a large trash bag. I had made about 20 different appetizers, enough to feed hundreds—so I thought—and enough iced tea for an army. We had pitchers of tea sitting on the round dinner tables and a buffet table of appetizers. I guess they thought that was dinner. They went to the tables, sat, and drank all of the tea. The men, being good hosts, came in to the house for tea refills and found me making salad in a large trash bag on the kitchen floor. Together we scooped the salad into very large salad bowls. We all laughed! The men were a real help. By the time the bread and lasagna were delivered, our guests were full. I learned the importance of communication. I also learned that hiring a caterer can sometimes be a very good idea. It adds to the cost but saves your sanity. That was the first of many such dinners.

The Christmas gatherings were for smaller gatherings, so I did the cooking. Several times we did theme dinners, and Chuck and I greeted our guests dressed according to the theme.

During those years, I learned a lot about planning and having fun at my own party. The more outside help I had, the more I enjoyed the evening. I had several friends who love to cook, and our three daughters helped with serving and clean-up. These events were family affairs. We tried during those years to teach our girls the joy of housecleaning for hospitality. At that age, they failed to feel the joy. Today, they are each planning their own events, both small and large. They have good skills on which to fall back. Most importantly, they have a heart to do hospitality.

The last years in our California home were a different season. We still welcomed large groups but began to devote ourselves to smaller gatherings. Most of the guests became friends. We had a monthly potluck and Bible Study share group for about twenty to twenty-five people. Now the dynamics changed. Deep relationship became more important. Smaller groups afford more time to share from the heart. Intimacy was the key. These gatherings were precious to our family. We all knew each others' strengths and weaknesses. When our family was called to Richmond, Virginia, these precious folks gave us amazing support and strength during our transition year, helping us let go and move on. Our hearts had become intertwined, and they still are many years later.

Now in Richmond, Virginia, having left thirty years of life investment in Southern California, we found ourselves spending a lot of time with people one on one or in smaller groups. Now we're talking heart to heart. There is no hiding behind a mask or business. Any props we might have had are gone. We have welcomed pastors and their wives in both small and large groups, building city-wide ministry relationships. Each season through which God has taken us has been a challenge full of joy in serving others with love. It is time to seek and reach once again—new focus, new needs, new opportunities...but always hospitality.

Ice Breakers

What is an icebreaker? An *icebreaker* is a question or game that helps people feel at ease and puts the focus on others.

Asking your guests to share a memory or special event in their lives starts conversation and helps people connect with one another. The questions can be geared to what you want to accomplish with each group setting. It could be a funny incident, a creative activity, or a shared memory. The question should take only a minute or two for each guest to answer.

When you have guests who don't know each other, your questions can help reveal personal history and interests. A good host begins by asking the question, then answering it himself first within the allotted time. This gives your guests opportunity to see what is expected.

A few suggestions:

- How did God bless you last week?
- What was the best thing about your week?
- What special talent has God given you?
- "People would be surprised to know that I _____."
- Name a vehicle that best describes you and tell why.
- What was the best compliment you have received?
- What are your three favorite activities?
- What is your favorite store? Why?
- What animal describes your personality?
- What was your favorite vacation?
- What is your most treasured memory?
- What is the most adventurous think you ever did?
- Tell us one thing you learned about yourself this year.
- How do you think people would describe you?
- What was your most embarrassing moment?
- What is the greatest blessing God has given you?
- What item you possess tells the most about you?
- When did you last feel the joy of serving someone?

- How has God used you recently?
- What are you trusting God for that only He can do?
- If you had to leave your home due to disaster, what three items would you try to save?
- What was your family's view of God?
- What do you consider your most important accomplishment?
- Where did you meet your spouse?
- How did you get engaged?
- Did you like your mate when you met for the first time?
- Share a favorite family tradition.

JERRY AND DONNA

These life-long friends had wonderful New Year's Eve parties. They put a lot of thought into this game. As each guest arrived, they pinned the name of a famous person to his or her back. The guest had a similarity to the famous person. Each guest had to ask a question of each of the other guests in an effort to obtain clues as to who it was whose name was pinned on the back. It was always so much fun to see the guest's reaction to the name on his or her back.

MIKE AND CHERYL

When these friends first moved from California to Virginia, they had a creative way of meeting new people. They asked one couple they met in their church to invite ten couples to their new home. Mike and Cheryl did the rest and made many new friends. Now that is what I call breaking the ice, even when you have no people connections whatsoever.

It's time now for you to break the ice, warming the lives of others through an open heart, an open hand and an open home. You can do it!

It's Time to *Plan*

Friendship with

God is facilitated by

fellowship formed in the

womb of hospitality.

HOSPITALITY MUST BE PUT ON OUR CALENDAR, because time slips away on other things. Good intentions don't count. I have a wonderfully honest friend. She was telling me she had been filling out a survey, and one of the questions was, "How often do you entertain at home?" She was really dismayed when she couldn't even check the last box, which read, "Less than twice a year." She had to ink in "None." When I asked her why, she said she really didn't have an excuse except fear. Fear has deprived her of so much enjoyment and fulfillment. Now, whenever she and her husband have opened their home, they have both enjoyed it immensely, and her husband loves to do hospitality.

It is time to get out the calendar and phone book. Just set a date and make those calls. It is amazing how the energy begins to flow. Put yourself on the line. This is part of the faith walk.

Hospitality is not a game of competition. Our society today is very competitive. The message that goes across the air waves and comes into our homes through printed word and advertisement and even in our schools is "Be better than the Joneses." We get caught in this trap before we realize it. Many of us just quit before we begin so we cannot possibly fail.

We all have preconceived ideas about hospitality. What thoughts come to your mind? It may be having a lovely home, serving wonderful, exotic food; being bubbly and vivacious: or spending a lot of money to impress others. Most of us become exhausted just thinking about it—so we don't think about it, or when we do, we feel guilty and inadequate. Most of us use the same excuse: "no time." "No time" is the most often used excuse by American Christians for not doing what we ought to do.

Gourmet Goals

Good hospitality does not just happen because you decide to have people over for dinner. Memory-making times with others usually require preparation. But don't let lack of plans frustrate impromptu opportunities to open your home on a moment's inspiration or notice. Such times can be a great blessing.

If you are having a few couples over for dinner, decide what your main objective of the evening is to be: to have lighthearted fun; to enjoy a quiet, elegant dinner to bring refreshment to the weary; to get better acquainted with new couples in your group; to allow a struggling family to see a solid marriage and Christ-centered family; to give a special relaxed evening to those who have worked hard for you on a committee; to meet and develop a relationship with your neighbors; to provide a family setting for those who do not have family in the area. The list is endless. The key is to think, plan, enjoy and evaluate.

After you have decided what you want to accomplish at your dinner and know who your guests will be, plan how you are going to accomplish your goals.

Main Goal:

<u>Relaxed evening</u> of fine dining to get to know two couples we do not know well and one couple we know is fun to be with. (Note: The same can be done with singles.)

How to accomplish the goal:

- Prepare a few topic questions just in case conversation drifts from your purpose.
- Focus on the new couple, how they met, how long they have been married, how many children they have, how they happened to come to your church and their interests during free time. This helps you get beyond the "Hi, how are you?" state of typical greeting. The next time you see them in church, you can genuinely ask how their situation is going in a given area and really care. You will know how to pray for them.
- Focus on your guests, not yourself, your home or your meal.
- Be a good listener. Then even if you serve beans, your guests will think you are a great host or hostess.

Setting the Atmosphere

Plan your table setting to set the mood and degree of formality of the evening. A pretty table, with little extras, such as place cards with a personal note inside or the meaning of their name, together with a pretty napkin fold, says to your guests (or to your own family), "You are special, and I enjoy going to the extra effort to bring pleasure to you."

A fresh flower on the napkins or an after-dinner mint by each place setting gives a nice touch and a special message of "I'm thinking about you" to each guest.

Edible centerpieces are always fun and often create conversation. Be creative with your table settings. An ice bowl with fresh rose buds frozen in the bowl can be filled with fruit as a center piece. Use two sizes of bowls, and place them in the freezer, one inside the other. Be sure to set it on a plate with an edge, because it will melt. Use flowers or greens arranged around the base after placing it on the table. Your guests will be very impressed and will feel honored.

If the weather is cooperative, an outdoor setting can create a very relaxed time for your guests. Candlelight is beautiful in a garden setting.

If you have chosen an informal dinner on a cold winter evening, consider moving your table in front of your fireplace. Dare to be creative! Your guests will get caught up in the excitement, and you have created an evening they will enjoy and always remember. You are not putting on a show. You are trying to create a memory maker they can enjoy many times over as they remember your willingness to be different and break out of a mold. Always ask yourself, "How can I bring pleasure?" "How can I touch the life of my guest?"

HOSPITALITY CAN INCLUDE...
- Dinners for one to more than one hundred
- Dessert and coffee
- Fun and fellowship over games
- Serious ministry of Bible studies, prayer gatherings, or counseling with one or with a hurting couple
- Spontaneous dinner after church with visitors
- A phone call of encouragement to a friend or someone who is hurting
- Notes and cards of encouragement (It is not what you spend, but what you say)
- Hosting overnight guests or long-term house guests
- Using your car to help those without transportation
- Outreaches in your home
- Open house for neighbors
- Holiday get-togethers

- Driving an elderly person to the doctor, or a drive in the country to help someone out of a rut
- Babysitting for a neighbor or friend who needs time alone for relaxation
- Cookie exchange: each guest brings two plates of cookies, one to sample and one to give. Each guest leaves with a few of each cookie brought.
- Caroling party: serve hot cider and dessert, sing carols and have each guest share what Christmas means to them. (This is a great way to get to know your neighbors and share the meaning of Christmas. Get a group together to carol at a retirement home and return to hot cider or a chili dinner to sooth a sore throat while sharing favorite Christmas memories.)

How To Get Started

Begin with prayer. Ask God to plant a desire in your heart to do hospitality, to reach out and love others right where they are. Sit down with your family and talk about hospitality. List your strengths and what each family member has to contribute to the ministry of hospitality in your home. Even the little ones have something to contribute: perhaps it's a happy heart while the rest of the family is getting ready.

Talk about the different ways you would enjoy doing hospitality as a family. How can you best serve others? What gifts and talents does each person have—from creative ideas to laughter and a happy heart or a listening ear? Look at the areas you would like to improve. What will you do to work toward improvement in those areas?

Decide as a family what kind of hospitality you would like to do to begin. Invite another family for dinner or a pool party. Perhaps begin by reaching out to the newest guest in your church fellowship. Maybe you would enjoy a dinner for six and let the kids do the serving. Remember neighbors. Help everyone to get to know one another. Create a sense of unity in the neighborhood.

1. **Plan the event.**
2. **Plan goals for the event.** Is your goal to get to know your guests better, or just to have fun with friends? Is it to create the opportunity to share the love of the Lord through example to nonbelievers? Is it to introduce a new couple or family to some of your friends to expand their relationships and build community?
3. **Decide what is necessary to accomplish that goal.** A little thoughtful planning helps you reach your goal.
4. **Decide what each family member will do** to get ready for the event and what part they will have during the event. Good planning keeps broken expectations of who should do what and when at a minimum. Clearly communicate your expectations, but always in the spirit of the Lord.

Early in the season of our larger-group hospitality efforts, we ran headlong into broken expectations and emotional exhaustion due to lack of planning together. Chuck was chairman of the Christian Business Mens' Committee in Pasadena for a number of years. In the beginning, he decided we'd have a summer outreach dinner at which each of the men would invite unsaved businessmen and their wives in our community for a garden dinner party with entertainment and a prominent Christian giving his testimony.

This began our journey of hospitality to one hundred (or more) guests. Relax, God probably won't require you to open your home to such events. But this was part of the Crismier journey of serving through hospitality.

The guys planned the event and contacted the guests. All I had to do was set-up, serve, sometimes cook, decorate (which I love) and clean up. No problem! It took me two such events to realize that my husband seemed to disappear the day of the event for long periods, doing last-minute things, and wasn't around. I found myself becoming angry at being left to face problems by myself. He would manage to return just before our guests arrived.

After such events, we sat down and discussed how I needed him to be there the day of the event, mainly for emotional support, but also in case of last-minute problems. After that, our events were much more pleasurable, and we learned to work together. We discussed and defined our expectations. We assigned people to help setup and others to help cleanup. Large gatherings soon became commonplace for our family, because we had worked out the "bugs" of responsibility. The entire family was recruited for these events, and each person knew his or her part and when it was expected to be accomplished.

This type of hospitality requires a lot of detail planning, if you want to enjoy your guests and keep your family happy during the process. No one wants to feel abused or put upon.

5. **Evaluate after your event.** After your guests have gone, discuss whether your goals were accomplished. If not, how could you better accomplish them next time?

You can set goals for a cup of coffee with a friend. Breathe a prayer of "Use me, Lord, to meet the need of this friend today." We want our conversation always to be pleasing to God. If we dedicate our times together with others and let the Lord nudge us, we will be sensitive to His nudge when things drift toward gossip.

Pray that God will help your guests feel his presence in your home and be blessed for having been there. Ask God to prepare your heart to be sensitive to the needs of your guests. Most people who accept an invitation of hospitality are not coming to visit your home; they are looking for relationship. They are looking for God's satisfying love that should flow through each of us.

Dinner Music

Music helps establish a mood. For a formal dinner, piano or string background music is very peaceful and quieting to one's spirit. It can be used in any setting where you desire a restful atmosphere. Keep the volume low. Use a tape or CD.

Greet Guests

How you greet your guests also sets atmosphere. Try welcoming your guests with a hug, and bring them in to be seated where the lighting is adequate. Have a snack ready. Your guests are special; show them by having fresh flowers in a vase. Your guests will feel so welcome and know you are trying to make them feel comfortable. They will be glad they are in your home. The basic needs we all share are to be loved and to be accepted. How can you and your family make your guests feel loved and accepted in your home? Plan. Then let it happen.

Once your guests arrive, it is time to stop thinking about the house, the food, and the table. Concentrate on your guests. Be willing to make mistakes. Remember, "Love covers a multitude of sins."

Evaluation of Goals

After your guests have gone, evaluate to see if your goals were accomplished. If not, how could you better accomplish them next time? We learn through evaluation. It is okay if the time together takes a different direction than you planned, as long as people are enjoying themselves and God's purposes are being accomplished.

If your goal was for each person to have an opportunity to talk, but one or two people monopolized the conversation, next time you might want to put a question under each plate requesting that each guest answer the question in two or three minutes and move around the table, allowing each guest to answer the question under his plate.

Never forget that your heart, hand and home are God's heart, hand and home extended. Friendship with God is facilitated by fellowship formed in the warm womb of hospitality. Let your home be the place, your heart provide the promise, and your hand fulfill the purpose.

HOSPITALITY PLANNER

EVENT:		STYLE/THEME:	
DATE:	TIME:	PLACE:	NO. OF GUESTS:

GUEST LIST/RSVP:	YES	NO

NOTES:

MENU	RECIPE SOURCES & GARNISHES	THINGS TO DO
Appetizers:		One Week Before:
Soup/Salad:		
		Three Days Before:
Entree:		
Side Dishes:		The Day Before:
Breads:		
		On The Day:
Dessert:		
Beverages:		Last Minute:

Table
Settings

Breakfast Table Settings

1. Toast Plate
2. Syrup Pitcher
3. Water
4. Glass
5. Fruit Bowl
6. Fruit Bowl Saucer
7. Service Plate
8. Fork
9. Knife
10. Teaspoon
11. Coffee Cup & Saucer

Luncheon Table Settings

1. Bread Plate
2. Water Glass
3. Soup Bowl
4. Soup Saucer
5. Service Plate
6. Fork
7. Knife
8. Teaspoon
9. Soup Spoon
10. Coffee Cup & Saucer

Dinner Table Settings

1. Dinner Plate
2. Knife
3. Soup Spoon
4. Dinner Fork
5. Salad Fork
6. Bread Plate
7. Water Glass

Dessert Table Settings

1. Dessert Plate
2. Coffee Cup & Saucer
3. Water Glass
4. Dessert Fork
5. Coffee Spoon

Standing Fan

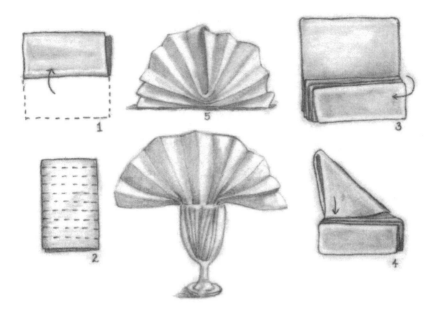

Standing Fan
1. Fold napkin in half.
2. Pleat into 1" accordion pleat up to 4" from top.
3. Fold in half with pleats outside.
4. Fold loose corner down and tuck in.
5. Carefully lay napkin crease side down on plate, allowing fan to open.

Fan
1. Fold, accordion pleat to end, slip end into glass and spread out.

Fleur-de-Lys

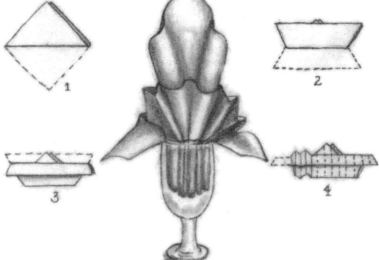

1. Fold napkin in half diagonally.
2. Fold bottom edge up to meet top point.
3. Fold the edge back on itself, leaving one inch at the bottom.
4. Fold in one-inch-wide accordion pleats from left to right.
5. Pinch the pleats together at bottom and slip into glass. Pull out the side "leaves" and let top fan out.

Bishop's Hat

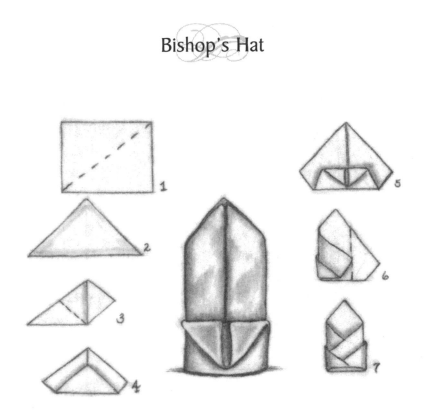

1. Fold napkin in half diagonally.
2. Place the fold along the bottom edge.
3. Fold the right and left corners up to the top corner.
4. Fold up the bottom point to within one inch of the top point.
5. Fold the same point back to the bottom edge.
6. Turn the napkin over and fold the left side toward the center.
7. Fold the right side over the left side, tucking the point into the left fold. Stand the napkin up.

Opera House

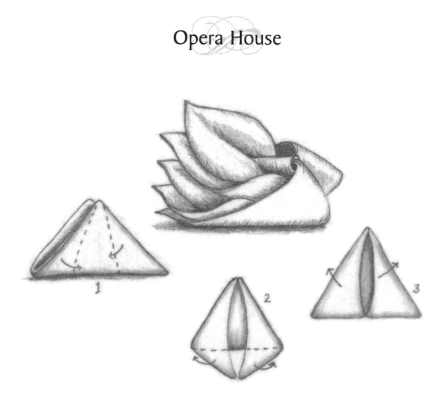

1. Fold into quarters and fold again diagonally. Fold sides to meet at middle.
2. Fold under bottom points.
3. Fold back on middle crease.
4. Position on plate and pull up points.
5. May secure underneath with clip.

*P*reparing for *O*vernight *G*uests

Where there is

room in the heart,

there is always

room in the house.

NOW YOU ARE READY for overnight guests or perhaps hosting a speaker or traveling missionary. You want to make your guests comfortable.

A well-decorated and equipped room will serve you and your guests for many years to come. Once decorated and furnished, all it needs is regular cleaning and a few special touches before the arrival of each guest. Remember, all that you do is as unto the Lord.

Make sure your guest room always has clean sheets and towels and is ready for last-minute guests.

One day I came home late after being gone for several days and found Chuck had an in-studio guest on his broadcast. His guest lingered, asking about hotels in the area. I was so glad our guest room was ready and clean. We took our guest to dinner, not having time to prepare at that late hour, and he was thrilled to have a nice room and a warm breakfast in the morning. We received a real blessing in getting to know this very interesting man from another country. You never know how God will bless you when you open your heart and home.

A number of times we have been the recipient of overnight hospitality in others' homes. It is such a thrill to stay in a home where they have planned for us. The little extras are special hugs from God. We have made friends wherever we have spoken when they have shared their homes with us.

Assisting Your Guests

When you provide a place for speakers, remember that they need quiet time... time to prepare their hearts. When you host a speaker, he is not there primarily to minister to you. Be prepared to give him space. Offer to provide transportation to and from meetings if he has no car.

Let your guests know when meals will be served and the plans you have made for them. Whether the guest is a friend or guest speaker, it is nice to give them maps of interesting places to see in your area. We live in historic Richmond, Virginia, where there is so much to see and do. We provide the brochures and help guests plan what to see and do. We offer to direct them and often meet them for a meal. We cannot go to all the sights each time we have guests. We visit while they are in our home and give them the freedom to make their own plans for sightseeing.

Before your guests arrive, pray over their room and for their time in your home. Pray that they will feel the presence of the Lord and be refreshed by their stay.

YOUR GUEST ROOM

Hospitality is preparation of your heart and home. Everyone who has a guest room needs to spend the night in it and use the bathroom your guest will use.

- Is the bed comfortable?
- Are the blankets sufficient?
- Is a reading light located near the bed?
- Is an alarm clock available?
- Do you have a night light in the bedroom and bathroom?
- A chair is a welcome addition if there is room.
- Your guests will feel welcome if you provide a snack basket with a written greeting.
- Fresh flowers always say "You were in our thoughts."
- A few books and magazines, as well as a Bible, are a nice touch for your guest's quiet moments alone.
- Provide hangers, closet space and a place for his or her suitcase.

Other nice additions might include:

- Laundry basket
- Radio with CD player and worship CDs
- Small refrigerator
- Small TV for news broadcasts
- A small writing desk
- Coffee maker with cups, cream and sugar

YOUR GUEST BATH

Preparation is so important to ensure your guest bathroom is comfortable and welcoming. Most important is absolute cleanliness. You want your guests to know you respect them and have considered their needs and desires. Go the extra mile when possible. Here are a few essentials for the bathroom.

- Bath soap
- Hand lotion
- Small tube of toothpaste
- Extra toothbrush in package
- Shampoo and conditioner
- Hair dryer
- Razor
- Bottled water
- Several bath towels
- Hand towel
- Washcloth
- Tissues
- Toilet bowl cleaner
- Extra toilet paper
- Band-aides and needles and thread.

Upon your guests' departure, pray a blessing over them. You will have sent them on their way with God's protection and presence. We cannot give a greater gift to others.

Make Your Home a Refuge

When you dedicate your home to the Lord and ask Him to use it and bring those who need refreshing, stand back and watch who God brings into your life. My friend, this truly is ministry, when you invite others into your home for rest and refreshment.

Our challenge to you is to use your home and your things, sharing with others—especially the Body of Christ—for rest, refreshment and joy in relationship.

Use your home as a refuge. People learn through example. When they see how husband and wife respond to each other in real-life situations and how your children treat each other, showing love and care for your guest, it can speak volumes. You may change someone's life forever through your love and commitment to God's ways of hospitality.

Chapter *23*

*P*lanning *Y*our *M*eal

Until we break

bread together, we are

virtual strangers.

ALMOST EVERYONE LOVES TO EAT. It is one necessary activity we all have in common. Breaking bread together binds us together like few other activities. So invest time, talents and treasure in this wonderful opportunity to build relationships.

For your own peace of mind, prepare foods you have fixed before and have confidence in preparing. Plan ahead, and prepare new dishes for your family and close friends.

I like to invite close friends when I am experimenting with new dishes. Some of my favorite recipes have come from friends and acquaintances. When I discover a wonder dish they have served me, then I know what it looks and tastes like. I then feel more comfortable in reproducing it for my own guests, passing along the blessing, and, of course, giving credit where credit is due.

Plan your meal with color, texture and richness, considering how it will look on the plate. Avoid serving all your favorite rich foods from each category at one meal as I once did. My poor guests were ill before the evening was over.

Plan ahead! I have learned it is far less stressful if I plan to make as much of the meal as possible ahead of time. Some things can be prepared several days ahead. Avoid last-minute preparation of an entire meal, unless you are a professional chef. You will enjoy your guests more if you are relaxed and feel in control.

Write It Down

You might find it helpful to write down the things you need to do during the week and what you will do each day. That was my common practice for years. Sometimes I would actually write down the time when I needed to do certain tasks. For instance, I would write down when a dish was to go into the oven and when it was to be removed. I no longer need to be quite so specific. However, if I am planning for a large group, I still like to make my specific time lists to avoid forgetting any details or unwittingly leaving in the refrigerator dishes which should have been cooked or served. Do as much as possible before the day of your dinner or event to alleviate stress. You want to enjoy your guests.

Consider Buffet Style

We often use Buffet Style when serving eight or more guests. That way, the host and hostess are not jumping up every few minutes to serve. Guests want to enjoy your company, too. Nothing is worse than having a hostess waiting on you hand and foot, never sitting long enough to carry on conversation. Remember, Jesus had to rebuke Martha for doing that. Relationship is the real goal. Guests feel they are inconveniencing you if you must constantly leap from their presence.

I try to keep a pitcher of water and the coffee on a buffet in the dining room. That way, I do not have to leave the conversation area. I hate to miss out.

Fold Others Into the Process

If you have a friend who loves to cook, you can help each other with food preparation and even with serving at dinner parties. It is a great way to deepen relationships and share your talents. Or, if you hate to cook and a friend enjoys the culinary arts, swap services.

Children love to help, especially when they are young. Our girls did pretty napkin folds and helped set the table. They learned at very young ages how to bless others with an attractive table. Sometimes they became very creative with place cards. They learned to value blessing others at an early age. We looked for ways to make our dinner for guests special. Then we as a family prayed for the evening—that all would go smoothly, that our guests would be refreshed, and that we would be calm to minister as unto the Lord.

Early in our marriage, I thought I had to cook everything from scratch, wax the floors and polish everything in sight. I ended up with migraines. I later learned to put my energy into the things I enjoyed most. I love to decorate, so I could set my table days ahead. Then I learned where to get the best rolls or bread in town. Occasionally, I have called upon friends who are renowned for making great rolls or other dishes to join me in a collective expression of hospitality. They love it! Sometimes I even bought a great dessert. When the pressure of cooking everything from scratch was removed, I learned to enjoy the food preparation I did choose to do. My guests then received a greater blessing—a peaceful and attentive hostess.

Plan Details

Plan when you will clean your house. You may want to schedule your week so you know all you want to do and when you will do it. Leaving everything to the last few days when you are first getting started may put you into stress overload.

Plan what table settings you will use and what your centerpiece will be. Remember to keep it low so it does not hinder you from seeing the faces of your guests. No matter how beautiful your table, if your centerpiece blocks everyone from clearly seeing one another, it becomes a great irritation.

Decide how the dinner will be placed on the table, how the serving dishes will be passed around the table and how plates will be positioned in the kitchen and served. Do you need help serving? If so, upon whom will you call? If your meal is casual, you may wish to ask your guest to help. If it is formal, you may need to enlist the help of a friend.

Decide where you will place your dishes. Is there enough room on either the table or the buffet? Plan what serving pieces you will use. Place cards will help you seat your guests and avoid any last-minute panic and confusion. Perhaps you can set your table the day ahead to leave time for food preparation, as well as leave time to relax just before your guests arrive.

Remember to choose soft background music without words. Words get in the way of conversation.

What lighting gives the atmosphere you want to create for the evening? Candles always add a special touch. You may want to assign a family member to be in charge of music and candles. I enjoy putting the music on long before my guests arrive. It is relaxing for me and helps me prepare my heart for their arrival.

Greeting Your Guests

You may want to serve appetizers or something to drink as guests arrive. It helps people relax and begin conversation. It also helps to bridge awkward moments before the meal is ready or while you await the arrival of all invited guests.

Plan who will greet your guests at the door, who will take their coats and where you will put them. Let your guests know where you have put them in case they should need them during the evening. It is very nice if both husband and wife greet guests. It lets them know you are glad they are there. It also binds husband and wife into the shared experience of hospitality.

Invitations Are Important

If you have mailed invitations, you may need to call anyone who has not responded so you will be prepared. Unfortunately, in our society, we no longer consider one another as we should, so requested R.S.V.P.'s often are not received. A true follower of Christ would always respond timely to an R.S.V.P. request, wouldn't we, because we love our neighbor as ourselves?

Respond to Cancellations

I learned many years ago how easy it is to remove a few place settings if, at the last minute, someone is unable to attend. I have also learned to think quickly when someone extra shows up. If my heart is to serve others, God has the freedom to give me creative ideas in an instant. If it is all about my beautiful table and how the seating will be thrown off, or fear that there will not be enough food, I may find both my evening and that of my guests ruined. They will pick up on my emotional mood. Those given to hospitality learn to respond graciously to the unexpected. Remember, God is equipping you both to will and to do His good pleasure.

I once had four people cancel at the last minute. I had to quickly remove a small table I had added to the dining table and rearrange all the place settings. I learned later what a testimony that was to one of my guests. I did not want four empty places that might cause the rest of my guests to feel uncomfortable. That pastor's wife saw how easy it was to go to plan B and then plan C without a hitch.

Planning is important, but it is perfectly alright to change your plan. Above all, be able to laugh at anything that goes wrong. It puts everyone at ease, including you!

Dine in Creative Places

Practice makes perfect. So, invite people into your home often and try dining in different places. We had our seventy-five-member Sunday School class over for a Christmas dinner and had to put a round table for eight in each bedroom, which was decorated for the occasion. People were running upstairs to see where we put all our guests. What a fun evening that turned out to be.

No room is beyond use! I once heard of a party in a one-room flat. They put a large piece of plywood over the tub and covered it with a cloth and used it as a serving table. They placed a large fern on the toilet and placed ice in the sink for soda cans. Let's get creative and use whatever we have to bless others. It is not about how much work we go to, but about relationship. Find ways to have fun and enjoy your guests. Everyone enjoys the extra touches of thought that we put into an evening. But remember, its about relationship! Our beautiful home or our culinary skills are only backdrops to the main event—people.

Assign Responsibility—Take Risks

It helps to assign family members things to do. Who will remove dishes? Who will clean dishes? Who will ensure beverages are kept flowing? If the family has expectations, all will run smoother when every member has a role and an investment in serving your guests. It becomes a family event.

It is important to teach your children how to set the table properly, serving from the left and removing dishes from the right. Children enjoy having interesting people at the table. You can teach your children about the history of other cultures by inviting people from another country. The active involvement of your children and grandchildren will extend *The POWER of Hospitality* in ways you may not expect. Take the risk. Invest *The POWER of Hospitality* with the next generation that God has entrusted to you.

Let your children help. Teach them by precept and example. Later, they will become a great resource, to both you and the Kingdom of God. My married daughters have come back to lend a hand on occasion when we've hosted large events. I trained them young, and each one now enjoys welcoming people to her home because they learned early.

Remember the Goal

Remembering our goal is to bless our guests and not "show off" is the greatest stress reliever of all. People want to be loved and accepted where they are, not for what they do or what you do. Focus on others, and let God knit your hearts together for His purposes.

MEAL PLANNING CHECKLIST
- ____ Determine your goals for the gathering.
- ____ Determine how formal or casual your gathering will be. Advise your guests.
- ____ Determine the number and names of guests to be invited.
- ____ Invite the guests.
- ____ Determine where the meal will be served.
- ____ Plan the menu.
- ____ Plan the table centerpiece and place settings.
- ____ Purchase the ingredients.
- ____ Plan what you will do on the days leading up to your event.
- ____ Plan what will be each family member's responsibility.

_____ Choose the appropriate music.

_____ Make place cards if you are going to use them.

_____ Decide on the lighting you will use in each room.

_____ Set the table a day ahead.

_____ Prepare the day before as much as you can, even if it is only chopping and storing, so you can mix ingredients the day of the event.

_____ Place coffee and water in the coffee pot early, ready to turn on just before dessert.

_____ Have cream in a pitcher in the refrigerator and sugar in bowl, ready to pull out when it is needed.

_____ Remember to serve from the left, remove from the right.

_____ Pass serving platters and bowls from left to right.

_____ Remove dinner dishes, serving dishes and salt and pepper before serving dessert.

_____ After dessert, remove the dishes. If you plan to visit longer, serve more coffee and tea, or remove to another room.

If Doing a Buffet Table

If you are using a buffet table, it is more interesting to place foods at different heights. Use boxes to raise a platter and drape the box with a pretty cloth. Place serving pieces ahead of time so you know where every item will go and if you have enough room. Your centerpiece can be elevated on a tall, draped box to add interest to the table.

Our Favorite Recipe

Here is a recipe we first experienced nearly thirty years ago in the home of new friends, Barry and Twyla Hartz, who were then on staff with Campus Crusade for Christ. It was a "hit" with us, and it has been a "hit" every time we have used it since, from coast to coast. It is not formal, is served buffet style, fosters fun and facilitates wonderful fellowship.

JAVANESE DINNER (SERVES 12)

2 stewed chickens in clear gravy (debone chicken and make gravy, add some curry powder)

12 c. cooked rice

1 c. chopped green onions

1 c. finely chopped celery

2 c. shredded cheddar

2 c. coconut

2 cans crushed pineapple (do not drain)

1 can peanuts

1 can chow mein noodles

SERVE AS FOLLOWS:

Each item should be in a separate dish on serving table

Put rice on plate and pat down.

2 Tbsp. stewed chicken (use ladle)

1 handful noodles

1 Tbsp. gr. Onions (use soup spoon)

1 Tbsp. celery (use soup spoon)

2 Tbsp. cheese (use soup spoon)

2 Tbsp. coconut (use soup spoon)

2 Tbsp. pineapple (use soup spoon)

2 Tbsp. nuts (use soup spoon)

Cover with gravy

Each guest is asked to bring one ingredient, which the hostess describes with necessary precision. Expense for the host and hostess is minimized. Guests wonder how their contribution will fit with the whole meal. All participate and marvel at the amazing combination as plates build high with the mountain of ingredients. Just ensure your guests are not allergic to coconut or peanuts. They should refrain from adding those to their plates. Enjoy!

Chapter

It's Your Turn

But be ye doers of

the word, and not

hearers only....

YOU CAN DO IT! Now it is your turn. But maybe you still need an extra nudge of hope to get you going as did my friend, Judi Reid, the wife of our state legislator. Her cry for help, while awash in feelings of inadequacy, was one of the extra nudges I needed to provide hope for others through this book. Her brief story may provide just the encouragement you need.

From Intimidation to Inspiration

"Mother, may Nancy spend the night with me this week-end?" I asked as a young girl.

"If she *has* to!" Mother moaned. "Make sure the mono-grammed, scalloped sheets and matching pillowcases are clean. Get out the good guest towels. Pick up everything around the house. And talk to Janie (our family cook) to make sure we have enough food for her to eat! You'll have to be quiet so you don't disturb your father!"

It makes me exhausted just remembering what an ordeal it was to invite someone into my own home as I was growing up. As you can imagine, offering hospitality was rare.

When I became a mother, my desire was to have our house be a real *home*, unencumbered by perfectionist show-casing. I had not learned to cook or do housework. When we bought our first microwave, I even had to make a recipe card with directions on *How to Boil Water in a Cup for Coffee*. Decorating was a disaster. Clutter was constant. But I had love and the courage to begin to break the cycle of erecting barriers to allowing my children to have friends drop in whenever they wanted.

This open-door attitude did not, however, apply to *my* friends! I was fearful of criticism about my weaknesses as a housekeeper and hostess. Yet, I was so honored when I was invited to someone else's home. The less elaborate the event, the more relaxed and connected I became. Something in my spirit yearned to be able to replicate those special times within the four walls of my own home.

Then came my breakthrough. Almost ten years ago I was invited to dinner at the Crismiers' with my husband and several other couples. Even from the outside, I noticed they had a huge, beautiful house. As we walked through their interior, I could feel myself cringing with inferiority.

When Kathie announced dinner, we proceeded into her well-appointed kitchen. I immediately relaxed. She had everything laid out on the countertops so beautifully, but simply. This was going to be fun! We each picked up a dinner plate and progressively heaped food from various bowls to create our individual culinary masterpieces. Somehow Kathie had preplanned the timing so the elements of the meal would look delectable, stay hot and be easy for us to serve ourselves—and with not a trace of a used pot or pan. She made it look so easy. The atmosphere was immediately jovial and without the *hostess tension* that I was prone to experience. When we all sat around her dining room table, although everything was elegant, we were able to be casual. The focus was on the fellowship.

To this day, I am moved almost to tears by the lessons I learned that night.

- Keep it simple.
- Focus on showing Christ's love from your heart to your guests.
- Hospitality is about connecting with the people who accept your invitation.
- The visibility of the hostess' gifts and talents for elegant decorating and entertaining are to be valued.
- A lack of similar skills does not negate the heart of the hostess.

Kathie's God-given gifts are extremely creative, enhanced by the genuine warmth of who she is. Once I moved from personally- inflicted intimidation to appreciation, I was able to receive, from a softened heart, God's blessings of the evening.

My God-given gift is encouragement. Before I left, I urged Kathie to write a book—for people like me—who dread even the thought of entertaining in their own home—who feel so inadequate and inferior—overwhelmed with anxiety that the whole family is *victimized* by the preparations—who need tools to create a connection of Christ's love through food in a relaxed home atmosphere.

Thank you Kathie and Chuck! May your book bless, encourage and provide hope and practicality for those whom God wants to use through this wonderful ministry of hospitality.

With thanks,

Judi Reid

Don't Forget

Give yourself to hospitality. Remember, it may well be the closest you will ever get on earth to the face of God. You may even entertain angels unawares. Most certainly you will be blessed and you will be a blessing. Think hospitality! Plan. Get started. And don't forget that God's grace is sufficient for you, for His strength is made perfect in your weakness.

As you now open your heart, hand and home in hospitality, write to let us know how God is working in and through your life in reaching to others. Let your life and testimony open the door of hope for yet another to experience *The POWER of Hospitality*.

Appendix 1

$\mathcal{P}$astor-to-$\mathcal{P}$astor

Preparing a City
for
Covenant Community

THE PURPOSE:

To build covenant relationship between pastors preparing and revealing a Covenant Community of believers ready for the move of God to save, heal, and reconcile your city or Metro area.

THE PLACE:

Pastors' homes

THE PEOPLE:

Pastors and their wives

THE PLAN:

Gather in homes not less than monthly in groups of six to twelve for breaking of bread together, encouragement, exhortation, and personal prayer.

THE PRINCIPLES:

- God's power is revealed and released when his people come together in one accord. *Acts 2:1.*
- We can walk together with the Lord and one another only when our hearts are in agreement as revealed by our relationship with one another. *Amos 3:3.*
- The hallmark of the early church was, "Behold how they love one another." *John 15:12, I John 4:7-8.*
- Our eyes, minds, and hearts are opened to the Lord and to one another as we break bread together. *Luke 24:30-35.*
- The fellowship of believers is centered in the "temple" for teaching and corporate worship, and for celebration of the work of the ministry taking place "from house to house" where believers gather for prayer, fellowship, exhortation, discipleship, and outreach. *Acts 2:45-47.*
- It is essential to all ministry that we give ourselves to hospitality. *I Timothy 3:2.*
- We cannot effectively lead the flock until we ourselves are revealing God's truth in relationship. *John 1:14 I Peter 5:1-5.*

Breaking Bread—Breaking Barriers

Pastoral Guidelines to Facilitate Pastoral Relationship

FACILITATING RELATIONAL MINISTRY

1. Encourage pastors to dress casually—no ties or clerical collars—preferably sweaters rather than coats.
2. Encourage intentional inclusion of pastors of differing race and denomination in <u>each</u> gathering.
3. Encourage use of round tables for eating whenever possible.
4. Encourage groups to a more relaxed, comfortable setting after eating, if at all possible; i.e., den or family room.
5. Encourage contact between group gatherings—phone, lunch, handwritten notes, etc.

CONDUCTING RELATIONAL MINISTRY

1. Encourage relationship by sharing what is happening in the lives of those present. The facilitator should preferably call on people by name to share.
2. Encourage a designated member of the group to lead in prayer for a specific need or situation, and especially in an area of his/her own need. Pray at moment need is revealed.
3. Encourage transparency and vulnerability by being transparent and vulnerable.
4. Encourage exercise of gifts—BUT—in love and in gracious recognition that not all share your experience, exuberance, or readiness.
5. Encourage informal praise and worship in song, while avoiding a fixed format.
6. Encourage active involvement by everyone, sensitively drawing all involved to risk relationship.
7. Encourage ministry of and around the Word by emphasizing the "doing" of the Word in the relationship of the group rather than extended teaching or telling *about* the Word.

FRUSTRATING RELATIONAL MINISTRY
(Avoid the Traps that Trip Relationships)
1. Allowing one or two personalities to dominate.
2. Allowing details involving others not present to be discussed and displayed, in the name of prayer, when they are really "gospel" gossip.
3. Allowing breaches of confidence—either from within the group or from without.
4. Allowing "puffing" about one's ministry.
5. Allowing "religion" to prevail over "relationship."
6. Allowing unnecessary vocal display of gifts—especially tongues—in a group setting. Remember Paul's admonition in I Corinthians 13:1…"Tho I speak with the tongues of men and of angels and have not love…"
7. Allowing cliques of familiar faces or persuasions within a meeting.
8. Allowing polarized discussion of theology and theological differences.
9. Allowing group to exceed 12 people without expanding to two or more groups.
10. Allowing meeting form to frustrate deep fellowship.

God is working His Spirit of Hospitality in us and through us…
To Reconcile men to God
To Reconcile us to one another.

Hospitality is reaching to "strangers"…even pastors of other races and denominations. Let's go for it! Let's build a Covenant Community that will reveal the glory of God to a broken nation.

Relationships Revealing Righteousness

Pastor-to-Pastor

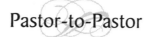

Risking

Relationship for

Revival and

Reconciliation

A SIMPLE PLAN

1. Pastors and their wives (4-6 couples) gather in a pastor's "cell" group for 9-12 months—at least once per month—moving "from house to house."

2. After 12 months, the group divides into separate groups of 2 pastors each and their wives. Each pastor invites at least one or two other pastors and their wives to join them at the next gathering, following the basic pattern for relational ministry. At this stage, there should be at least 4-6 such groups with 8-12 pastors/wives each.

3. After 12 months, the same pattern would again repeat.

4. At the end of the first 18 months, a weekend fellowship retreat could be scheduled involving all those who have participated.

Keep it Simple Saints!

Appendix 2

$\mathcal{P}$ortrait of a Covenant Community

JOHN WINTHROP

A Model of Christian Charity

Perhaps the best expression of what
America was to be and become.

A Prescription for Healing America's Broken Heart
Presented by
Save America Ministries

A Voice from the Past
A Vision for the Future
John Winthrop,
a Godly attorney and governor

HIS WORDS REMAIN A MODEL of what life in America was meant to be.

"We must delight in each other, make others conditions our own, rejoice together, mourn together, labor and suffer together, always having before our eyes, our community, as members of the same body."

One of the most distinguished members of the Massachusetts Bay Colony was the Puritan John Winthrop, who left England with his followers in four ships on March 22, 1630, and, after a delay of several weeks in Yarborough, arrived in Salem on June 12. Winthrop had given much thought to not only his personal decision to leave England but also the goals, both religious and civic, that he thought the Puritans should pursue in their new community. Before debarking from his flagship, the Arabella, he wrote a statement of the working principles upon which the colony would be built. Titled "A Model of Christian Charity," it is perhaps the best expression of the Puritan ideal of what America was to be and become. It reveals the seed from which America was conceived, the spiritual womb from which the nation was born. It is, in short, the American Vision—a vision for a covenant community, born of a heart of hospitality.

GOD ALMIGHTY, IN HIS MOST HOLY AND WISE PROVI-
DENCE, has so disposed of the condition of mankind, as in all times
some must be rich; some poor; some high and eminent in power and
dignity; others mean and in subjection.

The Reason Hereof: first, to hold conformity with the rest of His
works, being delighted to show forth the glory of His greatness in
that, as it is the glory of princes to have many officers, so this Great
King will have many stewards, counting Himself more honored in
dispensing His gifts to man by man than if He did it by His own
immediate hand.

Second, that He might have the more occasion to manifest the
work of His spirit; first, upon the wicked in moderating and restrain-
ing them, so that the rich and mighty should not eat up the poor, nor
the poor and despised rise up against their superiors and shake off
their yoke; second, in the regenerate in exercising His graces in them,
as in the great ones their love, mercy, gentleness, temperance, etc.; in
the poor and inferior sort, their faith, patience, obedience, etc.

Third, that every man might have need of others, and from
hence they might be all knit more nearly together in the bond of
brotherly affection. From hence it appears plainly that no man is
made more honorable than another or more wealthy, etc., out of any
particular or singular respect to himself, but for the glory of his
Creator and the common good of the creature, man. Therefore, God
still reserves the property of these gifts to Himself, as [in] Ezekiel
16:17; He there calls wealth His gold and His silver, etc; [in] Proverbs
3:9 He claims their service as His due: "Honor the Lord with thy
riches," etc. All men are thus (by Divine Providence) ranked into two
sorts, rich and poor; under the first are included all men such as are
able to live comfortably by their own means duly improved; and all
others are poor according to the former distribution.

There are two rules whereby we are to walk one toward another;
justice and mercy. These are always distinguished by their act and in
their object, yet may they both concur in the same subject in each
respect, as sometimes there may be an occasion of showing mercy to

a rich man in some sudden danger of distress; and also doing of mere justice to a poor man in regard of some particular contract, etc. There is likewise a double law of grace, or the moral law or the law of the gospel (we may omit the law of justice as not properly belonging to this purpose otherwise than it may fall into consideration in some particular case). By the first of these laws, man…is commanded to love his neighbor as himself. Upon this ground stand all the precepts of the moral law which concerns our dealings with men. To apply this to the works of mercy, this law requires two things: first, that every man afford his help to another in every want or distress; second, that he perform this out of the same affection which makes him careful of his own good, according to that of our Savior (Matthew 7:12) "Whatsoever ye would that men should do to you…."

The law of grace or the gospel has some difference from the former as in these respects: First, the law of nature was given to man in the estate of innocence; the law of the gospel in the estate of regeneracy. Second, the law of nature propounds one man to another, as the same flesh and image of God, the law of the gospel as a brother in Christ also, and in the communion of the same spirit, teaches us to put a difference between Christians and others…. The law of nature could give no rules for dealing with enemies, for all are considered friends in the state of innocence, but the gospel commands love to an enemy…. "If thine enemy hunger, feed him; love your enemies; do good to them that hate you" (Matthew 5:44).

This law of the gospel propounds, likewise, a difference of seasons and occasions. There is a time when a Christian must sell all and give to the poor as they did in the apostles' times. There is a time also when Christians (though they give not all yet) must give beyond their ability…. Likewise, community of perils calls for extraordinary liberality and so does community in some special service for the Church. Lastly, when there is no other means whereby our Christian brother may be relieved in this distress, we must help him beyond our ability, rather than tempt God in putting him upon help by miraculous or extraordinary means.

This duty of mercy is exercised in…giving, lending and forgiving.

Question: What rule shall a man observe in giving in respect to the measure?

Answer: If the time and occasion be ordinary, he is to give out of his abundance—let him lay aside, as God has blessed him. If the time and occasion be ordinary, he must be ruled by them.... Then a man cannot likely do too much, especially if he may leave himself and his family under...means of comfortable subsistence.

Objection: A man must lay up for posterity; the fathers lay up for posterity and children, and he is worse than an infidel that provides not for his own.

Answer: For the first, it is plain that the statement is made by way of comparison and must be meant for the ordinary and usual course of fathers and cannot extend to times and occasions extraordinary, for in another place the apostle speaks against those who walk inordinately, and it is without question that he is worse than an infidel who through his own sloth and voluptuousness shall neglect to provide for his family.

Objection: "The wise man's eyes are in his head," says Solomon (Ecclesiastes 2:14), "and foreseeth the plague," therefore we must forecast and lay up against evil times when he or his may stand in need of all he can gather.

Answer: Solomon uses this very argument to persuade to liberality. Ecclesiastes 2:1: "Cast thy bread upon the waters...for thou knowest not what evil may come upon the land"; Luke 16 "Make you friends of the riches of iniquity." You will ask how this shall be? Very well. First, he that gives to the poor lends to the Lord, who will repay him even in this life and a hundredfold to him or his. The righteous man is ever merciful and lends, and his seed enjoy the blessing; and besides we know what advantage it will be to us in the day of accounting, when many such witnesses shall stand forth for us to witness the improvement of our talent. And I would know of those who plead so much for laying up for time to come, whether they hold Matthew 6:19 to be gospel: "Lay not up for yourselves treasures upon earth." If they acknowledge it, what extent will they allow it? If only to those primitive times, let them consider the reason whereupon our Savior grounds it. The first is that treasures are subject to the moth, rust, and the thief; the second is that they will steal away the heart; where the treasure is, there will the heart be also.

The reasons are of like force at all times; therefore, the exhortation must be general and perpetual, which applies always in respect of the love and affection for riches and in regard to the things themselves, when any special service for the church or particular distress of our brother call for the use of riches; otherwise it is not only lawful but necessary to lay up as Joseph did, to have ready upon such occasions as the Lord (whose stewards we are) shall call for them from us.

Christ gave us an instance of the first when He sent His disciples for the ass and bade them answer the owner thus: "The Lord hath need for him" (Matthew 21:2-3). The Lord expects that when He is pleased to call for anything we have, our own interest must stand aside till His turn is served. For the other instance, we need look no further than John 1 "He who hath this world's good and seeth his brother in need, and shuts up his compassion from him, how dwelleth the love of God in him?" Which comes punctually to this conclusion: If your brother is in want and you can help him, you can have no doubt as to what you should do. If you love God, you must help Him.

Question: What rule must we observe in lending?
Answer: You must observe whether your brother has present or probably or possible means of repaying you, or if none of these, you must give to him according to his necessity, rather than lend to him as he asks. If he has present means of repaying, you are to look at him not as the recipient of mercy but by way of commerce, wherein you are to walk by the rule of justice. But if his means of repaying you are only probably or possible, then he is an object of mercy and you must lend to him though there is danger of losing it. Deuteronomy 15:7-8: "If any of thy brethren be poor...thou shalt lend him sufficient." That

men might not shift off his duty because of the apparent hazard, he tells them that though the Year of Jubilee were at hand (when he must remit it, if he could not repay it before), yet he must lend, and that cheerfully. Deuteronomy 15:10: "It may not grieve thee to give him," and because some might object, why so I should impoverish myself and my family, he adds: "With all thy work." Matthew 5:42: "From him that would borrow of thee turn not away."

Question: What rule must we observe in forgiving?
Answer: Whether you lend by way of commerce or in mercy. If he has nothing to repay, you must forgive him (unless you have a surety or a lawful pledge). Every seventh year the creditor was to quit that which he lent to his brother if his brother was as poor as he appeared…. In all these and like cases Christ gave a general rule in Matthew 7:12: "Whatsoever ye would that men should do to you, do ye the same to them also."

Question: What rule must we observe and walk by in the case of a community of peril?
Answer: The same as before, but with more enlargement toward others and less respect toward ourselves and our own right. Hence, in the primitive church they sold all and had all things in common, nor did any man say that what he possessed was his own. Likewise, in their return from captivity, because the work was great for the restoring of the church and the danger of enemies was common to all, Nehemiah exhorted the Jews to liberality and readiness in remitting their debts to their brethren, and disposed liberally of his own goods to those that wanted, standing not upon what was due him, which he might have demanded of them. Some of our forefathers did the same in times of persecution in England, and so did many of the faithful in other churches, and so we keep an honorable remembrance of them.

It is also to be observed both in the Scriptures and later stories of the church, that those who have been most bountiful to the poor saints—especially in…extraordinary times and occasions—God has left highly commended to posterity…. Observe again that the

Scripture gives no caution to restrain any from being overly liberal in this way, but recommends all men to the liberal and cheerful practice hereof by the sweetest promises.... Isaiah 58:10-12:

> *If thou pour out thy soul to the hungry, then shall thy light spring out in darkness, and the Lord shall guide thee continually, and satisfy thy soul in drought, and make fat thy bones; thou shalt be like a watered garden, and they shall be of thee that shall build the old waste places.*

On the contrary, most heavy curses are laid upon those who are illiberal toward the Lord and His people....

Having already set forth the practice of mercy according to the rule of God's law, it will be useful to lay open the grounds of it; also being the other part of the commandment, and that is the affection from which this exercise of mercy must arise. The apostle tells us that this love is the fulfilling of the law (Romans 13:10). Not that it is enough to love our brother and no more.... Just as, when we bid a man to make the clock strike, he does not lay his hand on the hammer, which is the immediate instrument of the sound, but sets to work the first manner or main wheel, knowing that it will certainly produce the sound which he intends, so the way to draw men to the works of mercy is not by force of argument on the goodness or necessity of the work, for though this course may persuade a rational mind to some present act of mercy (as is frequent in experience), yet it cannot work the habit of mercy into a soul so that it will be prompt on all accessions to produce the same effect except by framing the affections of love in the heart, which will as natively bring forth mercy as any cause produces an effect.

The definition which the Scripture gives us of love is this: love is the bond of perfection (Colossians 3:14). First, it is a bond, or ligament. Second, it makes the work perfect. There is no body that does not consist of parts, and that which knits these parts together gives the body its perfection, because it makes each part so contiguous to the others that they mutually participate with each other, both in strength and infirmity, in pleasure and in pain. To instance the most perfect of all bodies: Christ and His church make one body. The several parts of this body considered apart before they were united were as disproportionate and as much disordered as so many contrary qualities or elements, but when Christ came and by His spirit and love knit all these parts to Himself and to each other, it became the most perfect and best proportioned body in the world....

For patterns we have first our Savior, who out of His goodwill and in obedience to His Father became a part of this body, and, being knit with it in the bond of love, found such a native sensitivity to our infirmities and sorrows that He willingly yielded Himself to death to ease the infirmities of the rest of His body and so heal their sorrows. From like sympathy of parts did the apostles and many thousands of saints lay down their lives for Christ again, as we may see in the members of this body among themselves, and as we shall find in the history of the church in all ages: the sweet sympathy of affections in the members of this body, one toward another, their cheerfulness in serving and suffering together. How liberal they were without repining, harborers without grudging, helpful without reproaching, and all from this, that they had fervent love among them, which only makes the practice of mercy constant and easy.

The next consideration is how this love comes to be wrought. Adam in his first estimate was a perfect model of mankind in all generations, and in him this love was perfected.... But Adam rent himself from his Creator, rent all his posterity also one from another; whence it comes that every man is born with this principle in him, to love and seek himself only. And thus a man continues till Christ comes and takes possession of his soul, and infuses another principle—love to God and our brother....

The third consideration concerns the exercise of this love, which is twofold—inward or outward. The outward has been handled in the former preface of this discourse; for unfolding the other we must take...that maxim of philosophy, *simile simili guadet*, or, like will to like.... The ground of love is recognition of some resemblance in the things loved to that which affects it. This is the reason why the Lord

337

loves the creature to the extent that it has any of His image in it; He loves His elect because they are like Him; He beholds them in His beloved Son. So a mother loves her child, because she thoroughly conceives a resemblance of herself in it. Thus it is between the members of Christ. Each discerns by the work of the spirit his own image and resemblance in another, and therefore cannot but love him as he loves himself....

If any shall object that it is not possible that love should be bred or upheld without hope of requital, it is granted. But that is not our cause, for this love is always under reward; it never gives but always receives with advantage.... Among members of the same body, love and affection are reciprocal in a most equal and sweet kind of commerce.... In regard to the pleasure and content that the exercise of love carries with it, we may see in the natural body that the mouth receives and minces the food which serves to nourish all the other parts of the body, yet it has no cause to complain. For first, the other parts send back by secret passages a due proportion of the same nourishment in a better form for the strengthening and comforting of the mouth. Second, the labor of the mouth is accompanied by pleasure and content that far exceed the pains it takes, so it is all a labor of love.

Among Christians, the party loving reaps love again, as was shown before, which the soul covets more than all the wealth in the world. Nothing yields more pleasure and content to the soul than when it finds that which it may love fervently, for to love and be loved is the soul's paradise, both here and in heaven. In the state of wedlock there are many comforts to bear out the troubles of that condition, but let those who have tried the most say whether there is any sweetness...comparable to the exercise of mutual love....

Now make some application of this discourse to the situation which gave the occasion of writing it. **Herein are four things to be propounded: the persons, the work, the end, the means.**

First, for the persons, **we are a company professing ourselves fellow members of Christ.**... Though we are absent from each other by many miles, and have our employments at far distance, **we ought to**

338

account ourselves knitted together by this bond of love, and live in the exercise of it, if we would have the comfort of our being in Christ. This was common in the practice of Christians in former times; they used to love any of their own religion even before they were acquainted with them.

Second, **the work we have in hand is by mutual consent with a special overruling Providence, with a** more than ordinary **mandate from the churches of Christ to seek out a place to live and associate under a due form of government both civil and ecclesiastical.** In such cases as this the care of the public must hold sway over all private interests. To this not only conscience but mere civil policy binds us, for true rule that private estates cannot exist to the detriment of the public.

Third, **the end is to improve our lives to do more service to the Lord and to comfort and increase the body of Christ** of which we are members, so that ourselves and our posterity may be better preserved from common corruptions of this evil world in order to serve the Lord and work out our salvation under the power and purity of holy ordinances.

Fourth, the means whereby this must be effected are twofold. First, since the work and end we aim at are extraordinary, we must not content ourselves with usual ordinary means. Whatsoever we did or ought to have done when we lived in England, we must do that and more also wherever we go. **That which most people in churches only profess as a truth, we bring into familiar and constant practice. We must love our brothers without pretense; we must love one another with a pure heart and fervently; we must bear one another's burdens; we must not look on our own things but also on the things of our brethren. Nor must we think that the Lord will bear with such failings at our hands** as He does from those among whom we have lived, for three reasons: (1) Because of the closer bonds of marriage between the Lord and us, wherein He has taken us to be His own in a most strict manner, which makes Him more jealous of our love and obedience, just as He told the people of Israel, "You only have I known of all the families of the Earth; therefore will I punish you for your transgressions" (Amos 3:2); (2) Because the Lord will be sanctified in those who come near Him. We know that there were many who interrupted the service of the Lord, some set up altars to other gods before Him, others offering both strange fires and sacrifices; yet no fire came from heaven, or other sudden judgment upon them…; (3) When given a special commission He wants it strictly observed in every article….

Thus stands the case between God and us. We are entered into covenant with Him for this work. We have taken out a commission. The Lord has given us leave to draw our own articles; we have promised to base our actions on these ends, and we have asked Him for favor and blessing. Now if the Lord shall please to hear us, and bring us in peace to the place we desire, then He has ratified this covenant and sealed our commission, and will expect strict performance of the articles contained in it. But if we neglect to observe these articles, which are the ends we have propounded, and—dissembling with our God—shall embrace this present world and prosecute our carnal intentions, seeking great things for ourselves and our posterity, the Lord will surely break out in wrath against us and be revenged of such a perjured people, and He will make us to know the price of the breach of such a covenant.

Now the only way to avoid this shipwreck and to provide for our posterity is to follow the counsel of Micah: to do justly, to love mercy, to walk humbly with our God. For this end, we must be knit together in this work as one man; we must hold each other in brotherly affection; we must be willing to rid ourselves of our excesses to supply others' necessities; we must uphold a familiar commerce together in all meekness, gentleness, patience and liberality. We must delight in each other, make others' conditions our own and rejoice together, mourn together, labor and suffer together, always having before our eyes our commission and common work, our community as members of the same body.

So shall we keep the unity of the spirit in the bond of peace. The Lord will be our God and delight to dwell among us as His own people. He will command a blessing on us in all our ways, so that we shall see much more of His wisdom, power, goodness, and truth than we have formerly known. We shall find that the God of Israel is among us, and ten of us shall be able to resist a thousand of our enemies. The Lord will make our name a praise and glory. For we must consider that we shall be like a City upon a Hill.

If we deal falsely with our God in this work we have undertaken and so cause Him to withdraw His present help from us, we shall be made a story and a byword throughout the world; we shall open the mouths of enemies to speak evil of the ways of God and all believers in God; we shall shame the faces of many of God's worthy servants and cause their prayers to be turned into curses upon us, till we are forced out of the new land where we are going.

Now to end this discourse with the exhortation of Moses, that faithful servant of the Lord, in his last farewell to Israel (Deuteronomy 30:14-20).

> *Beloved, **there is now set before us life and good, death and evil, in that we are commanded this day to love the Lord our God, and to love one another; to walk in His ways and to keep His commandments** and His ordinance, **and His laws, and the articles of our covenant with Him,** that we may live and be multiplied, and **that the Lord our God may bless us in the Land** whither we go to possess it. **But if our hearts shall turn away so that we will not obey, but shall be seduced and worship other gods, our pleasures and profits,** and serve them; it is propounded unto us this day, **we shall surely perish out of the good land** whither we pass over this vast sea to possess it. **Therefore, let us choose life that we and our seed may live; by obeying His voice, and cleaving to Him, for He is our life and our prosperity** (Emphasis added).*

Endnotes

Chapter 1

1. Mary E. Patten, as quoted in "Quotable Quotes," Readers Digest, April 2000, p. 73.

2. Stephen Winzenburg, "Whatever Happened to Hospitality?" Christianity Today, May 22, 2000, pp. 87–89.

3. Taken from comments by H. B. London, head of pastoral ministries for Focus on the Family, in a one-hour interview on the author's daily radio broadcast, VIEW-POINT.

4. Robert E. Bellah, et al. Habits of the Heart (New York: Harper & Row, 1985), p. 37.

5. James Patterson and Peter Kim, The Day America Told the Truth (New York: Prentice Hall Press, 1991), p. 239.

6. David Brodes, "Viewed From Right or Left, Cultural Trends Are Alarming," Richmond Times Dispatch, February 16, 1994, p. A11.

7. George Gallup Jr., Forecast 2000, (New York: William Morrow & Co., Inc, 1984), p. 155.

Chapter 2

1. Rabbi A. James Rudin, in an address to the University of Richmond, as quoted by Will Jones, "Faith's Obligation: Offering Hospitality," Richmond Times Dispatch, September 23, 2000, p. B-6.

Chapter 3

1. George Barna, Virtual America (Ventura, California: Regal Books, 1994), p. 88.

Chapter 7

1. Henry Blackaby, "Awakenings," On Mission, May–June 2000, p. 11.

Chapter 12

1. Attributed to Paul Tournier.

2. Alexis de Tocqueville, Democracy in America, J.P. Mayer ed. (New York: Doubleday, Anchor Books, 1969), p. 506.

3. Robert N. Bellah, e. al., Habits of the Heart (New York, N.Y.: Harper and Row for Regents of the University of California, 1985), p. 37.

4. Ibid., p. 37.

5. Charles Crismier, Renewing the Soul of America, (Richmond, VA, Elijah Books, 2002).

Chapter 13

1. Margo Nash, Statue of Liberty, (Glendale, N.Y.; Manhattan Post Card Publishing Co. Inc., 1983), pp. 31, 48.

2. William Benton, pub., The Annals of America (Chicago, IL; Encyclopedia Britannica, 1968), pp. 109–115.

3. Gorton Carruth and Eugene Ehrlich, eds, American Quotations (Avenil, NJ; Wings Books, 1992), p. 109.

4. Attributed to psychiatrist Paul Tournier.

5. Frank S. Mead, ed., 12,000 Religious Quotations (Grand Rapids, Michigan; Baker Book House, 1992), p. 208).

6. Gorton Carruth and Eugene Ehrlich, editors, American Quotations, p. 278, quoting Josiah Gilbert Holland, "Home," Gold-Foil Hammered From Popular Proverbs, 1859.

7. Gorton Carruth and Eugene Ehrlich, eds., American Quotations, p. 278.

8. Ibid., p. 278.

9. Ibid., p. 278.

10. Ibid., p. 278.

11. The Bible, John 14:1–3.

12. Frank S. Mead, ed., 12,000 Religious Quotations, p. 229.

Chapter 17

1. Jim Russell, Awakening the Giant (Grand Rapids, MI: Zondervan Publishing House, 1996).

2. H.B. London and Neil Wiseman Pastors at Risk (Wheaton, IL; Victor books, 1993), p. 22.

3. Stephen Winzenburg, "Whatever Happened to Hospitality?" Christianity Today, May 22, 2000, pp. 78–79.

4. George Barna, The Barna Report (premier issue) (Waco, Texas: Word Publishing, 1996), p. 1.

5. H.B. London and Neil Wiseman, Pastors at Risk, p. 22.

6. William Hendricks, Exit Interviews (Chicago, IL; Moody Press, 1993), back cover.

About the Authors

From the womb of the South comes *The POWER of Hospitality*. Chuck and Kathie Crismier, together with their expanding family of three married children and seven grandchildren, reside in Richmond, Virginia.

Over the past twenty-five years, hospitality became a life message for the Crismiers. God, through thirty-eight years of marriage, led them from a my-home-is-my-castle mindset to a my-home-is-a-Christian-embassy heartset. Hospitality became a way of life now embraced also by their adult children. Their teaching on hospitality, from Southern California to Virginia, the birthplace of southern hospitality, has revolutionized the lives and congregations of people from coast to coast.

Chuck, in his own burning-bush experience, felt a profound call to leave his lucrative law practice in 1992, forming Save America Ministries to "Rebuild the Foundations of Faith and Freedom." Now, in full-time ministry, he hosts a national daily radio broadcast, VIEWPOINT: "Confronting the deepest issues of America's heart and home." Kathie, after two years as a teacher, has devoted her life to being a busy wife, mother and "nana," speaking on matters of the heart and home.

The Crismiers believe hospitality is at the heart of the Gospel and must be at the heart of our homes. As you begin to live out the pages of this book, may *The POWER of Hospitality* change your life as it has theirs.

Chuck and Kathie Crismier can be contacted by writing or calling:
P.O. Box 70879
Richmond, VA 23255
(804) 754-1822

or through the Save America Ministries web site
www.saveus.org

Additional copies of this book are available from your local bookstore or through Elijah Books.

If you have enjoyed this book, or if it has impacted your life, we would like to hear from you.

If you would like to use this book in groups through your church, ministry or other organization, please contact us for special case-lot pricing.

Please contact us at

ELIJAH BOOKS

P.O. Box 70879
Richmond, VA 23255
(804) 754-3000
or by email at
elijahbooks@comcast.net